Te Puna – A New Zealand Mission Station

CONTRIBUTIONS TO GLOBAL HISTORICAL ARCHAEOLOGY
Series Editor:
Charles E. Orser, Jr., *New York State Museum, Albany, New York*

A Continuation Order Plan is available for this series. A continuation order will bring delivery of each new volume immediately upon publication. Volumes are billed only upon actual shipment. For further information please contact the publisher.

Te Puna – A New Zealand Mission Station

Historical Archaeology in New Zealand

Angela Middleton

University of Otago, Dunedin, New Zealand

 Springer

Angela Middleton
University of Otago
Dunedin
New Zealand
angela.middleton@otago.ac.nz

ISBN: 978-0-387-77620-0   e-ISBN: 978-0-387-77622-4
DOI:10.1007/978-0-387-77622-4

Library of Congress Control Number: 2008926764

Cover illustration: (Figure 4.12 from book) Te Puna Mission Station, looking towards the east, c. 1839-1841 (Richard Taylor 1805-1873, Alexander Turnbull Library, Wellington, E-296-q-160-1)

Printed on acid-free paper

9 8 7 6 5 4 3 2 1

springer.com

Preface

This study is concerned with some of the central themes of historical archeology, those concerning colonization, cultural engagement, gender, ethnicity, and class. These themes are examined through the lens of mission archeology, and in particular through the case study of Te Puna, a nineteenth-century mission station situated in a remote location of Aotearoa/New Zealand.

Evangelical missionary societies have been associated with the processes of colonization throughout the globe, from India to Africa and into the Pacific. In late eighteenth century Britain the Church Missionary Society (CMS) for Africa and the East began its missionary ventures, and in the first decade of the nineteenth century sent three of its members to New South Wales, Australia, and to New Zealand, then an unknown, little-explored part of the world. The London Missionary Society had already made efforts to establish a mission in Tahiti, with uncertain success. Subsequently, the Wesleyans joined the field with their own society, but the different evangelical societies often worked cooperatively in the face of their common enemy, perceived as the devil, and personified for them in indigenous cultural practices. American efforts in Hawaii began in 1820.

In all of these locations, common themes of interaction with indigenous peoples, household economy, the development of commerce, and social and gender relations were played out. Across the globe, a common material culture traveled with its evangelizing (and later colonizing) settlers, with similar artifacts appearing as cultural markers, from Cape Town in South Africa to Tasmania and Victoria in Australia, and the even more remote Bay of Islands in New Zealand. After missionization, colonization occurred.

The New Zealand CMS mission station, Te Puna, was first settled in 1832 following the closure of the nearby Oihi mission, New Zealand's first station and first permanent European settlement. While the Te Puna mission had a comparatively short life, the much broader dramas of settlement, colonization, and culture contact were clearly reflected there, brought to life by the archeological and archival records. Despite its isolation, Te Puna was connected through its CMS networks, and through its material culture, with Sydney in New South Wales and London. Mission recruits traveled over networks that included these locations, as well as others in the Pacific, visiting Te Puna as part of their itinerary. Mission supplies were ordered from Sydney as well as from Great Britain. Staffordshire ceramics found their way to Te Puna, where they were recovered from the archeological context, as well as to other British colonies.

Daily life at Te Puna, revealed through the archeological record as well as through the archival sources, tells much about cultural engagement in the New Zealand context and missionary incursions into Maori life, as well as the ways in which missionary activity was defined and limited by Maori. In the early days, New Zealand missionaries were dependent upon their Maori patrons for food as well as for protection from hostile tribes. This demonstrates one important feature of the New Zealand situation, where colonization and culture contact were not unidirectional processes.

The New Zealand case study reflects local differences as well as common patterns in the role that missions played in globalization. The archeology of Te Puna brings to life the particularities of one far-flung outpost of early nineteenth-century British colonization, but its story resonates around the globe. New Zealand missions operated as small family households rather than the larger institutions as seen in parts of North America and Australia. However, in both types of missions, domesticity is revealed as a central, unifying theme of the "civilizing mission." This focus on domesticity can be identified in archival sources as well as in items of material culture associated with the maintenance of appearances and gender roles, and the processes of transforming and clothing indigenous people.

This work provides the first archeological examination of a New Zealand mission station. It situates the case study in a global context, examining the international field of mission archeology and shedding light on the material culture of the country's first European settlers, providing a point of comparison with other outposts of British colonization. The humble, austere artifacts that constitute the material culture of the Te Puna assemblage reveal the actual processes of colonization in daily life and everyday events, as well as the processes of the mission, such as schooling, the purchase of food and domestic labor, the purchase of land and building of houses, the stitching of fabric, and ironing of garments. These practices predate, but also anticipate the better-known grand historical dramas such as the signing of the Treaty of Waitangi, glorified but also critiqued as the defining moment of the relationship between Maori and European and of colonization.

Te Puna presented an apparently forgotten, abandoned landscape when I first visited it in 2001; even the better known site of Oihi, New Zealand's first mission station located in an adjacent bay, seemed to be little acknowledged for its significance as the place where the engagement between Maori and European really began. I hope that this study will assist in bringing the sites of Te Puna and Oihi into their true place of central importance in New Zealand's historiography, and that the processes of missionization in Aotearoa/New Zealand can be located within the global field of mission archeology.

Angela Middleton
Dunedin, New Zealand

Acknowledgments

Many people have assisted in this project over the last 7 years. It has also been supported with financial assistance from a number of organizations in its initial form as my Ph.D. thesis: the Department of Anthropology and the Graduate Research Fund, University of Auckland; the Green Foundation for Polynesian Research; the New Zealand Federation of Graduate Women; the Skinner Fund of the Royal Society of New Zealand; and Walter C. Mountain Landing Ltd. Thanks to the Department of Anthropology, University of Otago, for providing me with the resources in the recent months to finalize this manuscript. I also thank the following organizations for permission to reproduce their images: the Alexander Turnbull Library, Wellington, New Zealand; the Hocken Library, Dunedin, New Zealand; the Mitchell Library of the State Library of NSW, Australia; the National Library of Australia, Canberra; and the Auckland Institute and Museum, Auckland, New Zealand. Thanks also to the New Zealand Historic Places Trust for providing access to their collections and permission to photograph them.

The research would not have been possible without two essential teams of people, mostly students from the Anthropology Department at the University of Auckland: those who helped in the initial field surveying, many of whom continued with the subsequent excavation. Thanks are also to a number of other people, especially my Ph.D. supervisors, Associate Professor Harry Allen, and Associate Professor Peter Shepherd of the Department of Anthropology, University of Auckland, for their detailed reading of many drafts along the way, astute suggestions, support, and encouragement.

Thanks are also due to Peter Cooper of Walter C. Mountain Landing Ltd for providing access to Te Puna, making possible the fieldwork as well as the archeological investigation of the mission house site; the Mountain family, Bill, Avis, and Shane, for sharing information about family lands; and Sue and Fergus Clunie, for being available at the

Kerikeri Mission House and Stone Store for ongoing consultation, access to archives, comparison of material, and their excellent knowledge of missionary culture. I would also like to acknowledge those who have *mana whenua* at Te Puna, whose ancestors occupied the land before missionary arrivals and who welcomed those first Europeans to Te Puna, the *hapu* of Ngati Tore Hina at Wharengaere, in particular Whakaaropai Rihari for sharing knowledge and for support during fieldwork in January 2002, and Hugh Rihari and Herb Rihari for consultation.

Many thanks to Susan Lawrence of La Trobe University, Victoria, Australia. Susan has read and commented on drafts of this manuscript; her expert knowledge in the field of historical archeology has been a valuable source of encouragement and support over the last few years. And to my partner Ian Smith, special thanks for many things, but in particular for codirecting the investigation of the site of Te Puna Mission House in March/April 2002, and for our ongoing engagement with and shared passion for archeology and its dissemination.

Contents

Abbreviations Used in the Text and References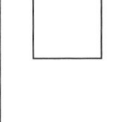

American Board of Commissioners for Foreign Missions	ABCFM
Alexander Turnbull Library	ATL
Church Missionary Society	CMS
Land Information New Zealand	LINZ
London Missionary Society	LMS
Minimum number of elements, i.e., the smallest number of anatomical elements necessary to account for all of the specimens in an assemblage	MNE
Minimum number of individuals, i.e., the smallest number of items/animals necessary to account for all the specimens in an assemblage	MNI
Number of identified specimens, i.e., the number of complete and fragmentary items identified to a category within an assemblage	NISP
New Zealand Historic Places Trust	NZHPT
New South Wales	NSW
Wesleyan Missionary Society	WMS

Section | 1

Introduction | 1

TE PUNA MISSION STATION

New Zealand's two main islands lie in the Pacific Ocean, forming the largest and southernmost landmass in the Polynesian triangle that extends to Hawaii in the north and Easter Island in the southeast. Known as Aotearoa by its Polynesian settlers, the ancestors of the Maori, who arrived in the thirteenth century, New Zealand formed the final outreach of Polynesian settlement into the Pacific (Higham and Jones 2005; Horrocks et al. 2007). Aotearoa/New Zealand was also the last outpost of the European expansion that followed some 500 years later. New Zealand was "rediscovered" by Captain James Cook in 1769, and from the 1790s became the focus of intense but ephemeral commercial exploitation for sealskins, whale oil, and timber. Most of this was conducted from or via New South Wales, Australia, some 1,500km across the Tasman Sea, where the British convict settlement was established in 1788. The first missionaries to New Zealand followed firmly on the heels of sealers and whalers. Formal British annexation did not take place until February 1840.

This research examines the nature of New Zealand's earliest mission stations within the wider context of such missions in other parts of the globe. In 1814 the first European settlers arrived in northern New Zealand, three "mechanic" missionaries along with their families and a small number of tradesmen, mostly "ticket of leave" convicts from Port Jackson (Sydney), New South Wales. John and Hannah King, William and Dinah Hall, and Thomas and Jane Kendall were members of the Church Missionary Society (CMS) mission station established by Samuel Marsden at Oihi (Figure 1.1), in the Bay of Islands under the auspices of a powerful local chief.

Sixteen years later, in 1832, the Oihi mission closed and the last two missionaries living there moved to houses they had built at the

A. Middleton, *Te Puna: A New Zealand Mission Station*,
DOI:10.1007/978-0-387-77622-4, © Springer Science+Business Media, LLC 2008

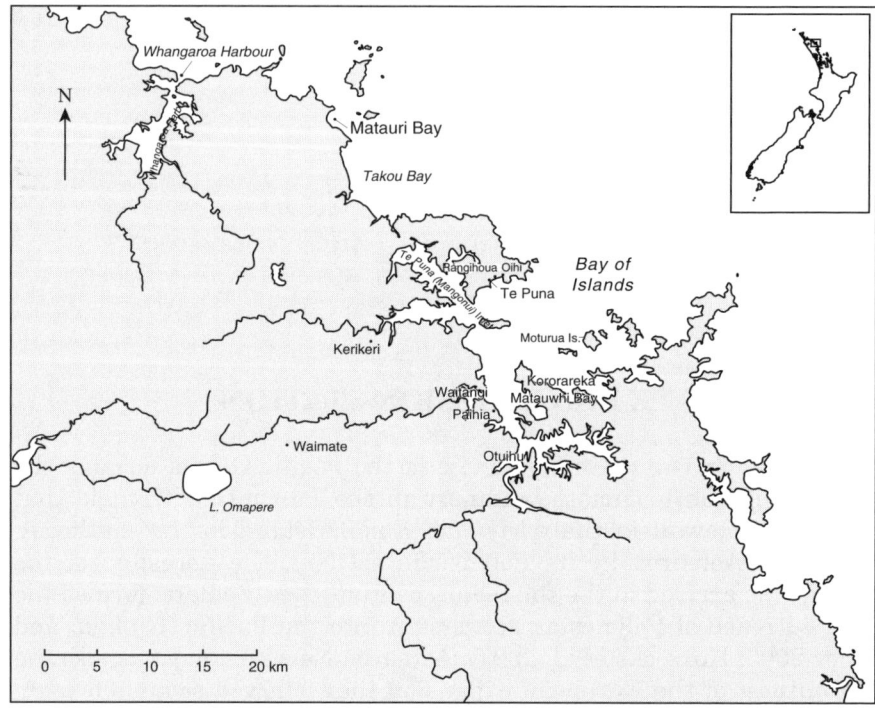

Figure 1.1. Location map

neighboring station of Te Puna. Te Puna itself was abandoned by about the early 1870s.

This study places the missionary household and economy at its center. It examines the archeology and domestic economy of the Te Puna mission household and looks back toward the archeology of the Oihi mission, shedding light on the material culture and economy of the first permanent European settlement in the country. Members of the household take their place as individual actors, considering the dynamics of gender, age, ethnicity, and class within the broader events of colonization. This contributes to an understanding of the details and particular circumstances of early New Zealand missions and to a New Zealand household and mission archeology. Deetz (1982) has pointed out that the household is effectively a microcosm of the culture of which it formed a part, and that it is able to inform us about that culture (Allison 1999a,b; Barile and Brandon 2004; Netting et al. 1984; Wilk and Rathje 1982). The archeology of the King household has the potential to inform about the larger society to which it belonged, that is the culture of the CMS, the culture of the settler society, and the archeology of contact. Archeological investigations of the household reflect functions of the most commonplace sort that can be projected beyond the household to the broader society. At the same time changes in the household and family over time reflect changes in the broader society. The archeology of the Te Puna mission house, integrated with historical documents, provides a detailed domestic context for wider events and changes in early nineteenth century New Zealand.

My approach uses the methods and theories of historical archeology (Deetz 1977, 1988, 1993; Funari et al. 1999; Noel Hume 1969, 2001; Orser 1996; Schuyler 1978, 1988, 1999), combining archeological investigation and the use of historical documents to produce a detailed picture of the domestic economy and material culture of an isolated rural household in the Bay of Islands in the first half of the nineteenth century. At the same time, this household was closely connected in a globalizing process with the economy of the CMS in both New Zealand and Australia, and ultimately in Britain. The synthesis of a number of sources – archeology, archives, printed material, and collections of material culture – brings archeology and history together to reconstruct the material culture of first European settlement in New Zealand, and European impact on the indigenous landscape. It may be considered an outcome of Orser's (1996: 183) refrain to "dig locally, think globally," or Beaudry's (2003: 294) call to produce "historicized studies of local contexts" that may lead to more subtle understanding of the plurality of colonizing processes.

A related question concerns the role of the CMS in the process of the annexation and colonization of New Zealand. Globally, missionaries have been identified with the advance of western colonization of indigenous worlds (Comaroff and Comaroff 1986, 1991, 1992; Graham 1998; Walker 1990). What were the specifics of this process in New Zealand? Samuel Marsden, chaplain to the British penal settlement of New South Wales in Australia, established the New Zealand mission on the premise that civilization should precede Christianity, that commerce should precede conversion through a "spirit of trade" (Elder 1932; Nicholas 1817: 18). According to Axtell (1982) and others (for example, Comaroff and Comaroff 2000b; Gould 2005; Marsden 2003) this was a wide spread belief in the colonial world. Marsden clearly saw Christianity as among the otherwise unacceptable ideas that might be carried along with the desire for material goods. He planned to introduce the ideas of Christianity to Maori, paving the way

> by creating artificial wants to which they had never before been accustomed, and which he knew must act as the strongest excitement to the exercise of their ingenuity. (Nicholas 1817: 17)

Binney (1969: 152) considered trade the "'Trojan horse' which carried...the otherwise unacceptable ideas into the Maori camp." I consider trade the "Trojan Horse" of colonization.

The focus of this book is the archeology, material culture, and economy of a CMS mission station in what was a remote "outpost of empire" in early to mid nineteenth century New Zealand, and the relationship between the mission and Maori. As such, it is not specifically concerned with the success or failure of the New Zealand CMS missions. The discussion below establishes a context for the New Zealand situation within the broader framework of late eighteenth and early nineteenth century mission activity in other parts of the new world, including the Pacific, Australia, North America, and South Africa.

THE CHURCH MISSIONARY SOCIETY

Both the London Missionary Society (LMS) and the Church Missionary Society were established in the 1790s, growing out of the Evangelical Revival that took place in Europe and North America, where it was associated with the Second Great Awakening, in the second half of the eighteenth century (Garrett 1982; Glen 1992; Stock 1899). While the Evangelical Revival was associated with figures like John Wesley, it also occurred within the bounds of the Anglican Church of England, that is to say, there were both Wesleyan and Anglican revivalists, the Wesleyans subsequently being identified with the Methodist denomination. Revivalism infiltrated many areas of life in Britain at this time, and pervaded British thinking throughout the first half of the nineteenth century (Smith 1985; Stock 1899). Some members of the East India Company were revivalists. William Wilberforce, a member of the British Parliament and fervent antislavery campaigner, was a vital member of the revivalist "sect" who corresponded with Samuel Marsden in Port Jackson and advised him about his plans within the CMS. Wilberforce was responsible for a chaplain, Samuel Marsden's predecessor, being sent with the First Fleet to Botany Bay. Other powerful revivalists include men such as Zachary Macauley, father of the historian. The premise of these revivalist societies was that the command of Christ was to evangelize the world, and they grew out of similar existing societies founded in the seventeenth century to promote Christianity in the New World of North America (Stock 1899).

Within the CMS women were perceived as playing a particular role. While mission work was considered the realm of the male, women were essential to the cause. In the early nineteenth century women held an idealized position, their domestic role accentuated within evangelical Christianity and the British middle class (Davidoff and Hall 1991; Johnston 2003). Changes brought about by the industrial revolution placed women within the home while men became breadwinners outside it; female "piety, purity, submissiveness, and domesticity" was emphasized in the "cult of true womanhood" or the "cult of domesticity" (Grimshaw 1989a: 22, 1989b; McClintock 1995; Langmore 1989b). Evangelical Christians believed that woman "had been created for man" and that the proper place for a woman was the home, "the first and chief scene of their mission" (Davidoff and Hall 1991: 115). The same ideas were seen at work in North American evangelism, for example at Five Points missions in New York city in the mid nineteenth century (Fitts 2001). The home was seen as the "nursery of virtue" where women could exert their moral influence not only over men but also over the whole family, including, in the nineteenth century, servants and associated household members. At the same time, while attendance at public meetings and similar events was unacceptable, women were perceived as having a limited role in the public sphere, in the area of social reform and conversion to Christianity, the one public field from which they were not excluded (Murray 2000). The presence of women was essential for the evangelizing, civilizing mission; "without them it was impossible to model the Christian monogamous family life that it was hoped could bring about a transformation of societies not yet influenced by the gospel" (Murray 2000: 69). The "family" was seen as a metaphor that extended into the mission station and beyond into the "family of empire" (Johnston 2003).

Men were encouraged, and expected, to marry before moving into the mission field in order to demonstrate this model of domesticity and to save themselves from the perils of indigenous women (Murray 2000; Gunson 1978; Johnston 2003; Middleton 2007a). The role of domesticity was central to the evangelizing mission, and to British imperialism; according to McClintock (1995: 35) the mission station became

> A threshold institution for transforming domesticity rooted in European gender and class roles into domesticity as controlling a colonized people. Through the rituals of domesticity, increasingly global and more often than not violent, animals, women and colonized peoples were wrested from their putatively "natural" yet, ironically, "unreasonable" state of "savagery" and inducted through the domestic progress narrative into a hierarchical relation to white men.

In 1792 evangelizing missionary voyages began with the first expedition to India. In 1795 Dr Haweis (after whom the ill-fated Tahitian missionary ship was later named) and others formed the nondenominational

LMS, and the following year the ship *Duff* sailed for the Pacific, reaching Tahiti in March 1797. At the same time, concern for similar objectives within the established Church of England, which accepted "Episcopacy and Liturgical worship" (Stock 1899: 64), that is, the government of the church by bishops and the use of "The Book of Common Prayer," led to the founding of the CMS for Africa and the East in 1799. The full title demonstrated the society's geographical areas of concern, and it was associated with the names of its founders, who also served as secretaries, such as John Venn, Basil Woodd, and Josiah Pratt. Women were not part of the CMS organization as it was considered quite improper for women to attend any public meetings, but at the same time attendance at the society's sermons was expected. The Wesleyan Missionary Society (WMS) was founded in 1818 (Langmore 1989a). There was no competition or schism between the LMS, the CMS, and the WMS; the societies co-operated and in the Pacific their efforts were co-ordinated by Samuel Marsden (Elder 1932; Garrett 1982; Marsden 1857; Stock 1899, 1913). This was reflected in the New Zealand situation where the CMS and Wesleyan missionaries worked together during the first decades of their missions. Conflict and competition over territory in New Zealand only developed toward the middle of the nineteenth century, particularly following the arrival of the high-church Bishop Selwyn (Owens 1974; Rogers 1961; Stock 1899, 1913; Williment 1985). Collectively, the revivalist societies were set up to counteract church hierarchy and selected humble, practical men to go into the mission field, who would be able to cope with an unknown environment.

The CMS advocated undertakings on a small scale, viewing perhaps with skepticism the early, virtual collapse of the LMS's Tahiti mission (Stock 1899), and its first ventures were into the mission field of Africa. The society looked for lay missionaries as well as men who were (or could become) ordained ministers, and in 1808 engaged two "Christian artizans...to go to New Zealand as pioneers of industry and civilization, though with the object, through these, of introducing the Gospel" (Stock 1899: 89). These were two single men, William Hall, a joiner and carpenter, and John King, a shoemaker.

As Stock (1899: 205) points out, at this time

> The Society was then still in its infancy. It had sent out exactly five missionaries, and these to a Mission-field comparatively near ... Now they were asked to send men to the Antipodes, to a land whence it would take twelve months to get an answer to a letter, to a race of warlike barbarians among whom no Europeans had yet settled.

Stock's language locates the mission within the framework of the Great Chain of Being where civilization was equated with Christianity and barbarism with a lower form of society (Stocking 1987). This framing of indigenous people as barbarians or savages replaced the earlier, late eighteenth century vision of the same people, portrayed in the voyages of Cook and other explorers of the age as the "noble savage" (Smith 1985; Harris 1990). This "noble savage" was now transformed into the "poor benighted Heathen." At the same time, evangelicals considered that within Britain there was "an uncivilized heathen land" of laboring poor (Thorne 1999). In New Zealand, Bay of Islands missionaries held similar attitudes toward seamen and some early European settlers, considering them in need of evangelizing as much as Maori. Missionaries held to popular beliefs of the time of the progression of societies from savagery to civilization, but there was uncertainty about whether savagery may also have been the result of degeneration from higher social stages (Smith 1985; Stocking 1987). Although members of the CMS and other societies considered the established church and state hierarchy as corrupt, they still held to a moral hierarchy in which they saw themselves (and the "civilized" Christian) above "barbarians" and "savages." In New Zealand, CMS missionaries were not egalitarian and thought themselves above both Maori (whom they had come for the specific purpose of "civilizing") and other Europeans such as sailors and "dissolute" settlers. One missionary wife, Marianne Williams, later articulated these ideas, noting that Samuel Marsden concurred:

> At present this noble though cannibal race of men, are fast bound in the cruel chains of Satan: & what can be a nobler ambition than to enlist beneath the banner of the King of kings, & in his strength to rescue them from their deadly foe? Often had I in the course of the day, pictured in idea our ancestors at the time of the conquest – Mr. Marsden had the same ideas, & many a noble Caractacus might we fancy we beheld as such these warlike, yet kindly looking savages." (Williams n.d.a)

Samuel Marsden (Figure 2.1) was appointed chaplain to the penal colony of New South Wales in 1794 after the first chaplain returned to Britain (Yarwood 1996). While he worked with the Tahitian mission, he is much better known for his long involvement with the CMS mission in New Zealand, which was established through his initiative. Marsden never lived in New Zealand, but visited seven times, and maintained a strong control of the Bay of Islands missions from his home in Parramatta (New South Wales) through his voluminous correspondence. From the beginning, his relationships with missionaries there were fraught with conflict and disagreement. This was due partly to his unrealistic expectations of the missionaries, in particular that they should be self-supporting. They were living in a strange land in situations that made unexpected demands of them, conditions that Marsden only experienced himself during brief visits to the mission. At times, his correspondence depicts him as an authoritarian bully, evocative of his reputation in New South Wales as the "flogging parson" (Hughes 1987).

The New Zealand mission, founded in 1814, can be contextualized in the framework of similar ventures into the Pacific of the same era in Tahiti and Hawaii. Connections were maintained between different stations, such as Tonga, Tahiti, and New Zealand with movement of missionaries between these locations and Port Jackson. Samuel Marsden maintained trading interests between these places, as well as a supervisory role, and came in for criticism for this (Elder 1932; Garrett 1982; Gunson 1978; Marsden 1857). The efforts of Catholic missions in the Pacific were also co-ordinated from strategic locations, but this occurred at a later time in the nineteenth century than the Protestant missions.

The remainder of this chapter considers mission archeology as a subdiscipline of historical archeology. I discuss the characteristics of two dramatically different types of mission stations, one that I have termed the "household mission" and the other the "institutional mission." It will be shown that these two types were found in different geographical locations, and that the institutional missions shared characteristics with similar institutions of reform. The following review considers limited geographical regions: the east and west coasts of the United States are followed by an examination of South Africa, Australia, and the Pacific. Other large regions such as Canada, China, and the complex history of Indian missions are not included. Due to the lack of archeological research, or its existence only within the "gray" unpublished literature, the section on the Pacific is limited to a review of the historical literature and a discussion of place.

"MISSION STATIONS": A DEFINITION

What constitutes a mission station? The Oxford dictionary defines a "mission" as a "body sent by religious community to propagate its faith." The question of definition is raised here as the Australian archeological and anthropological literature extends the term to include historical government organizations and institutions that were not religious or evangelizing in nature, Wybalenna being a particular example of this (Birmingham 1992; Harris 1990). Harris provides some explanation for the inclusion of government reserves and institutions as missions:

> Because for a century the only institutions for Aborigines were missions staffed by missionaries, the labels 'mission' and 'missionary' entered

Aboriginal vocabulary as designations for any kind of institution and those who supervised them, including the secular successors to missions and all government reserves. 'It was', said Jimmie Barker, 'a type of Aboriginal slang.' (Harris 1990: 583)

In her review of North American mission archeology, Graham (1998) notes that "the colonizing process, the spread of the Christian faith, and the enculturation of the Indians are common to all missionizing efforts," leading her to extend her definition to include not only a mission structure that is administered by a religious organization, but also, in a similar manner to Harris, to

communities with only visita [visiting] churches; to communities with limited resources and permeable boundaries; to the full range of Indian settlements, both Christian and non-Christian, and to colonial communities as well. (Graham 1998: 26)

Graham's definition gives some idea of the range and diversity of missions and research into this area in North America. In New Zealand, where the first mission was a private initiative without the involvement of the New South Wales government, there was not the geographical range of North America, nor did it incorporate the nonreligious government institutions included by Harris. I suggest that in New Zealand, Snow's (1967: 59) tighter definition applies:

A mission is an ecclesiastical unit of area of sufficient size, within which all activities (such as construction, farming, handicrafts, herding, recreation, etc) are administered by a ministry commissioned by, and dependent upon, a larger religious organization for direction or financial support.

MISSIONIZATION AND MISSION ARCHEOLOGY

The study of missions has been linked with the field of historical archeology in North America since the early years of the discipline, where those connected with the development of historical archeology in the United States were also associated with studies of North American missions (Deagan 1983, 1993). In the first volume of the journal *Historical Archaeology* Snow (1967: 58) highlighted the role of "mission site archaeology" in the examination of culture contact and the two-way process of acculturation.

Missions, the early crucibles where European and indigenous peoples encountered each other, provide a fertile ground for exploring these issues. Christianity itself was also transformed in this process.

"Mission archaeology" is a term devised by Graham (1998: 25):

> to focus attention on an archaeology of mission sites, and thereby on the
> light that can be shed on the process of the Christianization of the Americas
> by examining the material culture of missions.

Although not recognized as a subfield of anthropology, mission archeology has been undertaken for many decades in North America, prior
even to the seminal work of Deetz (1978) in the 1960s. The term is
derived perhaps from Snow's (1967, above) short discussion of "mission
sites archaeology." This term is also appropriate for the archeological
research undertaken at Te Puna, where the investigation is the first in
the field of "mission archeology" in New Zealand.

North America

Within North America there was a broad variation in missions types,
although the discussion here is limited to the Spanish Borderlands and
New England, an area consisting of a number of different settler colonies
in the seventeenth century (Beaudry 2006). While Catholicism arrived
with the earliest expeditions into La Florida in the sixteenth century,
further north on the Atlantic coast seventeenth century Puritan arrivals from Britain brought religious fervor with them and established
Protestant missions to the indigenous population. Gould (2005: 20) considers the history of evangelicalism in North America as "but one chapter in a larger story of British missions and missionary enterprise."

The Great Awakening in the American colonies of the 1740s and
1750s grew out of earlier evangelicalism and the establishment of
British societies such as the Anglican Society for the Propagation of
the Gospel in Foreign Parts (SPG, founded 1701) and the Society for
Promoting Christian Knowledge (SPCK, founded 1698), both these societies sending missionaries to New England. Despite the seventeenth
century phenomenon of John Eliot's southern New England "praying
towns" (Axtell 1982; Beaudry 2006; Mandell 1996; Silverman 2003;
http://www.fiskecenter.umb.edu/Magunco%20Hill.htm), Puritan missionary efforts were often met with obstacles, and success was slow,
although Thomas Mayhew Jnr, along with other evangelicals, success-
fully converted much of the Indian population of Martha's Vineyard and
Nantucket by the late seventeenth century (Salisbury 1992; Silverman
2003). During the eighteenth century preachers such as George Whitefield
and David Brainerd began the "itinerant evangelism" (equivalent perhaps to a traveling preacher) subsequently used by missionaries from the
later British evangelical societies, including the CMS in New Zealand,
and associated largely with the "household mission." Missionary

husband, wife, and family provided "cultural models" (Marsden 2003: 175) of the civilized mode of living to the indigenous population, demonstrated in the likes of Jonathan and Sarah Edwards at Northampton and John and Abigail Sergeant at Stockbridge, Massachusetts, where the mission house (built 1739) is still standing. The "Second Great Awakening" of the eighteenth century followed developing alongside the Evangelical Revival and the establishment of the evangelical missionary societies of the late eighteenth and early nineteenth centuries.

Archeological investigations into the site of one of John Eliot's Praying Towns at Magunco Hill, Massachusetts (the town also known as Magunkaquag, along with other names) have demonstrated "the continuing power of native identity in terms of technology and religion" through the maintenance of cultural practices alongside the presence of European manufactured goods (http://www.fiskecenter.umb.edu/ Magunco%20Hill.htm). As in the practice of "itinerant evangelism," this was a site that John Eliot and fellow missionary Daniel Gookin made occasional visits to, but was not a missionary residence.

As in other places, archeologists, historians, and ethnohistorians (for example, see Bragdon 1988, 1996a,b; Silverman 2003; Simmons 1979, 1986; Rubertone 2001) have found a rich source in missionary accounts of indigenous peoples in New England, often produced in order to describe the cultural traits they hoped most fervently to change and destroy. Rubertone's (2001) work on Roger Williams documents this controversial, significant historical figure, now considered the founder of Providence, Rhode Island, and his relationship with the local Narragansett. Sent into exile from Massachusetts to Rhode Island for his oppositional political and religious views, Williams was a somewhat ambivalent missionary figure, reluctant to undertake what may have been merely superficial conversions of Indians into a "less-than-pure Christian church" (Rubertone 2001: 92). Williams studied the Narragansett language in order to improve his ability to communicate with this people about religious matters and his "A Key into the Language of America" has served Rubertone as a useful tool to develop her interpretation of Narragansett graves at North Kingstown, Rhode Island. As with investigations at Magunco Hill, Rubertone's work sheds light on the archeology of an Indian population associated with missionization, concerned with the outcome of cultural engagement between Narragansett and the English. While this leads Rubertone to an interpretation of Narragansett lives and an archeology of the "processes of cultural entanglement" (Silliman 2005: 62), it does not provide an archeology of Williams' missionary work, as appears to be the case with many New England Protestant or Puritan missions. An explanation for this may lie in the less visible structure of Protestant missions, dependent as some were on the "itinerant" missionary.

The monumental architecture of Catholic missions of the Spanish borderlands appears more accessible and dominant in the literature of North American mission archeology. Examination of Spanish border-lands missions on both the east and west coasts of the United States demonstrates that these functioned as institutional missions in the manner of the "total institution" described by Goffman (1962; see also De Cunzo 2006). These Catholic missions were generally established as the controlling arm of Spanish colonization, with the aim of pacifying and transforming indigenous peoples into an "Hispanicized" peasant class of laborers (Lightfoot 2005: 59; Sandos 2004; Silliman 2004). Catholic missionaries accompanied the earliest Spanish expeditions into La Florida in the sixteenth century. In the same century Jesuits established missions in this area, followed by Franciscans a century later (Thomas 1990: 369; McEwan 1993; Graham 1998). It was more than two centuries afterward before the first missions were established on the West Coast in California in 1769. Christianity itself was also altered in different ways in its various regional interactions with the New World. As Graham (1998: 26) notes, "local conditions are critical in explaining the diversity of mission encounters." Graham's review of North American mission archeology examines literature from four areas of the Spanish Borderlands, as well as the Maya lowlands. Of these areas, La Florida on the East Coast, broadly equivalent to present-day Florida and Georgia has been the most extensively researched (Deagan 1983, 1993; Graham 1998; McEwan 1993; Saunders 1998; Thomas 1990, 1991).

While once again there was regional variation, in all areas mission buildings consisted of complexes, often with a central courtyard and usually including a church, convent or friary, kitchen, and other sleeping quarters. Churches were likely to have under-floor burials, with native inhabitants buried according to Spanish custom (Larsen 1993; McEwan 1993; Thomas 1993). In La Florida, missions encapsulated entire settlements,

> Defining a space in which tribal economies were reorganized, new crops and European methods of cultivation were introduced, and scattered native American groups were nucleated ('reduced') into new settlements where instruction included music, reading and writing. (Thomas 1990: 381)

Such studies often have an architectural focus due to the imposing monumental forms of mission complexes (Saunders 1993; Lightfoot 2005). Preservation and restoration occur to present a "romantic historical past," with archeology used to recover information to assist restoration (Graham 1998: 43; Deetz 1978), but reconstruction is not always accurate, as archeology can demonstrate (Trigger 1987). Reconstruction also takes place for the benefit and development of the tourist industry. The missions of La Florida followed the Hispanic plan, "a direct attempt to transplant a 'civilized' lifeway upon a wilderness highly 'frontier' in character" (Thomas 1990: 381), although none of this mission architecture remains standing now.

Within this North American monumental architecture, and inside the mission system, Native Americans were sometimes confined in a manner similar to slavery (Saunders 1993, 1998). Examination of skeletal remains from La Florida mission sites demonstrates that Native Americans inhabiting missions during the sixteenth and seventeenth centuries "experienced an overall decline in the quality of life and health status generally" (Larsen 1993: 347). Native labor was indispensable for the production of food, building construction and other projects, leading to severe labor demands on mission inhabitants. These demands are revealed in their effects on skeletal remains, with osteoarthritis and increased mechanical demands shown.

In North America, research programs and archeological investigations have taken place over a long period of time. Excavations at La Purisima, a Franciscan frontier mission in California, were first undertaken in the 1930s, and continued sporadically until a further program begun in 1962 by Deetz (1978). On the southeastern coast, efforts to relocate Spanish missions also began in the 1930s (Thomas 1993; Graham 1998).

Missions also provide an important focus for culture contact studies, as Snow had identified in 1967, given the seminal role they played in the interaction between European and indigenous peoples (Axtell 1982; Deagan 1983, 1993; Graham 1998; Larson et al. 1994; Lightfoot 2005, 2006; McEwan 1993; Saunders 1996, 1998; Silliman 2001; Thomas 1991; Trigger 1985). Deetz (1978: 160) points out that the work at La Purisima provided insight into the "acculturative process" through missionization among the Chumash Indians. On the other side of the continent, Deagan's (1983, 1993: 87) examination of the Spanish township of St. Augustine (not itself a mission) and the mission frontier highlighted a process of mutual accommodation between Indians and friars where the Spanish Franciscan missions "have long been recognized as the most important Spanish institution for effecting change in seventeenth-century southeastern Indian cultures."

On the west coast of the continent, the northern-most arm of Spanish colonization reached up the Californian coast in a chain of 21 Franciscan missions stretching from San Diego to San Francisco, the first of these built in 1769 (Deetz 1978; Lightfoot 2005, 2006), the same year when James Cook became the first European to explore the New Zealand coastline. As in Australia and on the East Coast of the

United States, these missions formed an arm of colonial control, with Spain relying on the padres to manage the transformation of the indigenous Indians from "coastal hunter–gatherer peoples into a peasant class of neophyte Catholics" (Lightfoot 2005: 3; Sandos 2004; Silliman 2004). Californian missions, developed as agricultural centers, were constructed on a similar plan to those of La Florida, with a central quadrangle or plaza close to an adobe church, and with a *convento* or priests' residence, dormitories or houses for neophytes, soldiers' residences, store rooms, and kitchens. Designed to be self-sufficient, from 500 to 1,200 neophytes (or converts) were housed and worked in these institutions, their lives firmly regimented and scrutinized by the padres, mission guards, and Indian assistants. The padres preferred to begin the indoctrination of children at an early age, separating them from their parents and wider family members. From the age of about seven, young girls moved into dormitories, often locked in at night, where they remained until marriage. According to Lightfoot (2006: 60), in many ways these missions resembled penal institutions, where "every aspect of the daily lives of the neophytes came under the controlling scrutiny of the padres." Severe punishment such as the use of solitary confinement, whippings, stocks and leg chains followed infringement of any of the stringent rules or work code. The six soldiers at each mission enforced regulations and tracked down any Indian deserters. Armed resistance to missionization was taken up with many refugees fleeing into the Californian interior.

For the Spanish, the desired outcome was a pacified Indian population able to function as peasant laborers, the women trained to carry out sewing and other suitable domestic tasks. By 1834 when the Franciscan missions were secularized, the gathering of all Indians into mission settlements was almost complete (Graham 1998: 45). Secularization was followed by the proliferation of private land grants, and a rising number of "ranchos", as well as the expansion of towns. Private land owners now had available the pacified labor force they required (Silliman 2004; Graham 1998).

Alongside this approach the place of indigenous women as "cultural mediators" or "negotiators of change" between indigenous and colonial peoples can play an important role (Sleeper-Smith 2000: 423, 2001). Deagan (1983, 1996: 149), in her examination of early Spanish settlements in Haiti and the Dominican Republic, as well as St. Augustine, notes that non-European traits were incorporated into the archeological record of Spanish colonial households in traditionally female areas such as "kitchen activities, diet, and household management" through the documented "domestic accommodations" of Spanish men and Indian women, while Indian men remain virtually invisible in the archeological record. Such encounters and transformations lead to new hybridized societies.

South Africa

The colonial history of South Africa is also a rich source for historical archeology (Hall 1993, 1994, 2000; Schrire 1988, 1992, 1995; Winer 1994, 2001; Winer and Deetz 1990), and provides some scope for archeological comparison with New Zealand, although this question has not yet been explored in any depth (see for example Klose and Malan 2000; Malan and Klose 2003). Historical archeology in South Africa has, to date, focused on sites such as the VOC (Dutch East India Company) fortifications (Schrire 1988, 1992), the archeology of slavery, and the urban archeology of Cape Town (Mitchell 2002a).

South Africa's mission history also has the potential for comparison with other areas of British evangelical influence, such as New Zealand, but it appears that little examination of mission archeology has taken place (Mitchell 2002a; Hall 1993), although Africa itself formed the focus of early CMS efforts, as the society's full title, the CMS for Africa and the East, demonstrated. The first LMS missionary arrived in Capetown in 1799, many following after him (De Gruchy 2000). Web searches suggest that the region has a complex mission history with the WMS and Moravians also establishing missions (see also Porter 1999). Mitchell's (2002b) review of South African archeology has no mention of any mission archeology but does discuss the Methodist settlement of Salem, the subject of Winer's (1994, 2001; Winer and Deetz 1990) research. Scott and Deetz (1990) followed this with further examination of the "creation of a distinctively British South African frontier culture," similar to that of colonial North America (Mitchell 2002a: 395). Brink (2004: 98) notes that Dutch colonists did not carry out any official mission work at the Cape, while the VOC was openly opposed to German Moravian missionaries.

Hall's (1993: 183) earlier review of the archeology of colonial settlement is broken into four themes, the archeology of impact, the archeology of the underclass, of the mind, and of the text. He considers missions as part of the "frontier," the "archeology of impact," and mentions two mission sites. The source for one of these is a brief article in *Digging Stick* (the newsletter of the South African Archeological Society) about Genadendal, South Africa's first mission station, established by Moravians in 1792, although an earlier missionary worked on the site for 6 years from 1738 (Brink 2004: 108; Humphreys 1989;

http://www.museums.org.za/genadendal/). The *Digging Stick* article is
not about the mission itself, but is more concerned with the Khoikhoi
long-term occupation of the area prior to the mission. The second mission site mentioned is Farmerfield, a Wesleyan farm station in the
eastern Cape, the results of recent excavations reported in a then-
unpublished paper (Hall 1993).

Jeppson's (2005: 1) work on the Farmerfield mission station is
concerned with "how one category of Industrial Age, European goods
– ceramics – becomes involved in the construction, reproduction, and
transformation of shared cultural beliefs and values during a time of
culture contact and change." Ceramics from the mission formed only
one component of assemblages examined from several different sites.
The mission was established to provide relief for landless indigenes and
former slaves, offering perhaps an alternative to a "colonial dominated
(structured) existence" (Jeppson 2005: 153). While Jeppson provides
some basic information about the mission it was not the focus of her
research, and the details of its organization are not given. The number
of residents was large, growing from 50 families in 1840 to about 500
residents in 1850, at least 150 of whom were converts. Inhabitants lived
in three hamlets located around a church and house of the catechist,
agricultural lands and pasture, with the population divided "on the
basis of perceived cultural and language differences" (Jeppson 2005:
11). Residents paid rent for land to build a house and graze animals,
and evidently became successful farmers who produced surplus crops
and traded for other goods. By the turn of the nineteenth century mission residents were traveling to Grahamstown to work, forming a labor
supply for local industry. Around the same time, much of the original
mission land was sold and remaining residents relocated closer to the
church. The mission continued to operate into the middle of the twentieth century until removal was forced by the South African government's land acts, when the remaining land was sold as private farms.
The church building still stands.

While there is little evidence of archeological research into South
African missions, other works discuss the intertwining of state policy and missionary efforts in the "civilizing mission" (Comaroff and
Commaroff 1992: 246, 2000b; McClendon 2004). The ethnohistorical
works of Comaroff and Comaroff (1986, 1991, 1992, 2000a,b) have
long been recognized and discussed in the field of mission studies
and anthropology. Comaroff and Comaroff have examined the role of
the evangelist London Missionary Society and Wesleyan Methodist
Missionary Society in South Africa. They consider that the "colonization of consciousness and consciousness of colonization begins
with the entry of evangelical Christianity onto the historical land-

scape" (Comaroff and Comaroff 1992: 236). Aspects of the Comaroffs' argument about the South African mission experience, where the reconstruction of the everyday world of the indigenous people was a primary intention, resonate with the aims and outcomes of the CMS in New Zealand.

Australia

Mission archeology has also been undertaken in Australia over the past four decades, but before reviewing this work it is useful to discuss the contextual history of Australian missions.

Although Britain established the convict colony of New South Wales in 1788, it seems that there was no missionary activity until the second decade of the nineteenth century. This can perhaps be explained by the fact that the settlement of Port Jackson struggled with famine, lack of supplies, and its huge distance from Britain in the first decades of its existence. It was not until 1825 that Marsden established a branch of the CMS in Sydney (Harris 1990). As Harris (1990: 42) notes, "the missionary movement virtually ignored Australia." Another factor in this may have been that the important evangelical movements, the CMS, the LMS, and the WMS, did not exist at the time the settlement of Port Jackson was founded.

There were missionaries to the Aboriginals prior to 1825. The efforts of Samuel Leigh (who established the first Wesleyan mission in New Zealand in 1822) led to the arrival of a Wesleyan missionary, William Walker, in Port Jackson 1821. His attempts to establish a mission north-west of Sydney were unsuccessful because of disputes with Samuel Marsden. According to Harris (1990: 51) "Marsden was negative about all efforts to assist Aboriginal people and doubly negative about efforts that he did not control," an attitude that Johnston (2003: 169) confirms.

Educational and similar institutions such as reservations are included in Australian historical, archeological and anthropological contexts as missions, although these did not function as Christian missions and were not founded on this basis. Australian institutions began with the Parramatta Native Institution, established in 1814 to educate Aboriginal children. By 1820 this had languished, but was replaced in 1822 with a similar institution at nearby Black Town (Harris 1990; Lydon 2005a). CMS missionaries George and Martha Clarke spent nearly 2 years working with Aboriginals at this Native Institution (from October 1822 to March 1824) before taking up their journey to the Bay of Islands, where they remained for the rest of their lives.

William Hall, among the first band of arrivals to the Bay of Islands in 1814, left New Zealand in 1825, unable to withstand "the rigors of another New Zealand winter" due to his poor health and "debilitated condition" (chronic asthma; Brook and Kohen 1991: 203). Hall then acted as supervisor of the Native Institution, from late 1826 until it finally closed in 1829. Several Maori children were counted among the total of around 14 living in the Black Town Native Institution (Brook and Kohen 1991).

These two institutions apparently marked the start of the practice of forcibly removing Aboriginal children from their parents to be raised within European establishments, precipitating Aboriginal fear of child removal and marking the beginnings of the "stolen generations" phenomena. Children were also taken into homes as "domestic experiments," to be raised as Europeans, training them in domestic tasks in order to work as servants in the expectation of "civilizing" them (Lydon 2005a: 204; Johnston 2003). Similar organizations followed, based on policies of assimilation and protection, such as Wybalenna on Flinders Island where George Robinson took the last of the Tasmanian Aboriginals in 1830 (Birmingham 1992; Harris 1990).

The New South Wales mission of Wellington was first established as a convict agricultural station in 1823. This closed in 1830 and in 1832 the CMS took over the station and its buildings, establishing a mission to the Wiradjuri people where their children were housed in dormitories while the rest of the population continued a nomadic existence, although food was provisioned from the mission. Indigenous populations in the area were subject to the usual settler depredations. Aboriginal women were abducted and numbers reduced by settler aggression. These events provoked outrage and concern from the British government and the CMS in Britain. The CMS considered that the Aboriginal population was likely to become extinct, mirroring concerns elsewhere in the Pacific and New Zealand that saw indigenous peoples as a "dying race." By 1844, after bitter internal divisions and conflict, the clergy had moved on to different locations and the mission closed, subsequently subsumed into the town of Wellington (http://www. nationalparks.nsw.gov.au/PDFs/CMPdraft_MayngguGanaiHS.pdf).

In the Australian colony of Victoria, Grimshaw and Nelson's (2001) analysis of the "civilizing mission" of evangelicals supports the argument for Australian missions as "total institutions" (Goffman 1962; Sutton 2003). In this state as elsewhere in Australia, the congruence of missionary goals and state agendas led to a situation where missions appeared to run almost as prisons, where "missionaries and managers appeared not to be their [inmates'] protagonists but their jailers. Religious and secular staff had acquired a capacity for surveillance, coercion and punishment...few outside Australia ever realized," where a "travesty of Christian humanitarianism" was demonstrated (Grimshaw and Nelson 2001: 297). Lydon (2005b: 29) found the same situation in Victoria's Moravian evangelical missions, where the religious agenda was gradually taken over by the secular interests of the colonial administration, resulting in an increasingly repressive regime. Missions and government reserves were nearly indistinguishable; Aboriginal lives in such stations were regulated by legislation that had deprived them of land and controlled their family lives, even to the point of once again forcing the removal of children. At the same time, missions could provide a sanctuary for Aboriginals faced with a hostile settler population avid for Aboriginal land.

In such institutions the contrast between the situation in Australia and New Zealand is demonstrated. In New Zealand, in the early days of the missions, missionaries were effectively captives of their indigenous patrons, while in Australia this was reversed, with the indigenous people virtually imprisoned within missions and government institutions like Wybalenna and Poonindie, established in South Australia in 1850 as a "native training institution" (Harris 1990).

Mission Archeology in Australia

While archeological research of Australian mission stations appears limited, given the scale and number of mission settlements (Harris 1990), investigations have been carried out with particular research questions in view.

Mission archeology in Australia began with Birmingham's (1992) seminal work on the Wybalenna Station, the original fieldwork undertaken between 1969 and 1971, the same decade as Deetz was working at La Purisima mission in North America. While Wybalenna was not a mission station it is regarded as such, demonstrating the diverse range of institutions included in the Australian mission literature. This was the place where George Augustus Robinson advised the British Government to settle the surviving Tasmanian Aboriginals, a remnant population of approximately 300 out of 4,000 estimated when the European settlement of Tasmania began in 1803 (Harris 1990; Birmingham 1992). Between 1827 and 1830 Robinson persuaded more than 200 of the Tasmanians to go with him to a new settlement on Flinders Island, a "barren and forbidding place" (Harris 1990: 97) off the north-east coast of Tasmania. Wybalenna had a structure similar to a mission settlement with obligatory church attendance, work, and education programs. The remnant Aboriginal population was effectively incarcerated on the island, without any autonomy or control over their lives.

Birmingham used documentary records alongside archeology to reconstruct the 15 or so years of Aboriginal occupation at Wybalenna. The investigations revealed the remains of five brick cottages out of a likely original total of 20, and the chapel that Robinson had built in 1837. A range of European items including transfer-printed ceramics, glass, buttons, clay pipes, nails and other metals, along with indigenous artifacts and faunal remains was recovered. Robinson's journal details daily events, rations and goods supplied such as clothing and building materials. The settlement closed in 1847 when the last 44 remaining Aboriginals moved to a new location close to Hobart (Harris 1990). Established to protect the last-remaining Tasmanian Aboriginals, Wybalenna was hardly a success. The balance of the over 200 people who moved there in 1832 died on the island. The period that the Wybalenna settlement was occupied, 1832–1847, corresponds with the main period of occupation of the Te Puna mission. This may account for some similarities in artifacts recovered from the two sites, as is discussed in more detail in Chap.5.

Birmingham's (2000) more recent work at the site of the Killalpaninna mission in the remote Simpson Desert uses historical and archeological data to test a set of theories relating to Aboriginal responses to culture contact at this mission: resistance, creolization, and optimal foraging. Killalpannina, established first in 1866 by Lutheran missionaries, closed in 1915. Birmingham found that all three of the models were confirmed at the mission, where European goods such as bottle glass and salvaged items were used in new, indigenous ways and the Lutherans themselves recorded the systematic Aboriginal exploitation of mission rations and goods.

Other recent academic work includes an examination of the Benedictine New Norcia Mission in Western Australia (Russell 2001). Russell found that the New Norcia mission, built in 1847 was modeled on similar institutions in Europe, where monastic missions have a traditional design and standardized form of settlement that includes economic self-sufficiency. Extensive landscape surveys revealed aspects of this traditional design at New Norcia, with a strong Mediterranean influence. Other missions that have been the subject of archeological analysis include the Hermannsberg Lutheran Mission (1877–1982) near Alice Springs, Manga Manda (1945–1955) in the Northern Territory (Davison 1985; Paterson and Wilson 2000), Lake Condah in Victoria (Rhodes 1986, 1996), and Poonindie in South Australia (Griffin 2000).

Of particular interest to the Bay of Islands is Yarwood and Douglas' (1994) unpublished report on the site of Rangihu Cottage, Marsden's seminary for Maori that was built in 1819. As the name suggests, Rangihu Cottage was named for Rangihoua Pa, and depicted the relationship between the two places. The seminary was situated on a point overlooking the Parramatta River, on a block of land that is today bounded by New Zealand Street and Rangihou Crescent. Douglas carried out an archeological survey of the area, finding several features that may have been associated with the seminary, while Yarwood (Samuel Marsden's biographer) contributed an historical overview of the seminary and Marsden's relationship with Maori. Marsden built the seminary with the plan of having young Maori men from the Bay of Islands stay there while they learnt methods of European agriculture and other skills. However, so many of the young men who lived there died prematurely from European diseases that Marsden ceased to use it for this purpose. The cottage continued to be used for accommodation for missionaries on their way to the Bay of Islands.

Jane Lydon's (2000, 2002, 2005c) approach differs from those noted above. She uses the large photographic archive of Coranderrk Aboriginal Station, near Melbourne to analyze the "civilizing" process that the Board for the Protection of the Aborigines undertook there in 1863. As with Wybalenna, this station was not a mission as such, but a government institution that aimed to discipline its residents through "surveillance and measurement," the imposition of discipline and a set of Victorian values. The station also exercised a "Christianizing" influence through its Presbyterian manager, in a similar manner to the influence of Robinson on Wybalenna. According to Lydon, while Christianity was the main theme behind the photographs, the images were also open to interpretation in a number of different ways. They could be seen to demonstrate the progress of civilization, but also "told stories" to Aboriginals and signified claims to land; the images present a "densely ambiguous nature" (Lydon 2002: 72).

Lydon et al. (2004) and Lydon (2005c) have more recently carried out excavations on the site of the former Ebenezer mission site in north west Victoria. This mission, established by Germans of the Moravian Protestant sect in 1859, consisted of a church, Aboriginal cottages, a kitchen, mission house and dormitories. It closed in 1904. Lydon and her team recovered artifacts of domestic family use at this site and, as will be demonstrated later of Te Puna (Chap.5), noted that luxury European goods were scarce commodities there. As in other locations, the role of Aboriginal women in creating a transformed domestic space was seen as an essential and revealing aspect of the missionizing and civilizing processes.

Anthropologists also see the relationship between missions and indigenous peoples as a rich field for the examination of issues relating to culture contact, and are concerned with the role of missions as a colonizing force, as Comaroff and Comaroff (1986, 1991, 2000a,b) have identified. A number of works and collected volumes use an ethnographic and/or historical approach to discuss the relationship between Aboriginal Australians and missionaries (Brock 1988, 1993; Brock and Kartinyeri 1989; Harris 1990; Lydon 2000, 2002, 2005b,c; McNair and Rumley 1981; Stevens 1994; Swain and Rose 1988). The work of Harris (1990) is useful for its exhaustive historical overview of Christianity's relationship with Aboriginal people since the first European settlement in 1788, and documentation of the development of mission stations throughout Australia.

Brock focuses on the consequences of policies of assimilation and protection that led to the institutionalization and segregation of Aboriginal communities within Christian mission stations and government settlements, brought about through legislation like the Queensland government's Aboriginal Protection Act of 1897 and used as a blueprint by a number of other states to control their Aboriginal population (Brock 1993; Brock and Kartinyeri 1989). Brock makes the point that while discriminatory and harsh, institutionalization contributed to the survival of many Aboriginal communities, which often developed a strong sense of identity within such organizations. Harris makes a similar point many times over, noting that nineteenth century missionaries often defended Aboriginal rights in the face of strong opposition from pastoralists and settlers, who sometimes participated in massacres of Aboriginals and were able by legislation to use them as virtual slaves. In this situation, mission stations were seen as a refuge from a hostile white population (Cole 1971, 1988).

Tahiti

Protestant missions in the Pacific began with the LMS voyage to Tahiti on the *Duff*, which left Britain in 1796 and arrived in Tahiti in the following year. This voyage, planned by the Rev. Haweis, was inspired by Cook's voyages to the Pacific, and later glowing accounts of the island published by Captain Bligh of *Bounty* mutiny fame. The work of the mission to Tahiti proved to be more challenging than expected, and was considered a complete failure in some circles (Davies 1961; Edmond 1997; Ellis 1859; Gunson 1978; Stock 1899). After only a year on Tahiti, 11 of the original 17 missionaries returned to the safety of Sydney, from where several, Cover, Hassall, and Henry, continued to promote the interests of the Tahitian mission, working in collaboration with Samuel Marsden. Marsden was appointed adviser and correspondent to the LMS in Tahiti from 1801 (Johnston 2003: 173). Hassall and Marsden were eventually connected by marriage, Hassall's son marrying one of Marsden's daughters.

Following the defection of another two, only four missionaries, single men, remained on Tahiti. Four reinforcements arrived on the *Royal Admiral* in 1801. Not surprisingly, the small band of missionaries was closely dependent on the goodwill of the monarch, initially Pomare I, who died in 1803, and after this of his successor, Pomare II. The missionaries on Tahiti had a difficult time of it. At the end of 1809, only two remained, all the others having returned to Sydney on a passing ship. Shortly after, Pomare II indicated his desire to convert to Christianity and by 1816 Christianity was commonly accepted. However, Pomare was not yet baptized as he was on a trial of good behavior. The arrival of a second group of missionaries in 1817 led to tension between the new and the older groups. In the same year Pomare's mission ship, the *Haweis*, was launched, and used to trade and procure supplies for both the Tahitian and New Zealand missions, as was Marsden's ship, the *Active*. The *Haweis* was later lost at sea in 1829, while CMS missionaries in the Bay of Islands waited anxiously for it to arrive with Charles Davis and his wife aboard (Gunson 1978; Davis n.d.).

Missionaries were dependent on the involvement of local people as advisors and informants whose knowledge of the marine environment was vitally important. Trade in coconut oil, arrowroot, pigs, and cotton developed to support the mission, and became a source of internal division and conflict, as it was in New Zealand (Gunson 1978). Pomare, finally baptized in 1819, lived only 2 years longer. After his death, followed by the death of his successor, the young Pomare III 5 years later, the missionaries had to come to terms with the reign of the "young and pleasure-loving" Queen Pomare IV (Garrett 1982: 28).

However, the position of the church established by the LMS under the patronage of the succession of Pomares was jeopardized by the arrival of French Catholic missionaries in 1836. Queen Pomare's initial rebuttal of the two French priests led to major French intervention and, in the early 1840s, to French "protection" following the quelling of Tahitian armed resistance. While the English missionary, Pritchard, traveled to Britain to seek support for Tahitian independence, recognition of French influence was traded "for French acceptance of British rights over New Zealand" (Garrett 1982: 255).

A connection between the Tahitian mission and the Bay of Islands was made soon after Marsden arrived in New Zealand in 1814 when the Ngati Manu chief Whetoi took the name of Pomare on hearing of the king of Tahiti. He named Matauwhi Bay, the location of one of his *pa* just outside Kororareka (the present-day town of Russell), for

Matavai Bay in Tahiti where the mission was located (Elder 1932). The bay is still known by this name. After his death in 1826 Pomare I's nephew took both his names (Whetoi and Pomare), becoming known as Pomare II. Pomare II presented something of a challenge to missionaries such as Henry Williams from his pa at Otuihu, a rival to the port of Kororareka, where he ran "grog shops" patronized by sailors and refused to entertain the idea of conversion to Christianity (DNZB 1998; Earle 1909; Middleton n.d.).

Sites associated with LMS as well as Catholic missionary activity in French Polynesia present an apparently rich but unexplored archeological field, in an academic milieu where prehistoric archeology is paramount and there appears to be no research being undertaken into the archeology of the historic period generally. Matavai Bay on the island of Tahiti has a memorial to its 1797 *Duff* missionary arrivals (as well as others to James Cook's observatory located there, and to the *Bounty* mutiny). Churches still occupy sites in Papeete, Papatoai on the island of Moorea, and Fare on Huahine, among other locations, where early churches were built in the 1820s. Missionary literature (for example, Davies 1961; Ellis 1859) describes locations where missionaries built houses, printed Bibles and held schools, little or none of this apparently surveyed.

Hawaii

Missionaries from the American Board of Commissioners for Foreign Missions (ABCFM), founded in Boston 1810, arrived in Hawaii early in 1820. The ABCFM, similar to the British evangelical societies and with Calvinist theology as its background, was stimulated by efforts of the LMS in the Pacific and the presence in the early years of the nineteenth century of several young Hawaiian men in New England. The missionary group of 14 Americans, mostly married couples, and three Hawaiians were instructed to subject themselves to chiefly authority. They found on their arrival that following the recent death of the king, Kamehameha I, Liholiho had succeeded to this role, with his mother, Kaahumanu, also playing a powerful role in the state in her own right (Kirch and Sahlins 1992; Garrett 1982; Zwiep 1991).

In Hawaii the LMS and the ABCFM worked together with the arrival in 1822 of the missionary Ellis and his wife as part of a deputation from the LMS. Ellis (1859) and his wife had been part of the Tahitian mission, and came with nine converts from that island. The Hawaiian mission was seeking reinforcements, frustrated by its slow progress. The chiefly Tahitian converts, one of whom made connections with a lost brother in Hawaii, contributed largely to the continuing success of the Hawaiian mission as they promoted Christianity to Kaahumanu and other royalty, and by the 1860s an indigenous Christian dynasty ruled.

Although, as in New Zealand, the missions were initially subject to the politically sovereign indigenous population, dependent on them for protection, food supplies, and shelter, missionaries subsequently held positions of political power. For example, the Reverend William Richards was the principal author of the 1840 Hawaiian Constitution, held an official position as advisor to the chiefs, and secured recognition of the kingdom's independence from Britain, France, and the United States (Kirch and Sahlins 1992 I: 115). A more notable (or infamous) missionary who played a powerful role was Gerit Judd. Judd held a number of key portfolios in the Hawaiian government, and according to one of the foreign merchant class (often the missionaries' adversary), "he rides us down to the dust. The king is nothing – nobody. Judd orders him as you would a boy" (Reynolds in Kirch and Sahlins 1992 I: 115). Herman Melville, visiting the islands in 1843, held the missionaries in similar contempt, describing them as "a junta of ignorant and designing Methodist [sic] elders in the councils of a half-civilised king, ruling with absolute sway over a nation just poised between barbarism and civilisation" (in Kirch and Sahlins 1992 I: 116). However, according to Grimshaw and Nelson (2001: 298) "while missionaries remained a considerable moral and indeed political force, Christian Hawaiians were in no sense answerable to their will before or after their conversion."

As was the case elsewhere in the Pacific, as later religious denominations arrived they sought the support of different local political factions in order to become established. This was the case with the Catholics who arrived in Hawaii in 1827 but were rebutted. A ban on Catholic teaching and the arrest of Catholics in 1839 was followed by strong protests from the French government, and religious freedom was granted in the same year after the visit of the French warship *L'Artemise* (Garrett 1982; Kirch and Sahlins 1992). By mid 1840 the Waialua Valley had seen an exponential growth of Catholic converts and schools, much to the dismay of the local Protestant missionary, Emerson. At the same time, Emerson complained about the rekindled "heathenism" and its similarities to "popery." New syncretic religious forms developed here as elsewhere, and as were seen in New Zealand's Bay of Islands.

Hawaiian missions followed the "domestic" model, the household mission station of the kind seen in New Zealand at Te Puna. Missionary couples established stations throughout the Hawaiian Islands, but none of these functioned in the role of the "total institution," although schools were held and literacy spread. The Hawaiian Missionary Society

(HMS) made an attempt to establish the same style of mission on the island of Nukuhiva in the Marquesas when three young missionary families arrived there in late 1833. They lasted only 8 months on the island before fleeing back to Hawaii (Wallace 2005). As Wallace (2005: 269) notes, "the Christian culture the three HMS families attempted to introduce to Nukuhiva was a domestic one, thoroughly embedded in the unassuming practices of daily life," with the domesticity created by mission wives essential. As elsewhere, wives played an important role in training women, especially chiefly women, in the domestic arts (Grimshaw 1989a,b; Kirch and Sahlins 1992 I: 110; Zwiep 1991).

In Honolulu, the Mission Houses Museum (www.missionhouses. org) consists of several buildings, the earliest of these built in 1821, and significant collections of associated materials relating to early Hawaiian mission families. Other extant mission buildings can be found at Hilo, built late 1830s (http://www.lymanmuseum.org) and Wai'oli, built in 1837 (http://www.hawaiimuseums.org). However, archeology relating to missions is more difficult to uncover, perhaps because mission history is quite visible in its standing architecture and related collections. Some of the archeology may be found in the less accessible "gray" unpublished literature relating to consultancy reports, for example the work of Puette and Dye (2003), a report monitoring a services trench at the Mission Houses Museum. Otherwise, it appears that there are no programs of survey or research relating to Hawaiian mission archeology.

Mission Station as Household – New Zealand and the Pacific

In New Zealand, missions consisted of humble wooden houses for the mission family, perhaps only one or two families forming the mission station, with a church or school building sometimes associated. Small numbers of Maori lived in the mission house with missionary families, and others may have lived in nearby dwellings, as was the case at the Waimate mission. Otherwise, the missionary "itinerated," walking or riding to distant villages where he preached, catechized, and taught the basics of reading and writing. While no public role was deemed suitable for women, the missionary wife's work was pivotal in teaching not only reading and writing but also the whole range of domestic skills seen as fundamental to the mission. In New Zealand, as in other locations in the Pacific such as Hawaii and Tahiti, "indigenous Christian converts or pupils did not live commonly with missionaries, or come under their personal command, but engaged as individuals or members of communities with them" (Grimshaw and Nelson 2001: 297). The household mission station was constructed around the concept of the family, projecting the essential links between this institution, Christianity, godliness, and civilization.

Missions in places like Tahiti and Hawaii confronted similar problems to those faced by the CMS in the Bay of Islands. Mission beginnings in all three places were fragile, dependent on the outside world and indigenous patrons for supplies, and pre-dated formal settlement and colonization (Barker 2005; Edmond 1997; Grimshaw 1989a,b; Middleton 2005a). The missions had to rely on powerful local protectors, and through this dependency could find themselves used as pawns in local politics. At the same time they were wracked by internal conflict, which did not necessarily improve with the arrival of later reinforcements. Indigenous people in all these locations developed syncretic forms of Christianity hybridized with traditional forms of religion, in an effort to control Christianity and incorporate it into traditional religious practices.

Such missions did not show the characteristics of the highly regimented institutions discussed below. There was no monumental architecture, no large structures, and no emphasis on punishment. Few indigenous people lived within the mission itself. Daily routines consisted of regular hours for schooling and regular church attendance, as well as a focus on the role of the family and household.

Mission Station as Institution – Australia and North America

The household mission structure, as seen in New Zealand, the Pacific Islands, and Protestant New England, was dramatically different to the kind of institutions that operated in Spanish Borderlands of North America and Australia. It has been argued (Sutton 2003) that in Australia missions formed "total institutions" (Goffman 1962; Lemert and Branaman 1997), the kind of structures that included locks, barred windows, barbed wire fences, regimented spaces, and segregated buildings. Punishment may form an important part of institutional life. According to Goffman (1962: introduction) a "total institution may be defined as a place of residence and work where a large number of like-situated individuals, cut off from the wider society for an appreciable period of time, together lead an enclosed, formally administered round of life." Such institutions include homes for the needy, prisons, asylums, boarding schools, large households with servants' quarters, and finally, according to Goffman, training institutions for the religious.

A key attribute of these institutions in Australia was the division between inmates and staff, and in Queensland officials and missionaries maintained almost total control over the movement of indigenous people (Sutton 2003). Many of the same features can be identified in North American Catholic missions. Farnsworth, for example, considers that North American Spanish missions shared many of the same characteristics as slave plantations (Farnsworth 1989, 1992; Silliman 2005: 65).

The characteristics of the "total institution" can also be seen in reform institutions (Spencer-Wood and Baugher 2001: 9) such as the Adelaide Destitute Asylum (Piddock 2001), the Ross Female Factory (Casella 2001a,b) and the Magdalen Asylum in Philadelphia (De Cunzo 1995, 2001, 2006). Such institutions shared a similar focus to evangelical missions, focusing on the "evangelical reform agenda" (De Cunzo 2001: 32). As De Cunzo expresses it, "a complex set of beliefs linking women, moral purity, Christian piety, motherhood and the family home evolved in [the early nineteenth century]…[Magdalen] Society members accepted these symbolic concepts as 'core symbols', thus necessitating the interplay of moral cleansing and redemption with domestic training in the reform program" (De Cunzo 2001: 25). Although De Cunzo has not articulated this set of beliefs as the "cult of domesticity," the description suggests that this was the ideology behind much of the reform program at the Magdalen Asylum. Female inmates at all the three reform institutions identified above were taught domestic work as preparation for employment in domestic service (Spencer-Wood and Baugher 2001: 13).

Reform institutions and institutional missions often encircled their structures with high walls. At the Magdalen Society home a 13.5ft wall enclosed the asylum's garden and kept its inmates in, separated from the outside world, while the walls of the Ross female factory also ensured the inmates seclusion (De Cunzo 2001; Spencer-Wood and Baugher 2001). Sutton (2003) records the use of high barbed wire fences around a number of Aboriginal reserves and missions in Australia, used particularly around dormitories (with locked doors and windows) to keep young women segregated and young men out. This can be contrasted with the New Zealand situation where walls were built around mission houses to keep pillaging Maori out and missionary families and garden produce safe within (Goldsbury 1986; Middleton 2007b).

The mission station itself (whether household or institution) was also a fundamental institution for transforming European domesticity founded in gender and class roles into a domesticity used as a tool of colonization and control (McClintock 1995: 35). Hence the "cult of domesticity" (Davidoff and Hall 1991; Grimshaw 1983, 1989a,b; Johnston 2003;

Middleton 2007a) and the associated focus on the family and the home as a pivotal element of the "civilizing (or reforming) mission" appears as a unifying concern throughout all three types of organizations.

The UNESCO World Heritage website (http://whc.unesco.org/exhibits/afr_rev/africa-r.htm) suggests that there were two styles of South African missions: "Mission settlements, of which there were many variations, [with] a civic nucleus consisting of a church and various social facilities surrounded by a settlement. Mission stations, on the other hand, were institutions which were not intended to be centers of settlement, but offered various social services to the surrounding areas. These missions consisted of only the nucleus without a surrounding or adjacent formal settlement." This suggests that missions in South Africa (and elsewhere on this continent) varied from the two models I have described above, and were neither institutional nor household but lay somewhere between the two.

HISTORICAL ARCHEOLOGY IN NEW ZEALAND

In 1988 Schuyler acknowledged the potential of historical archeology in the analysis of contact between indigenous and European cultures in the process of expansion, exploration, and colonization, noting "...that the field is deeply concerned not only with European and European colonial societies but also with transculturation between these groups and native cultures" (Schuyler 1988: 39; Little 1994).

Recent debates over the context of historical archeology have focused on the distinction between historical and prehistoric archeology, and whether the dichotomy created between the two fields is valid (Funari et al. 1999; Lightfoot 1995; Lightfoot et al. 1997). This dichotomy has been created through the association of historical archeology with the advent of European colonialism and the use of written records, in particular in the North American context (Deetz 1977; Orser 1988, 1996). This produces a beginning date for historical archeology in North America of 1492 but varying elsewhere, and in the New Zealand context dating to Captain James Cook's arrival in 1769 (Smith 1990).

Following Schuyler's emphasis on the potential for historical archeology's concern with cultural engagement between European and indigenous cultures, Smith (1990) highlighted the lack of archeological concern in New Zealand with Maori sites of the historic contact period. Subsequently Bedford (1996, 2004) followed Smith's sentiments, suggesting that New Zealand archeology perhaps considered that postcontact Maori archeology was "contaminated" by European influence, or was not worthy of serious academic attention, not "real" archeology.

Bedford points out that "culture contact" is an inadequate term for complex processes that continue into the present, a point that others (Torrence and Clarke 2000; Silliman 2005) also make. "Entanglement" (Silliman 2005: 59) may be a more suitable description for the political, social, and cultural processes that lead to the long-term intertwining of more than one cultural group.

As elsewhere in the Pacific, in New Zealand the idea that indigenous peoples would not survive the "fatal impact" (Moorhead 1966) of European arrival (or invasion) was common; but in all locations this concept was proven wrong. At the beginning of the nineteenth century, Maori entered into engagement with Europeans as sovereign agents, in control of political and economic choices. After British annexation with the signing of the Treaty of Waitangi in 1840, the dynamics of this situation altered, and by 1845 Ngapuhi Maori of northern New Zealand had taken up arms to fight for their independence, apparently unwittingly signed away with the Treaty, according to variations in translation (Orange 1987, 1997; Walker 1990). Land wars between European and Maori continued in other parts of the country up until the last decades of the nineteenth century, and resistance to land grabbing by colonial and later governments continues into the present in a variety of forms (Belich 1986; King 2003; Shoebridge 2006; Walker 1990; Ward 1974).

As in other "settler societies" (Torrence and Clarke 2000), the history of Maori and Pakeha (New Zealanders of European origin) in New Zealand has been characterized by battles over land and indigenous political sovereignty. At the same time, as Lightfoot (2005) and Lightfoot et al. (1997) found of the "multiethnic community" at Fort Ross, California, Maori and Pakeha were (and are) not monolithic ethnic groups. Maori were made up of different tribal and subtribal groupings, uniting, splintering, and reforming. Intertribal warfare was prevalent in the nineteenth century and earlier (Ballara 2003). It was only after the advent of Europeans that the term "Maori," meaning "ordinary" or "usual," was adopted to refer to Maori collectively, who previously identified themselves by tribe. Pakeha were not just British, but Scots, Irish, and English, as well as Portuguese, French, or American. Other groups also constitute this "other" immigrants from the Pacific Islands, Croatia, India and China (Smith 2004; Bozic-Vrbancic 2006). This has led Smith (2004: 260) to call for the understanding of the history of identity through the construction of "richer and more nuanced histozple strands of evidence to produce finely detailed pictures of different communities. Smith's approach echoes Hill's (1998: 149) discussion of "culture contact" as the "intertwining of two or more formerly distinct

histories into a single history characterized by processes of domination, resistance, and accommodation" (Hill in Silliman 2005: 61).

Such an approach is demonstrated in Phillips' (2000a,b) examination of "postcontact landscapes of change" in New Zealand's Hauraki
Plains, where initially Maori adopted an "entrepreneurial approach" in
engaging with European outsiders. The arrival of European trade goods
and plants such as potatoes and corn unfortunately also brought new
diseases. This resulted in deadly epidemics and large population loss,
exacerbated by the incursions of Ngapuhi war parties from the north,
armed with muskets, the new deadly weapon. A hiatus followed in the
occupation of Hauraki lands from 1822, when the tribe migrated to
safer territory belonging to allies, until 1830 when the people returned
to reclaim their former territory. The style of occupation now changed;
pa were smaller, and defended for musket warfare; houses were built
according to a more European plan and used squared rather than
rounded timbers; large amounts of goods such as dressed flax, timber,
potatoes, and pigs were produced in order to obtain muskets, until a
balance of power was established with tribes owning relatively equal
numbers of muskets, destabilizing Ngapuhi's former supremacy. While
the center of population moved to coastal settlements, where access to
shipping was easier, mobility across the landscape, providing access
to a wide range of resources, endured as an important aspect of Maori
life. Overall, the population declined, and after British annexation in
1840, the gradual purchase of land resulted in further attrition. While
the work of Phillips (2000a,b) and Bedford (1994) touched on the 1830s
CMS mission on the Hauraki Plains at Puriri, no evidence remained
of any mission structures, evidently destroyed by the construction of a
later nineteenth century farmhouse. The mission itself was abandoned
after only 4 years of occupation, because of its "unhealthy" location.

As Belich points out, in 1959 Wright (1959) "effectively shifted the
idea of 'Fatal Impact' from the eighteenth to the early nineteenth century" in the New Zealand context, by identifying the agency, assertive-
ness, and selective attitude of Bay of Islands Maori in the early years
of "culture contact" (Belich 1986; Bedford 1996: 417). Wright's ideas
took Linton's (1940) earlier work on acculturation into account. But
as Caroline Phillips (2000a: 79), and others in the North American
context (for example, Cusick 1998a,b; Lightfoot 2005; Rubertone 1989,
2000; Silliman 2005) have discussed, what exactly is the relationship
between the adoption of exotic technology and cultural change? Does
the cultivation of potatoes and the use of muskets mean the end of
Maori cultural identity? Both Phillips (2000a,b) and Bedford (1994, 2004)
found that on the Hauraki Plains, while change took place following

contact with Europeans, this occurred within a Maori framework, and demonstrated a continuity of the traditional practice of temporary abandonment and reoccupation of tribal lands. Moreover, as the Maori renaissance (Webster 1998) that began in the 1990s has demonstrated, the "impact" of cultural engagement was not fatal, but also led to a "hybrid vigor," where Europeans were incorporated into the Maori world, contributing to a more dynamic tribal population base for the future. This was especially so in the case of Ngai Tahu, the dominant tribe in southern New Zealand (Anderson 1991).

Historical Archeology in the Bay of Islands

The Bay of Islands is significant in New Zealand historical archeology because of the first interactions between Maori and European that took place there. It is also of interest to anthropologists such as Salmond (1991a, 1997, 2000) for similar reasons. Cook visited and named the Bay in 1769 (Lee 1983). Three years later, in 1772, two French ships, the *Mascarin* and *Castries* under the command of Marion du Fresne arrived (Kelly 1951; Kennedy 1969; Ollivier 1985; Salmond 1991a,b). On this visit du Fresne set up a hospital camp and ship settlement on the island of Moturua (Figure 1.1) for his ailing sailors. According to later writers, while the French were camped on the island they ignored and broke requirements of *tapu*, an offence for which many of the men including du Fresne were murdered and eaten by Maori at Assassination Cove on the mainland. The remaining French sailors sacked Paeroa Pa on Moturua Island in reprisal. Groube (1965, 1966) subsequently carried out excavations on the site of the pa in 1964–1965, looking for evidence of Maori settlement at the apex of "Classic" culture, at the first point of European contact. This was evidently an elusive quest. Continuous occupation of the pa into the nineteenth century had disturbed the "Classic" occupation period Groube was seeking, and he was not concerned with the nineteenth century material.

As part of the fieldwork associated with Groube's excavations of Paeroa Pa, Kennedy (1969) undertook one the first examples of "text-aided" archeology in the country, using methods subsequently identified with historical archeology. Kennedy applied information from textual sources to archeological remains of places in the Bay associated with the visit and subsequent demise of Marion du Fresne, in an effort to understand "protohistoric Maori" in the Bay of Islands. Kennedy (1969: 172) independently articulated the aims and methods of historical archeology at the same time that the field was developing in North America:

Documents and tradition can be studied in their own right. The conclusions reached may be valid in terms of documentary and traditional evidence, as archaeology may reach independent and equally valid conclusions. The fusion of evidence from these discrete sources of information is necessary. It is possible only when the significance of each kind of information can be understood in terms of the others, and thus integrated into a whole that transcends history, tradition and archaeology.

Mission Archeology

Little archeological work relating to missions in New Zealand is available in published form. Most archeological analysis relating to this field can be found in reports written for the NZHPT as a result of piecemeal investigations undertaken as a requirement of the Historic Places Act 1993, when earthworks or building projects may destroy or modify an archeological site, often associated with the conservation of NZHPT buildings. Research questions are not often addressed as a part of this process.

Archeological fieldwork has been carried out at the site of Pompallier's first Catholic mission at Purakau in the Hokianga, founded on Pompallier's arrival there in 1838 (Best 2000; DNZB 1998). Excavation uncovered the site of the chapel that stood on a point overlooking the harbor until the early twentieth century. The remains of the mission school, which continued to function until the early twentieth century and was standing until 1999, can be found close to the chapel. Limited archeological investigations have also been carried out at Pompallier House in Russell, built by Bishop Pompallier in 1841 after his move to the Bay of Islands from the Hokianga (Best 2001; Clunie 1998; Maingay 1993).

Another NZHPT heritage site, the former CMS Kerikeri Mission House and Stone Store, provides archeological evidence and items of material culture that more closely related to the CMS mission at Te Puna. Investigative archeological work was undertaken during the restoration of the Stone Store between approximately 1995 and 1998, and as required when any other earthworks or building restoration has been undertaken (Best 1995, 1997, 2003a; Clunie personal communication 2002; McLean 1994). Artifact finds from these investigations are displayed at the Mission House and Stone Store, presented along with the history of the mission, as at Pompallier House. Waimate Mission House, located further inland from Kerikeri, is another source of material comparative with the Te Puna mission. Little archeology has been carried out. Only one of the three original mission houses remains standing, built over a cellar of similar dimensions to that at

Te Puna. Both Waimate Mission House and Kerikeri Mission House display artifacts in their collections from the Te Puna mission house donated by members of the King family. The material recovered in the course of limited archeological investigations at these places and in the NZHPT collections will be referred to further in Chap.5, along with the discussion of material from the Te Puna investigation.

The New Zealand Comparison with Australia

While the indigenous peoples of Australia and North America were confined within missions, the situation was very different in New Zealand, where Maori could not, or would not be restricted to the missions. Buildings were inadequate to house large numbers of people, although schools sometimes accommodated small numbers of pupils. During the early years of the missions in New Zealand, missionaries were virtually prisoners of their Maori patrons, entirely dependent on them for their safety and for a large part of their food supplies.

The historical, archeological, and anthropological literature demonstrates that there are few similarities between the history and development of missions in Australia and New Zealand, although the presence of Samuel Marsden at Parramatta, who exerted such a strong influence over the New Zealand missions throughout his life, might at first glance suggest otherwise. Given his founding role in the New Zealand mission, it is useful to compare missionary and colonist thinking in the two countries, and Marsden's work in Australia, where he set up institutions at his home base in Parramatta for Maori from the Bay of Islands, but was reluctant to work with Aboriginals. There were major differences in the nature of indigenous and European interactions in the two countries. Australian missions demonstrate many of the qualities of the "total institution," as described above, often acting as a hand of the state in exercising social control through regimented systems that came close to incarceration. Other differences are demonstrated in scale and chronology. While by 1848 "all of the first generation of missions in the Australian colonies had been abandoned as failures" (Woolmington in Johnston 2003: 175), at this time in New Zealand the Bay of Islands missions were still functioning, while in the south of the country missions had only recently been established (Purchas 1914).

Christian missions in Australia were established considerably later than in New Zealand. This can be attributed to attitudes toward Aboriginal people, typified by the ideas Samuel Marsden and other missionaries expressed. Marsden established the New Zealand mission because of his connections with the New Zealand chiefs Te Pahi and Ruatara; however, he had limited involvement in missionary activity within New South Wales. Marsden held to popular thought of his time, in which Australian Aborigines were believed to represent the lowest form of social life in the Great Chain of Being (Harris 1990; Johnston 2003; Stocking 1987). Botanist Peter Cunningham placed Aboriginals "at the very zero of civilization, constituting...the connecting link between man and the monkey tribe" (quoted in Harris 1990: 26). Many elements in Australian settler society considered Aboriginals little better than animals, providing justification for ill treatment, dispossession of their lands, and even extermination.

Marsden considered Maori "in many respects...one of the finest aboriginal races with which the English have come in contact" (quoted in Stock 1899: 9). In 1819 Marsden wrote to the secretary of the CMS, arguing that Aboriginals should not be "received into" Rangihu Cottage, the "seminary" he had built at Parramatta for young Maori men from the Bay of Islands (Yarwood and Douglas 1994). For the previous 4 years, Maori had lived with Marsden at his own home. The New Zealanders, who Marsden considered superior "civilised Heathen" (Harris 1990: 79) "would never be induced to live with them [Aboriginals] if it were possible to contain them," Marsden argued. He considered that

> The natives of the Colony...cannot be induced to live in any regular way, and as they increase in years they increase in every vice, and particularly drunkenness, both men and women, and still go naked about the streets. They are the most degraded of the human race...their conduct is so disgusting altogether, as well as their persons...The time is not yet arrived for them to receive the great blessings of civilization and the knowledge of Christianity. (Elder 1932: 231–232)

New Zealand missionary wife Marianne Williams also considered Maori presented a more worthy proposition than Aboriginals, as she described on her arrival in the Bay of Islands in August 1823:

> The men who rowed the boat were fine, intelligent, active-looking lads, talking with great animation...and in comparison with the sleepy, degraded and disgusting looking natives we had just left at Port Jackson, they appeared quite astonishing. (Marianne Williams quoted in Gillespie 1996: 95)

The New Zealand missions were part of a globalizing network with its main center located in England. Marsden, based at Parramatta, formed another node in this network, where Port Jackson (Sydney) was the source of some of the stores for the Bay of Islands missions. Stores were also ordered through the CMS in Britain. Connections between New Zealand and Parramatta were also maintained as missionaries landed first in Port Jackson on their way to New Zealand from Britain.

Once there, some were delayed for long periods, or moved between Tahiti, Port Jackson, and New Zealand. Antipodean arrivals such as Henry and Marianne Williams spent several months at Parramatta before moving on to New Zealand, while Maori from the Bay of Islands also traveled there to live with Samuel Marsden or to stay in his "seminary." Wesleyan missionaries moved between these locations. The point is that although the New Zealand missionaries may have lived in an isolated part of the globe, they existed within a mission network with close links to New South Wales and parts of the Pacific such as Tahiti, and extending ultimately back to Britain (Marsden 1857; Stock 1899).

FROM CONTACT TO ENTANGLEMENT

Although the Dutchman Abel Tasman skirted the New Zealand coastline in 1642, desperate for provisions, he made no landing. Tasman beat a hasty retreat to the north, heading toward Tonga and back to Batavia after an encounter with "treacherous" Maori at Murderers Bay in which four sailors were killed (Salmond 1997: 22, 1991a,b; Anderson 2001: 89). However, his name for the country persists. When James Cook explored New Zealand shores over a century later, in 1769 and returned again in 1772 and 1777, the cultural engagement between Maori and European began in earnest. Cook's expedition members included naturalist Sir Joseph Banks, botanists George and Johann Forster, and artist Sydney Parkinson, among others, leading to the beginning of a prodigious tradition of collecting, botanizing, describing, and illustrating (Salmond 1991a, 1997); this material provides a rich source for archeology and ethnographic historians, as much current work demonstrates (for example, see Phillips 2000a,b; Walter et al. 2006). Cook was also the first to introduce new foods such as the white potato, although this was not immediately incorporated into the local economy. During his 1769 expedition Cook visited the Bay of Islands, but did not return there on the later voyages (Edwards 1999). On this visit Cook described the Bay as a fertile area rich in resources. He found large, well-kept gardens often lined with stone, much of the landscape covered with *aruhe* or fern root. At around the same time, the Frenchman de Surville stopped on the coast just north of the Bay of Islands; Cook later found that his ship and de Surville's had probably passed within about 25 miles of each other during a storm off North Cape. While relations with local Maori were cordial for most of the 14 days de Surville spent at anchor, this altered in the last 2 days following the supposed theft of the ship's boat. Reprisals followed, and when the ship left de Surville took prisoner a local chief, Ranginui, who had been

A. Middleton, *Te Puna: A New Zealand Mission Station*,
DOI:10.1007/978-0-387-77622-4, © Springer Science+Business Media, LLC 2008

particularly hospitable toward the French visitors. Although Ranginui was well treated, he suffered from scurvy and died at sea on 24 March 1770 (Dunmore 2006; Salmond 1997).

A more infamous fatal encounter took place in the Bay 3 years later. In 1772, two ships forming a French expedition under the command of Marion du Fresne took refuge in the Bay of Islands, setting up a hospital camp for many of the crew who were suffering from scurvy. Following some transgression of *tapu*, Marion du Fresne and 24 seamen were killed and eaten. The remaining men under the command of du Clesmeur took revenge, sacking a neighboring pa and killing its inhabitants, then fleeing back to Europe (Salmond 1991 a). A similar event that had consequences for those living in the Bay of Islands took place in 1809, when the *Boyd*, anchored in Whangaroa Harbor, was sacked, and all the Europeans on board killed and eaten, apart from four passengers. Once again, this was reprisal, this time for the beating and ill treatment of the chief George, who was working his passage home from Port Jackson on the *Boyd* (Salmond 1997).

These visits typified exchanges between Maori and European of increasing intensity and sometimes hostility. When the first mission was established in 1814, it was a small, ephemeral settlement located on the margins of a Maori fortification, dependant on the protection and patronage of this *pa* and its chief. At this time, while sealers had been left ashore in the far south of the South Island, staying there for short periods of time while they collected seal skins (Smith 2005b), there were no other European settlers in the country. There were no like settlements the missionaries could flee to in times of stress, no military support or British legal system.

Te Pahi and Samuel Marsden

The New Zealand mission itself largely grew out of the friendship between Samuel Marsden, chaplain to the colony at New South Wales, and Te Pahi (Figures 2.1–2.3), the renowned chief of Te Puna and Rangihoua Pa (Elder 1932, 1934; Salmond 1997). It is important to examine the beginnings of the New Zealand mission in the context of exchanges between these two, which accounts for the location of the first mission at Oihi, and establishes it firmly under the auspices of the chief of Te Puna and Rangihoua Pa, the most prominent location in the Bay of Islands at the beginning of the nineteenth century.

Exchanges between Maori from the Bay of Islands and Europeans in the colony of New South Wales began after Philip Gidley King,

Figure 2.1. Samuel Marsden, c. 1837 (From Havard-Williams, 1961. *Marsden and the New Zealand Mission*)

governor of Norfolk Island, made repeated requests to the British Admiralty to bring New Zealanders to Norfolk Island to teach convicts and settlers to process flax growing on the island, badly needed to manufacture fabric for clothing for the colony. In 1793 off the east coast of northern New Zealand the *Daedalus* raised the ship's sails and left the coast with two young Maori men on board, Tuki and Huru, while they were entertained, unsuspecting, below decks (McNab 1908, 1914; Salmond 1997). Tuki, a priest, and Huru, a warrior, spent 7 months on Norfolk Island living with Governor King and his family, but they were not the right people for this task, flax weaving being women's work in the Maori world. Later in the same year, King responded to their entreaties to be sent home, sailing with them on board the *Britannia* to the Bay of Islands. Off the coastline of New Zealand, Tuki and Huru's relatives greeted their kinsmen, and exchanges of gifts (as well as names) were made between the two parties, Maori presenting Governor King with adzes and flax garments, while King gave Tuki and Huru axes, tools, spades, maize, wheat, potatoes, and pigs. King

TIPPAHEE
A
NEW ZEALAND CHIEF
From an Original Drawing by G. P. Harris.

Figure 2.2. Te Pahi, chief of Rangihoua and Te Puna, c. 1805 (Artist G. P. Harris, 1775–1840. Alexander Turnbull Library, Wellington, New Zealand. A-092-007)

had plans to extend the colony at New South Wales to New Zealand, and promised his Maori friends that he would come back.

King's dreams of this settlement never developed, as he was recalled from Norfolk Island to England, but his gifts of potatoes and pigs were redistributed, beginning an important trade for Maori in provisioning whalers in the Bay of Islands. By the first years of the nineteenth century European visitors to the Bay of Islands such as Savage (1973 [1807]) remarked on the quantities of potatoes grown at Te Puna for trade with the shipping, under the auspices of Te Pahi, principal chief of the Bay at this time. In fact, Savage considered Te Puna the "capital" of the Bay of Islands:

> The capital of this part of the country, which is situated partly on the main land, and partly on a small island, is called Tippoonah, and consists in the

Figure 2.3. Te Pahi, drawn in NSW, 1808 (Artist James Finucane, Mitchell Library, State Library of New South Wales, Australia. Sv/Mao/Port/14)

whole of about an hundred dwellings. On the main the dwellings of the natives are surrounded each by a little patch of cultivated ground; but the island is appropriated to the residence of a chieftain and his court, where no cultivation is carried on. Tippeehee, the chieftain, has a well constructed dwelling on this island, and a large collection of spears, war mats, and other valuables. (Savage 1973 [1807]: 22)

Te Pahi was absent from Te Puna in Port Jackson at the time of Savage's visit and his brother, Tiarrah, was "governing" in his place. Genealogies such as that by Sissons et al. (2001) make no mention of this brother of Te Pahi. His name is more likely to have been Te Ara. According to Savage, at the time of his visit only potatoes were being cultivated at Te Puna, because of the value in trade with the shipping:

> The mode of bringing potatoes to the ship is in small baskets, made of green
> native flax, and of various sizes, containing from eight to thirty pounds in
> weight... The potato is the only vegetable cultivated by the natives; they
> have had the seed of several others, but as they are found ill calculated for
> trade, they have been neglected. (Savage 1973 [1807]: 63)

Savage's observations confirm Te Puna as the most important
location in the Bay of Islands for trade between Maori and European
in the earliest years of this interaction. Here, Te Pahi expanded agriculture, growing the European-preferred potato, and producing pork
from the animals Governor King had sent to him, in order to supply the
demands of whaling ships arriving in the Bay (McNab 1908).

In December 1804 Te Pahi had sent his son Matara to see the
English settlement at Port Jackson, Matara returning some months
later in 1805 with presents of pigs and goats (McNab 1908; Salmond
1997). In the same year, Te Pahi made the return journey to Norfolk
Island on the ship on which Matara had arrived, then traveled on to visit
Governor King at Port Jackson, in order to explore the European world
there for himself (Elder 1932; McNab 1908, 1914; Salmond 1997).

At Port Jackson, Te Pahi presented Governor King with gifts
of mats and weapons, explaining that his visit came about through
the reports of Tuki and Huru, at the request of his father, and "at
the prospect of procuring other benefits for the country, such as had
eventuated from the introduction of the potatoes by Tuki and Huru"
(McNab 1914: 105). During his time in Port Jackson Te Pahi made a
strong impression on Samuel Marsden, who reported that Te Pahi
was "the first New Zealand chief I had seen at Port Jackson, and
with whom I had formed a particular intimacy," considering him "a
man of high rank and influence in his own country. He possessed a
clear, strong and comprehensive mind, and was anxious to gain what
knowledge he could of our laws and customs" (Elder 1932: 205, 59).
Marsden's meetings with Te Pahi led him to make immediate plans
for a Christian mission to the Bay of Islands, to be founded under the
patronage of the chief.

After 3 months living with Governor King at Government House,
Te Pahi returned to the Bay of Islands in 1806 on the *Lady Nelson*, with
gifts including an inscribed silver medal, as well as maize and other
goods from the government store, and gifts from other individuals.
The ship's carpenter erected a European-style house on Te Pahi's
home, the small, fortified island just off shore at Te Puna (see Fig. 4.2).
In return for the hospitality there, Te Pahi sent back to Port Jackson
"great quantities of valuable native curios, some fine seed potatoes,
and some equally fine spars" (McNab 1914: 108), the seed potatoes
being especially welcome in the colony where famine was endemic.

Two years later, Te Pahi made a second journey to Port Jackson. The intervening period of increased trade had not brought benefits for the people of Te Puna. A number of disastrous events occurred, including the kidnapping of Te Pahi's daughter Atahoe and her husband George Bruce. On the return voyage to Te Puna in 1806, English convict Bruce was also on board the *Lady Nelson* with Te Pahi and his sons. When the *Lady Nelson* left the Bay, Bruce remained behind at Te Puna, evidently at the request of Te Pahi (Bruce n.d. [1817]). Bruce stayed at Te Puna for 18 months, during which time he married Te Pahi's daughter Atahoe and received a full facial tattoo. The tragic story of Bruce and Atahoe's kidnapping, travels to India and back to Port Jackson, and Atahoe's death there have been documented by a number of writers (Bruce n.d.; McNab 1914; Salmond 1997). Bruce, however, played an important role for Te Pahi at Te Puna, becoming "his factor and interpreter between all the shipping that touched there," acting as the chief's agent in trade (Dening 1974; Nicholas 1817: 372). It was while Bruce was organizing a valuable cargo of timber for Captain Dalrymple of the *General Wellesley* that he and Atahoe were kidnapped by Dalrymple and taken to Penang.

The potato grounds at Te Puna were now the target of pillaging by ships' crews and captains. On one occasion Captain Walker of the *Mercury* raided Te Pahi's potato gardens, taking what they could get of the immature crop and later trying to loot the storage houses. Unjust treatment was commonplace with Te Pahi himself having been tied to the rigging of the *Elizabeth* after a basket of potatoes disappeared, later found in the hold of the ship. On another occasion Te Pahi was flogged when an axe went missing, probably traded for a mat (Salmond 1997).

In Port Jackson on his second visit, Te Pahi found that his complaints about these events and his warnings about the ill treatment of Maori crewmembers on European ships were not heard. King was no longer governor, but had traveled back to England on the same ship as Samuel Marsden, who had sailed to Britain in 1807 to gain the support and resources of the CMS for a New Zealand mission. While Te Pahi stayed briefly at Government House, he was soon left to make his own way, "cruelly neglected and ill-treated," according to Marsden (Havard-Williams 1961: 27). On this visit he featured in the journal of James Finucane, secretary to Lieutenant Joseph Foveaux. Finucane lampooned Te Pahi as "king of New Zealand," and caricatured him in an unflattering portrait (Fig. 2.3) (Bell 1980; Whitaker 1998).

Te Pahi's concern was with the development of a mutual relationship with the European officials at Port Jackson, such as King and Marsden, in order to develop benefits through trade. Unfortunately, he was cheated and taken advantage of by unscrupulous Europeans who stole his crops and meted out unjust treatment to him and his people. On his second visit to Port Jackson, he found those in power (Finucane and Foveaux, following the mutiny against Governor Bligh) treated him with contempt, and that his earlier connections with King and Marsden were disregarded. However, it was Samuel Marsden's friendship with, and esteem for, Te Pahi that spurred Marsden to visit England in order to gather resources for the New Zealand mission. By the time Marsden returned to Port Jackson, Te Pahi was dead.

In March 1810, Marsden and his family arrived back in Sydney with two recruits for the New Zealand mission, William Hall and John King. On board the *Ann* on the return voyage Marsden found Ruatara, nephew of Te Pahi. This young chief was well traveled, and had experienced many difficulties and injustices in the European world (Elder 1932, 1934; McNab 1908, 1914; Nicholas 1817; Salmond 1997). Ruatara was coughing blood and close to death after rough treatment at the hands of a ship's captain, but with Marsden's care his health improved. On arrival in Port Jackson, Marsden found that he could not proceed with the planned mission. At the same time news had arrived of the burning of the *Boyd* in Whangaroa Harbor, 20 miles north of the Bay of Islands some months earlier; nearly all those on board had been killed and eaten in revenge for earlier depredations by the captain of the *Boyd*. The *Sydney Gazette* (1810a) reported Te Pahi as the chief responsible for this, fingered by Tara, a rival chief from the south of the Bay, and identified in a letter by Alexander Berry. Colonel Foveaux and James Finucane were about to leave the colony for Britain. Their ship put in at the Bay of Islands, meeting there with six other vessels where rough justice was dispensed at the hands of the captains and crew of the ships. According to Finucane's journal:

> I set out yesterday morning with some of the captains of the ships at present here and 60 seamen well armed for Tippoonah where we arrived before day light, and on landing…were received with a discharge of musketry and spears by which we had one man killed and some wounded. We soon cleared the island of its inhabitants. A few were killed and the remainder throwing away their arms leaped into the sea and swam to the mainland, leaving their king's house with the presents he had at various times received from our Government and from individuals as a booty to the invaders. (Whitaker 1998: 99)

Te Pahi, wounded in the attack, swam to the mainland where he died shortly after. Sissons et al. (2001), however, state that Te Pahi survived this attack but was subsequently killed fighting against the Ngati Pou of Whangaroa. Finucane reported 70 killed on the island and mainland. Subsequent statements of seamen to the Thames Water Police pointed out that the crew member was killed by friendly fire;

the attack on the island and the people of Te Puna was described as a "wanton piece of business" (Barnes n.d.), and in September 1810 the *Sydney Gazette* (1810b) published a further article exonerating Te Pahi from all responsibility in the sacking of the *Boyd*.

Both Maori and Europeans exacted *utu* (loosely translated as balanced return, good returned for good, bad for bad) in this situation. Initially, Maori responded to the unjust cruelty of the captain of the *Boyd* when he flogged the Maori crewman, George, as the ship sailed for Whangaroa; Europeans from Port Jackson responded with no less violence to the sacking of the ship when they took unjust revenge against Te Pahi and his people for the loss of the ship and her crew.

New Zealand was no longer considered a safe place to visit; plans for the mission were now delayed indefinitely. Ruatara remained with Marsden at Parramatta for some 18 months, learning about European methods of agriculture. He returned to Rangihoua in 1812 with the intention of developing the agricultural economy first undertaken by Te Pahi, and planned to export wheat to Port Jackson, where food supplies were scarce at times (Elder 1932, 1934; Nicholas 1817).

While Te Pahi's part in the *Boyd* affair has been debated since the year of his death (McNab 1908, 1914; Salmond 1997), Marsden believed implicitly in his innocence (Elder 1932). Salmond (1997) suggests that Te Pahi's celebrity status had aroused the jealousy of less powerful people at Port Jackson in 1806. His profile and visibility in the European world made him an accessible target, as did rivalry and inter-hapu warfare in the Bay of Islands, where in 1805 Savage named Te Puna the "capital" of that part of the country.

Te Puna was also a place at which some of the earliest Europeans to live in New Zealand resided. Another lesser-known European resident of Te Puna in the first decade of the nineteenth century was Charlotte Badger, one of two convict women on board the *Venus*. In 1807 the *Venus*, a brig from Port Jackson, was taken by convicts when the ship was out of Tasmania. It sailed on to the Bay of Islands, where Badger, her child and another woman, Catherine Hagerty were left on shore with several of the men. Hagerty died at the Bay, while Badger is said to have lived a number of years at Te Puna before sailing on to Tonga (DNZB 1998; Salmond 1997; *Sydney Gazette* 1807).

Te Pahi was the motivator behind Marsden's plans to establish a mission in New Zealand. Te Pahi "planted the acorn [of the mission] but died before the sturdy oak appeared above the surface of the ground," Marsden's intentions being to establish a mission within Te Pahi's jurisdiction at Te Puna (Marsden quoted in Elder 1932: 201). In the following years, the landscape of Te Puna evoked the presence of Te Pahi for Marsden, Kendall, and later generations of missionary

families, particularly his abandoned island standing just offshore at
Wairoa Bay, *tapu* since the attack in 1810 (Elder 1932; Kendall n.d.a;
Middleton 2003; Williams, Henry junior n.d.).

INTO THE MAORI WORLD: MANA, TAPU, AND UTU

In New Zealand, missionaries entered a world of Maori values of
which they largely remained ignorant, until they were faced with this
difference. These values infused the landscape and affected everyday
behavior (Middleton 2003; Allen 1996). Primary concepts organizing
the Maori world, in particular those of *mana*, *tapu*, and *utu*, confused
Europeans and created conflicts. Missionaries considered these to be
superstitious ideas, which were to be broken down and overthrown, but
they were forced to bow down to them or suffer consequences.

The concept of *mana* is complex and not easily explained or translated from the Maori world into the European. Hohepa (1999: 196)
notes that it is "the driving force to ensure the happiness and good
existence of the tribal nation," a "nonvisible measure" possessed by all
things, consisting of "ancestral or spiritual inheritance, prestige, power,
recognition, efficacy, influence, authority, and other positive virtues."
Mana is closely connected with *tapu* (sacred or set apart under religious restriction) and *utu* (Hohepa 1999). The mana of a person can
grow or be diminished, depending on the actions of that person or others toward him or her. Breaking of *tapu* brought loss of *mana* and the
possibility of retribution, supernatural or otherwise. The *hau*, "wind
of life" or "spirit of the thing given" (Salmond 2000: 39), was central
to *utu* and the relationship of reciprocal return and the maintenance
of *mana*. According to Salmond (2000: 41), *hau*, the breath of life, per-
vades the kin group as the breath of the ancestors; "gifts or insults to
any part of the group thus affected the *hau* of the entire kin group." It
was this kind of connection the missionaries entered into with Maori,
as Marsden engaged with Te Pahi at Port Jackson and looked after
Ruatara on board the *Ann*.

Utu provides a mechanism for maintaining *mana*, by balanced
return, good returned for good, bad for bad. Infringements of tapu,
both of the body and of the land were punished by *utu*. Maori exacted
utu on both Maori and missionary as a means for maintaining *mana*
and *tapu*. European "justice" or revenge was also exacted for Maori
transgressions, in a continuing cycle that marked the early decades of
the nineteenth century. Some of this has been touched on above, with
the sacking of the *Boyd* followed by the killing of Te Pahi and 70 of his
people at Te Puna.

For Maori, concepts such as *mana* and *tapu* charged both the landscape and the body of high ranked persons with cosmic ancestral powers essential for eminence and fertility. This relationship between land and body was clearly demonstrated when chiefs named prominent features of conquered lands after parts of the body (Allen 1996). The infringement of *mana* and *tapu* either through the body or possessions of the chief, or desecration of sacred elements of the landscape brought the possibility of sickness or defeat to those who had allowed the infringement to occur, while *utu* created a return to the status quo (Parsonson 1981).

Into this landscape stepped missionaries, whalers and administrators, confounded and unnerved by these concepts, and confident of the spiritual and economic superiority of their own practices. However, in the early decades of missionary settlement, through their close association with and dependency on Maori, they were forced to submit to the usual, or in some cases, a reduced form of punishment for infringements of *tapu*, carried out by *taua muru* (plundering parties). In this manner, the transformations between Maori and missionary were mutual, and not the one-way process missionaries anticipated. On his arrival in the Bay of Islands in August 1823, Henry Williams appeared acutely aware of the missionaries' subjection to Maori. The decision about the location of the new mission station (eventually sited at Paihia) where he and his wife Marianne would reside "occupied many days, and required great caution, as the missionary becomes one with the tribe with which he is connected. After many pros and cons we decided on the place where we are now at" (Williams, Henry n.d.a October 24 1823). Missionaries, concerned with the sacred which was not of this material world, denied the concept of *tapu*, apart from the use of the term *wairua tapu*, a translation of "Holy Spirit." For them, the landscape was profane, until they had stayed long enough for children or other family members to be buried close by, creating an attachment to place.

Ngapuhi: Whanau, Hapu, and Iwi

The concepts discussed above were organizing principles in the Maori world. In the Bay of Islands and inland toward the Hokianga Harbor on the other, west coast, Ngapuhi, the primary *iwi* or tribe was made up from a number of *hapu*, or subgroups and *whanau* (families) (Ballara 1973; Lee 1983; Munn 1981; Shawcross 1967; Sissons et al. 2001). The principal operational unit of Maori society was the *hapu*, coalescing as a number of family groups. Within the Bay different *hapu* were based at primary locations, with intersecting access to resources and land interwoven in a network of traditional and seasonal rights. Such interwoven rights providing access to different resources of the land (such as fishing, horticulture, and snaring birds and rats) was paralleled in the social world by a "mosaic of local groups which at any time could split up or coalesce into higher order social entities" (Allen 1996: 671; Phillips 1994, 2000 a,b).

Sissons et al. (2001) illustrate these primary locations from about the years 1815 to 1819, and names those chiefs associated with *hapu* and specific places. While Savage had identified Te Puna as "the capital of this part of the country" in 1805, this was no longer the case after the death of Te Pahi in 1810. Tara, of the Ngati Manu *hapu*, was Te Pahi's rival across the bay at Kororareka (Fig. 1.1), and it was Tara who identified Te Pahi as responsible for the sacking of the *Boyd*, an easy means to have his rival taken out. Sissons identified Hongi Hika, who was born at Kaikohe, near Waimate, with three different *hapu* (Binney 2007; Sissons et al. 2001; Sissons 2007). Hongi's areas of influence extended from his gardens at Te Puna, to Kerikeri, and inland from there toward Waimate. After Hongi's death in 1828, his relatives Rewa and Moka were based at Kerikeri where Rewa was the leader of the *hapu* and pivotal to relations with the mission (Elder 1932, 1934; Easdale 1991; Binney 2007). Sissons et al. (2001: 36) point out that

At the most general level, the hapu of the Bay of Islands were related in terms of a political triangle – northern alliance, southern alliance, and Ngare Raumati

The *hapu* located at Rangihoua and Te Puna formed part of the northern alliance. Within these alliances of Ngapuhi itself there was a degree of inter-*hapu* rivalry and conflict, and change of control of strategic trading locations, focused in particular on Kororareka as this port came to have increasing importance for provisioning ships. This conflict and rivalry appeared as an "ebb and flow of kin and strangers across the landscape" (Munn 1981: 22), a series of renegotiations of control of important places characteristic of Maori society at the time of European contact. This was before 1840 when the signing of the Treaty of Waitangi projected Maori tribal groups into a new legal environment and fixed tribal boundaries. The ebb and flow during the early period is demonstrated in the ongoing rivalry between different *hapu* and intermittent skirmishing for control of the main trading centers such as Kororareka and Paroa Bay (Earle 1909; Lee 1983; Shawcross 1967; Sissons et al. 2001). There were a number of battles, as the northern alliance appeared to struggle for supremacy even after Hongi's death, among others, skirmishes for Paroa Bay in 1828 and Kororareka in 1830. At the same time, Ngapuhi *hapu* would coalesce as a tribe under chiefs such as Hongi Hika and Te Morenga to wage war against *iwi* in other parts of the country.

In the first decade of the Oihi mission, Rangihoua Pa and the beach below Oihi was the regular gathering point for Ngapuhi war parties traveling (and returning) by canoe to the south, moving against the *iwi* of Tamaki, Hauraki, and the Bay of Plenty. Missionaries saw all conflicts, both inter-*hapu* and inter-*iwi*, as a challenge and attempted to intervene for peace, a role that was subsequently identified with Henry Williams (Carleton 1948; Elder 1932, 1934; Rogers 1961, 1998).

John and Hannah King

Samuel Marsden employed John King at a time when he believed that "mechanics," that is to say, craftsmen or tradesmen were the most useful people to establish the New Zealand mission. In this respect, King may be typical of the converts the Evangelical Revival produced in the early years of the nineteenth century, literate, but only just, and of humble origins.

King was born in Swerford, a small farming village in England, in 1787, the fourth of seven children of John and Sarah King (nee Holloway). John King's father, also John King, was a shoemaker, a skill that his son learnt. While there was no school in the Swerford parish, there was a schoolroom attached to the church at Nether Worton, where John King junior lived for a time, so it may have been here that he learned to read and write (Higgins 2001). King's lack of fluency was of some concern to him, and in his New Zealand journals he later expressed concern about his inability to write well, and his determination to improve this, as his later journals and letters demonstrate. At Nether Worton, John King came under the influence of one of the leading evangelical Anglicans of early nineteenth century in Britain, Daniel Wilson, later Bishop of Calcutta (Berry 1981; Higgins 2001; Stock 1913). Wilson, a tutor at Oxford from 1804 to 1809, was also curate of the Wortons (including Nether Worton) at this time, whose sermons were known for attracting crowds from miles away, in the manner of the Evangelical Revival. John King and his friend Thomas Wheeler were "driven to their knees" and converted to the Evangelical cause after listening to Wilson, who subsequently appears to have acted as mentor to John King in the missionary field (for example, see Wilson, Daniel n.d.). Wilson recommended King to the CMS, and Marsden, on his visit to England in 1808, drove through a snowstorm to interview him at Nether Worton. King was subsequently instructed in flax-dressing, twine-spinning, and rope-making skills, which Marsden hoped would be useful in passing on to the New Zealanders. John King left Britain in August 1809 with Samuel Marsden and William Hall.

On arrival in New South Wales in 1810, King lived at Parramatta, while Marsden waited for a suitable time to send the missionaries to the Bay of Islands. It was here that King met the young Hannah Hansen, born in 1792, the daughter of Captain Thomas Hansen and his wife, also Hannah. The family had sailed to the colony of Port Jackson in 1807 on board Thomas Hansen's ship, the *Duke of Portland*, when Hannah was aged 15, along with her older brother Thomas (Berry 1981; Martin 1990). Hannah Hansen and John King were married at Samuel Marsden's parish church, St. John's, in Parramatta, on November 10 1812, with Thomas Hansen and Dinah Hall (wife of William) acting as witnesses. Their first child, Philip Hansen King, was born in August 1813. Hannah gave birth to another 11 children in New Zealand, nine of whom survived to adulthood (Berry 1981; Evans 1989). Their Christian names all reflect John and Hannah King's family connections, with the names of John King's siblings, mother's maiden name, and his friend Thomas Wheeler given to the next generation.

OIHI 1814

In 1814 Marsden considered that the dangers associated with the sacking of the *Boyd* had abated. He sent out William Hall and Thomas Kendall, who had arrived in Port Jackson in 1813 to join the New Zealand mission, on a reconnaissance voyage to Ruatara's territory in the Bay of Islands. On their arrival at Rangihoua William Hall explained to the people of the *pa*

> That we would come and live with them and bring our wives and families if they would not injure them, and I told them that I was a Carpenter and that I would build them large houses and fine Canoes, and they seemed very much pleased with the Idea and expressed their joy by saying, "Nuee nuee rungateeda pakehaa" – a very great Gentleman white man. (Hall in Salmond 1997: 436)

Salmond (1997: 21–22) discusses varying origins and early uses of the term Pakeha, describing Europeans. One version states that it followed the Maori term for pale-colored flax used to make garments, while another gives its origins from the pre-European word "pakepakeha," after an ancient light-skinned people. Maori, used to identifying themselves to each other by tribal affiliation, came to identify themselves as "Maori," or ordinary, in the context of the presence of Pakeha. While Maori at Rangihoua used this term to refer to the missionaries,

Figure 2.4. Oihi mission station (at *right*) and Rangihoua pa (*left*), 1827 (Artist Augustus Earle, 1793–1838. Rex Nan Kivell Collection, National Library of Australia. PIC T176 NK12/139)

the missionaries did not identify themselves or other Europeans as "Pakeha" at this time.

Hall (n.d) and Thomas Kendall (n.d.a) returned to Port Jackson with favorable reports. In November 1814, the *Active* sailed again for Rangihoua, with the full complement of those for the mission. The ship anchored off Rangihoua Pa on December 22 1814, Marsden having decided that the mission should be established close to the pa under the protection of both Hongi Hika and Ruatara, close relatives of the deceased Te Pahi. As Marsden (quoted in Elder 1932: 206) expressed it, "Tippahee being dead, and Shunghee [Hongi] promising, with Duaterra [Ruatara], that he would take care of the missionaries, they came, and were placed under their protection by me." The missionaries were clearly under the control of those in the pa, incorporated into the Maori world through the relationship of *utu* that began with Marsden's friendship with Te Pahi and developed with his care for Ruatara on board the *Ann*. The mission, located alongside the *pa*, is depicted in an 1822 map of the district (Fig. 2.4) and in an 1827 watercolor by the English artist Augustus Earle (Fig. 2.5).

Rangihoua was an important *pa* during the first years of contact between Maori and European. Sissons (2001: 38) states that Te Hikutu was probably the principal *hapu* located there, with Ngati Rua also present. Others name Ngati Rehia as the main *hapu* (for example, McCormick 1966; Spencer 1983), while today the *hapu* of Ngati Tore

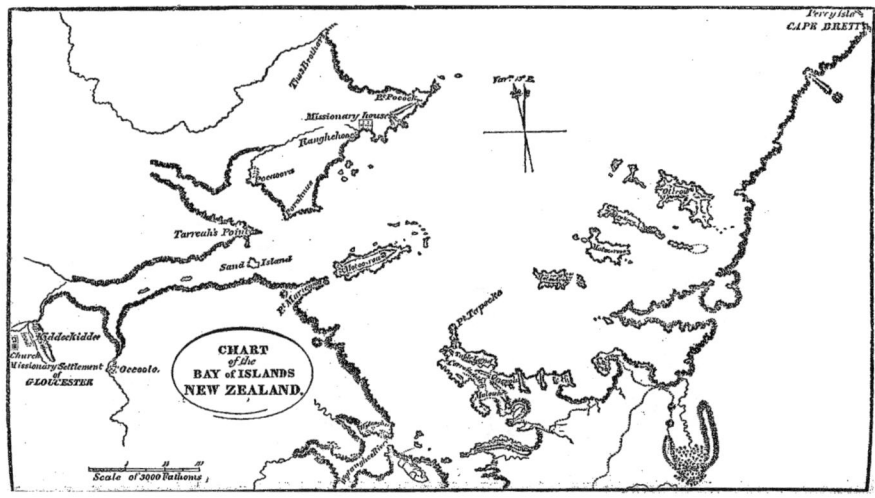

Figure 2.5. Chart of the Bay of Islands New Zealand, 1822 (CMS *Missionary Register* 1822)

Hina is considered to have *mana whenua*, dating back to Te Pahi and earlier times (Whakaaropai Rihari personal communication September 2002). While Ruatara may also have had closer links to other *hapu*, Sissons notes his connections to Te Hikutu. Marsden (1932: 459) states that Waikato and Wharepoaka, Ruatara's brother-in-law were both Hikutu. Rakau, Ruatara's father-in-law and father of Wharepoaka, was the *tohunga* and principal chief of Rangihoua (Cloher 2003; Sissons et al. 2001). Te Paea Waiawa Riwhi, an elder recorded in the minutes of the Maori Land Court, states that Te Pahi "was of several tribes. He could have been Ngapuhi, Tahawai, Ngati Ruanui" (Department of Conservation n.d: folio 48). Through cognatic descent Maori could have links to a number of different *hapu* on either the male or female line, maintaining stronger links to perhaps only one or two of these (Allen 1996; Salmond 1991b).

The CMS missionaries consisted of John and Hannah King and their eldest son, Phillip Hansen King, William and Dinah Hall, and Thomas and Jane Kendall and their five children. Hannah King, heavily pregnant at the time, was lowered from the missionary ship *Active* to a waiting boat seated in a wooden chair. Hannah King also had other family members with her. Her father, Thomas Hansen, was captain of the *Active*, and his wife, also Hannah, as well as their oldest son Thomas were on board. There were a number of tradesmen such as sawyers, a brick maker, and a blacksmith, some of these "ticket of leave" convicts from the colony of New South Wales under the supervision of Marsden and the missionaries. Marsden (Elder 1932) records a total of 25 Europeans left at Oihi, the original number increased by one by the birth of the Kings' second son on February 20 1815, under somewhat grueling conditions. Three days after their arrival Marsden celebrated the first Christmas and church service in New Zealand, Christmas Day falling on a Sunday on that occasion (Bawden 1976; Elder 1932).

None of the missionaries were ordained ministers. They were artisans, chosen according to Marsden's belief that nothing could "pave the way for the introduction of the Gospel but civilization, – and that can only be accomplished among the Heathen by the arts" (quoted in Stock 1899: 206). Thomas Kendall, schoolmaster, was the nominal leader of the group, but was quickly challenged and criticized by Hall and King (n.d.c; Marsden n.d.a; Pratt and Bickersteth n.d.). Marsden (quoted in Elder 1932: 224) listed his instructions to the missionaries in a letter to the secretary of the CMS:

> Mr. Hall was to procure a cargo of spars for the *Active* against her return. Mr. King was to collect the flax which the natives brought for sale, and Mr. Kendall was to devote himself to the school. Messrs. Hall and King were also to instruct the natives in agriculture or anything they could for their general improvement.

The *Active* set sail to return to Port Jackson on 25 February 1815, taking Marsden and a number of chiefs from the Bay of Islands back to Parramatta. Three days before his departure Marsden purchased 200 acres of land adjacent to Rangihoua, from "the two nephews of the late Tippahee," Te Uri o Kanae and his brother "Warree" (Elder 1932: 123; Nicholas 1817: 192). "Kana" had been injured along with Te Pahi in the raid on the island in 1810, but had survived after swimming to the shore (Sissons et al. 2001: 18). Te Uri o Kanae (Fig. 2.6) signed the deed with a copy of his *moko*, and Thomas Kendall and John Nicholas signed for the CMS.

The main part of the deed stated:

> I, Ahoodee o Gunna, King of Rangheehoo,...do give ... and sell unto the Committee of the Church Missionary Society for Africa and the East...all that piece and parcel of land situate in the district of Hoshee, in the Island of New Zealand, bounded on the south side by the bay of Tippoona and the town of Rangheehoo, on the north side by a creek of fresh water, and on the west by a public road into the interior. (Elder 1932: 123; Nicholas 1817: 194)

Marsden paid 12 axes for the 200 acres, the first purchase by a European of any land in New Zealand. By this time Ruatara was dangerously ill with a fever, perhaps the result of his earlier illness on board the *Ann*. However, the missionaries do not specify this illness beyond a

Figure 2.6. Te Uri o Kanae, chief of Rangihoua, c. 1814 (Artist J. W. Lewin 1770–1819.
Alexander Turnbull Library, Wellington, New Zealand. A-327-042)

general "fever," or a "cold with inflammatory symptoms" according to
Nicholas (1817: II, 150). Nicholas (1817: I, 23–24) described Ruatara at
this time as

> In the full bloom of youth,...a man of tall and commanding stature, great
> muscular strength, and marked expression of countenance: his deportment,
> which I will not hesitate to call dignified and noble, appeared well calcu-
> lated to give sanction to his authority

The missionaries first came into conflict with Maori values when they
wanted to visit Ruatara on his sickbed with food and drink, but were
only allowed to do so after much negotiating on their part. King reported
that Marsden finally threatened to "fetch the big Guns and blow up
the Town and set it all on fire, with this the natives permitted Mr. M
to see [Ruatara] and give him a little refreshment" (King n.d.c July
4 1815; Pratt n.d.). Ruatara was considered highly *tapu*, as was anything he touched. Maori were concerned that any breaking of this *tapu*
by the Europeans would exacerbate his condition (Elder 1932, 1934).

Thomas Kendall wrote to Marsden in March, telling him that a few days after the *Active* left, Ruatara "was conveyed from the village [Rangihoua] upon a kind of bier to a hill at Tippoona upon which in his lifetime he had proposed to you a town should be built, a shed having been previously prepared for his reception" (Elder 1934: 75). Ruatara died there a day later, his wife Rahu hanging herself soon after Ruatara's death. Both their bodies lay in state on a stage erected on this spot, enclosed by Hongi with a board and railing fence, until being moved later to a burial place (Elder 1934: 83). On his deathbed, Ruatara told his wife to ensure that the people of Te Puna continued to be kind to the missionaries after his death, no doubt in order to continue the relationship of reciprocity that was first established by Marsden and Te Pahi, and continued with Marsden's care for Ruatara when he was sick on board the *Ann*. Salmond (2000: 39) has analyzed the events around Ruatara's death as a clash of Maori and European cosmologies, brought about by the intermingling of the *hau* (breath, or "wind of life") of Marsden and Ruatara during Ruatara's illness on board the *Ann*.

The role of protector of the missionaries largely fell upon Hongi from this point on, while Waikato, Wharepoaka, and Te Uri o Kanae, chiefs of Rangihoua and Te Puna continued to be closely involved with the mission, as well as the elderly *tohunga* Rakau (Elder 1932, 1934; Sissons et al. 2001; Cloher 2003). Te Uri o Kanae moved from Rangihoua to the Kawakawa area in 1819 (Elder 1932: 169). Hongi Hika was uncle to Ruatara, of the same generation as Ruatara's mother. Both were descendants of Te Wairua, and some generations further back, of Rahiri, the founding ancestor of the Ngapuhi *iwi*.

On arrival at Oihi, the missionaries and men from the pa set about constructing a large building out of *raupo* (reed) that would house them all. This shelter, 14 ft. by 60 ft., was divided into four sections, one for each family (Elder 1932). Samuel Marsden and the mission tradesmen were also housed there. John King's letter of 15 February 1815 to the Rev. Daniel Wilson describes their conditions at Oihi:

> We arrived at this Port and are in good health, but our House or Hut is made with flags by the natives it has no Chimney in it it will neither keep wind nor rain out, we have no window in it Mr. M [Marsden] gave orders to have it made he says it is very comfortable indeed it will do very well, This is a very wet Day it has been so for this three days on Sunday last Feb 12 it rained very much the water came through upon our wheat rice bed clothing and the water was half over my shoes in our bedroom from the wetness of the durt floor as our hut is on low flat ground our clothing damp & tho we do all we can to keep them dry we have no fire to dry them when it rains as our fire is out of doors for my own part I am in good health but it is uncomfortable indeed for my wife and Child in the state she is in, it will be a great blessing

indeed if it does not make her suffer exceedingly as she has taken a severe
cold already. (King n.d.d).

A few days later the Kings' second son was born, John King noting:
"Mrs. King was put to bed on Monday 20th with a son." John Nicholas,
Marsden's companion, recorded his futile efforts not to laugh "though I
desired him to desist from so unseemly a detail" as one of the men from
Rangihoua Pa, "servant" to Hannah King's mother Hannah Hansen,
mimicked her cries in labor, mocking the response of this European
woman to such an everyday event as childbirth (Nicholas1817 I: 171).
King's remarks about Marsden's attitude toward this inadequate
house point to the on-going conflict the missionaries at Oihi experienced with him.

The *Active* was sent to the Kawakawa district on the opposite side
of the Bay for timber for more permanent buildings, little being available near Rangihoua. The carpenter, William Hall, was paid to start
building houses for Kendall and King, and a schoolhouse, but by July
1815 Kendall was writing to Marsden asking for another carpenter for
the settlement, doubting that William Hall would ever be able to finish
the structures (Elder 1934: 90, 103). Houses for individual families, as
well as the schoolhouse, were eventually completed. William Hall (n.d.)
noted in his journal for 18 May 1816 "This week Mr. King and Thomas
Hansen have both shifted out of the thatched huts Mr. King's house
was built by Thorn the carpenter." Missionary journals refer to individual houses, and De Blosseville, from Duperrey's expedition on *La
Cocquille*, noted four missionary houses at Oihi on a brief visit in 1824
(Sharp 1971; Spencer 1983). Cruise (1974), visiting 4 years earlier, had
also commented on the English style of the houses.

However, there were problems with the location of the mission
that continued throughout its occupation. Both Kendall and King
had objected to the site of Oihi from the beginning, situated in a narrow, steep valley where there was little flat land suitable for gardening (Elder 1934: 98). Marsden had insisted on this location because
the little valley was in close proximity to the pa, Rangihoua, which he
believed was an essential factor in protecting the mission from attack
from other tribes.

THE MISSION: ORGANIZATION AND TRADE

The New Zealand mission's ultimate governing body was the Church
Missionary Society's London committee, the organization that Samuel
Marsden had traveled to England to see in 1809 in order to gain their
permission to establish the New Zealand mission. The New Zealand

missionaries were required to send copies of six monthly reports and daily journals to the London committee, with the committee responding to any queries or requests in a process that could take a year or more for a reply through irregular shipping channels. Correspondence was generally written by the committee's secretary, with names such as Josiah Pratt and Samuel Bickersteth featuring prominently in this role. Samuel Marsden, closer to the Bay of Islands at Parramatta, took a firmer controlling hand with his New Zealand mission and its finances (Stock 1899; Standish 1962). In the Bay of Islands, all the missionaries, both ordained and layman, participated in a local committee, but the mission was run according to rules fixed by the London committee.

When William Hall and John King left London with Marsden in 1809 the committee instructed them, among other things to "guard earnestly the sacredness of the sabbath-day; never to omit family worship, and to perform it as publicly as possible, by reading Scripture or singing loud enough to be heard by a passing Native." They were to converse with the Natives about sin and salvation "when employed in planting potatoes, sowing corn, or in any other occupation." As regards civil conduct, they were told to "spend no time in idleness" but to "occupy every moment set apart for labor in agriculture, building houses or boats, spinning twine, or some other useful occupation... If you indulge in idleness, you will be ruined." They were to "make themselves independent in respect of provisions, by cultivating grain and rearing pigs and poultry," a regulation that was very difficult to carry out and caused hardship. On no account were they to be drawn into local wars. "Tell them you are forbidden by the Chiefs who sent you out" (Stock 1899: 206–207). A superintendent or nominal leader was established. Thomas Kendall was given this role in 1814, but his actions caused much conflict between himself and Hall and King. In 1820, Rev. John Butler became superintendent, but was dismissed in 1823, the same year that Rev. Henry Williams arrived to become the first effective leader of the CMS in New Zealand.

Missionaries (that is, unordained missionaries, called "settlers" according to Marsden) were paid a fixed salary of £20 for each man and woman and £10 for each child in the family. In 1820, "Rules for the Settlement" detailed weekly provisions from the mission store:

For every man
8 lb Flour
5 lb of Salt Pork or 7 lb of Fresh meat
1 lb of Sugar
2 oz Tea & 1/4 lb Soap

For every woman
8 lb Flour
4 lb of Salt Pork or 6 lb of Fresh meat
1 lb of Sugar, 2 oz of Tea & 1/4 lb Soap
And for every child
4 lb Flour
4 lb of Salt Pork or 5 lb of Fresh Meat
1 lb Sugar, 1 oz of Tea & 2 oz of Soap (CMS n.d.c)

The superintendent could increase the provisions if it seemed necessary. Whale oil for lighting and lamp cotton were also included in the
quarterly rations. Supplies were ordered from Port Jackson as well as
London by the storekeeper at Kerikeri. All other missionaries were
subject to the superintendent, who could make binding decisions about
mission matters. Missionaries were to obey the superintendent's directions "according to their several offices, Trades and calling, and shall
account to him for all their labor and time" (CMS n.d.c, undated, but
c. 1820). Each person (or family) permanently engaged by the society
was entitled to a house, yard, and garden to be cultivated "for their
private individual benefit." No member of the mission was allowed to
acquire or hold any private property, other than that granted to them
by the Society. No private trade was to be undertaken with Maori or
with any ships, except for the "general account and benefit of the mission." All stores, including goods acquired from Maori (such as additional food supplies) or from any other sources were to be deposited
in the mission store and distributed to those engaged in the mission
"according to their wants" (CMS n.d.c).

William Colenso, who arrived in Paihia in 1834, later recalled
that

> The weekly allowance of foreign rations was very small ... it was said to have
> been the same in quantity as the convicts' allowance in Sydney; a single
> ration not being sufficient for one person (as in my own case), but a number
> coming together – as in a large family where all received rations, did better.
> (Colenso 1888: 28)

The superintendent (as chairman) was to call monthly committee
meetings, with reports of activities and finances submitted quarterly,
although it appears that the frequency of meetings changed from the
later 1830s, with only quarterly and occasional "special" meetings held.
All the missionaries (men, but not their wives) attended meetings,
whether ordained or not. The committee made decisions about the day-
to-day running of the missions such as whether a member could build
a house, the expenditure of committee finance for such things, the relocation of personnel between missions, and the setting up of schools.

While members submitted reports and accounts to quarterly meetings that were copied into the minutes, reports and journals were also sent back to the CMS in London, where excerpts were published annually in the *Missionary Register*.

A blacksmith, Walter Hall, came with the mission families in 1814. Marsden directed Thomas Kendall to keep "an exact account" of all the work the blacksmith did. He considered the smith "the principal person for procuring by his labor, pork, fish, potatoes and such things as they want from the natives. Nothing could be done without the smith.... A pious smith or two would be a great blessing" (Marsden n.d.a to the Secretary Oct. 26 1815). The blacksmith was an essential member of the mission, important for his skills in manufacturing metal trade items (Middleton 2007d). However, by 1827 the preferred trade goods had changed from hardware to blankets due perhaps to a decline in the demand for muskets in the Bay of Islands from about 1823. In this year, the committee requested the CMS in Britain "to send in future three-fourths of the amount of trade usually sent out, in Blankets weighing 4 lb each" (CMS n.d.a August 1827). The issue of missionaries trading on their own accounts, forbidden by the Society's rules, was often a cause of disagreement and continuing conflict, setting up the potential for a "black" economy to operate outside the firm control of the CMS.

Although Henry Williams used hard currency to pay for stores from ships (Rogers 1961), it does not appear to have been in consistent local use until after annexation in 1840. At times missionaries were tempted to exchange muskets for food, the most acceptable trade goods for Maori. In 1823, Marsden (n.d.a) wrote to the secretary Josiah Pratt, blustering that "the missionaries had fallen into another serious error. Some of them had purchased provisions from the natives with dollars....I saw this evil would be as great as the other [trade in muskets], as this would furnish the natives with the means of purchasing muskets either from the ships or Port Jackson." Marsden considered that Maori would never accept "iron" if they could trade in dollars. In the same letter, he insisted that the missionaries

> want for nothing. No persons can have more of the comforts of life than they enjoy. The difficulties the missionaries have met with in New Zealand originate from their perverse tempers, their pride, envy and a secular spirit. (Marsden n.d.a)

At the same time, in a demonstration of his lack of consistency, Marsden had founded the mission on the premise that "commerce" or consumption of goods was the means to introduce Maori to "civilization" and Christianity. While he suggested that the CMS should both encourage and control commercial enterprise in New Zealand, Maori were in control of trade and missionaries had to accept trade on their terms, which led to trading in muskets (CMS n.d.c; Elder 1932, 1934).

These conditions set the Oihi mission on a course of potential conflict with Samuel Marsden. The missionaries, poorly resourced, struggling with difficult conditions, terrified at times by threats and plundering by war parties gathering on the small beach in front of their homes, still managed to fulfill Marsden's instructions. School was taught initially in Kendall's home. The schoolhouse was opened in August 1816 with 33 pupils aged between seven and seventeen. By April 1817 the roll had risen to 70 (Elder 1934: 128). Reports from Oihi in the 1820s note the numbers being taught, sometimes only six boys and the same number of girls, at other times sixteen boys and about the same number of girls, children from the neighboring Rangihoua Pa. It seems that while the boys attended the school, girls were taught by the missionary wives in their homes (CMS n.d.a). By early 1825, the year he returned to Port Jackson, William Hall (CMS n.d.a) had built another school house "20 ft. by 12 ft. convenient to Mr. King's dwelling so that he may have the boys more immediately under his eye at all times." The pupils were fed and clothed at the school, presenting some problems for the scant resources of the mission. In 1816, Kendall was writing to the CMS in Britain, requesting trade articles that could be given to pupils, including thimbles, needles, knives, hair combs, and boys' whistles, in return for school attendance.

King (Elder 1934: 99) also fulfilled his missionary duties:

> It is my full intention to take one or two boys to learn to spin and to make shoes, to read and do anything else that may be useful. Mrs. King will have one or two girls to instruct in writing, sewing, making any sort of clothing, to knit and spin. These things she is well qualified to teach them, and to wash and clean the house.

These were the kind of activities that John and Hannah King carried out during their years at Oihi and Te Puna. At the same time, the small community was plagued by dissent.

A Community in Conflict

Within the first year, Thomas Kendall was writing to John King to heal a breach between them over materials for housing and iron items from the smith that could be used to trade with Maori. Journals detail ongoing conflict between Hall, King, and Kendall, while letters from Samuel Marsden demonstrate his own antagonisms, not only toward Kendall, who Marsden dismissed from the CMS in 1823, but also toward King, Hall, and later, other missionaries (Marsden n.d.a, n.d.b). Letters detailing this conflict traveled at the slowest speed from Hall, King, and Kendall to Marsden and onward to the CMS in London. In November 1816, King (n.d.c) wrote to his old mentor, Daniel Wilson, asking him to "Accept, Dear Sir, of my thanks for your kind and faithful reproofs" after Wilson (n.d.) wrote a highly critical letter to King for not following Marsden's authority, accusing him of being "at ease in worldly security" and exhorting him to "meekness, forbearance, obedience, prayer." In March 1818, Josiah Pratt wrote reprovingly to King:

> It does not appear to us that you are zealously exerting yourself, as you should be, in promoting the objects of the Society. You must entirely conform to Mr. Marsden's directions or return to Port Jackson and provide for yourself independently of the Society. (Pratt and Bickersteth n.d.)

Pratt accused King of unchristian conduct, pointing out "Mr. Kendall has not complained of you, as you evidently do of him." This conflict appeared to simmer for a number of years, while the missionaries at Oihi struggled to obtain necessities; the time taken up with "secular concerns" (Shepherd in CMS n.d.a April 1827) often meant they were unable to take up their religious pursuits to the extent required of them. In his letter to Daniel Wilson in November 1816, King complained that they had been without tea and sugar since July, "and should have been without wheat if we had not got a little from a friend." By the following year King had fenced in two acres of land and sowed most of this in wheat, but did not expect a prolific crop. In 1823, the disputes with Marsden were still simmering. At the end of 1822 John King had returned a quantity of shoe leather to the mission store "having declined making shoes" (CMS n.d.d). Marsden wrote to King in November of 1823, when he was visiting the Bay of Islands:

> In consequence of what passed last evening between you and myself relative to your instructing some of the native youths (one or more) to make a pair of shoes, allow me to address a few lines to you upon the subject ... It is my duty to point out to you what you ought to do, as well as to all others employed in the service of the Society. It rests with you whether you will obey or disobey. (Marsden n.d.a)

Neither Marsden nor King provides any further details of what had taken place "last evening." Marsden accused King of disobedience and disrespect which "originated from highmindedness, from that abominable spirit of pride, which has so disgraced the mission," and in the process demonstrated the autocratic style of leadership that so often brought him into conflict with those in the New Zealand mission.

Missionaries depended on supplementary pork and potatoes, supplies they needed to procure by barter from local Maori. These were often difficult to obtain. Maori preferred to deal with the ships anchored

in the Bay, whose captains traded more desirable items such as muskets for pork (Elder 1934: 100). Timber for building had to be towed
from the south of the Bay. Internal conflict was also fuelled by individual trade with shipping, rather than pooling resources for the mission. There were continual accusations among the missionaries about
who was dealing in muskets for food supplies and who was indulging
in too much alcohol.

Throughout the early years of mission settlement in the Bay
of Islands missionaries were within Maori control. Marsden (Elder
1932, 1934) felt vindicated in his decision to place the mission at Oihi
when in 1815 William Hall moved to Waitangi, a more appealing location with flat, arable land 10 miles up the harbor from Oihi. Hall
and his wife were only there long enough to establish their house,
when they were attacked, robbed of their possessions and Mrs. Hall
knocked unconscious. They fled back to the Oihi settlement immediately. These events can be related back to the early friendships of
Marsden with Te Pahi and Ruatara, and the early incorporation of
the mission into the tribe at Rangihoua, where it was protected from
real harm, even though the missionaries were threatened at times by
strange tribes gathering at the beach to join war parties traveling to
other areas.

THE EXPANSION OF THE MISSION: KERIKERI, PAIHIA, AND WAIMATE

From 1819, missionary numbers in the Bay of Islands increased
and other stations were slowly established (see Fig. 1.1). In the same
year the Wesleyan Samuel Leigh, who had first arrived in New South
Wales in 1815, made a brief visit to the Bay of Islands, sailing immediately afterward for Britain to gather resources for a Wesleyan mission
to New Zealand. His time in Britain coincided with the visit of Kendall,
Hongi Hika, and Waikato. Leigh introduced Hongi to the WMS and
Hongi stayed some time with Leigh (Cloher 2003; Owens 1974). Leigh
and his wife arrived back in the Bay of Islands early in 1822. They lived
with William and Dinah Hall at Rangihoua for 18 months before moving to set up the Wesleyan mission further north at Whangaroa Harbor
(Owens 1974; Elder 1932, 1934).

In 1819 Samuel Marsden returned to the Bay of Islands, on board
the same ship as Samuel Leigh. Marsden brought with him the first
ordained missionary to New Zealand, the Rev. John Butler and his
family, along with other new recruits, James and Charlotte Kemp, and
Francis Hall. Butler, Kemp, and their families, along with Francis Hall

Figure 2.7. Kerikeri stone store and mission house, 2003

were established at a new station at Kerikeri (Fig. 2.7), close to Hongi's main settlement.

Butler soon fell out with Marsden, and was dismissed by him in 1823 for drunkenness. Other factors may have been behind this, though, Butler himself accusing Marsden of gun running (Butler n.d.).

The Kerikeri station continued to thrive without Butler, acting for a time as the center of missionary activity. Hongi's neighboring *kainga* near the pa of Kororipo ensured the mission's importance (Binney 2007; Middleton 2007c). The mission store was located at Kerikeri, with supplies dispersed from there to other stations. New arrivals were accommodated in the houses already built. George Clarke, his wife, and infant son arrived from New South Wales (having left the Parramatta Native Institution) in April 1824 on board the French corvette *Coquille*, moving into the house Butler had built in 1822. Butler had come under further fire of extravagance from Marsden, for building such an unnecessarily large, commodious dwelling (Barton 1927). The Kemp family eventually settled in the house after the Clarkes moved to Waimate. The house still stands, now known as the Kerikeri Mission House (Fig. 2.7; Binney 2007).

In August 1823 Henry and Marianne Williams arrived in the Bay with Samuel Marsden, on his fourth visit, establishing a third mission station at Paihia. Williams, an ex-naval lieutenant and an ordained minister, was installed as the leader of the missions in the Bay of

Islands and was joined 3 years later by his brother William Williams and his wife Jane. The latter two, after some years at Paihia, moved to the East Coast. Both Williams' families became influential figures in the CMS (Carleton 1948; Fitzgerald 2004; Porter 1974; Rogers 1961, 1998; Rountree 2000).

In 1830, the CMS committee decided to set up a fourth station at Waimate which they hoped would become an agricultural center and make the missions generally independent of the parent body of the CMS for food, as had been unrealistically expected at Oihi (Elder 1932, 1934; Hargreaves 1962; Harris 1984; Standish 1962). Bay of Islands missions all held schools for Maori, where the children were clothed and fed, and each missionary household apparently had its Maori members who often carried out the duties of paid domestic servants, while there were also independent households of Maori families who were loosely attached to the mission, employed to carry out tasks such as sawing timber and assisting with building.

By 1826 John King and James Shepherd, who had joined the Bay of Islands CMS in 1820, along with their families, were the only residents at Oihi. Hall had returned with his family to Port Jackson in 1825, due to his chronic ill health, where he acted briefly as superintendent of the Parramatta Native Institution after the Clarkes' move to the Bay of Islands. Marsden had dismissed Kendall in 1823 after some years of disagreement; one of Kendall's initial conflicts with the CMS was caused by his journey to England with Hongi Hika and Waikato, Hongi's relative from Rangihoua, in 1820, without the consent of the Society or Marsden. Kendall's wife Jane and eight children remained at Oihi. The party returned from Britain in 1821, Hongi with 300 muskets to add to his Ngapuhi arsenal. During this visit the three were painted by the artist James Barry (Fig. 2.8; see Bell 1980). In September of that year, Hongi and his war parties left to attack those in the south, armed with over 1000 muskets, unmatched by any other tribe in the country. Kendall was accused of trading in muskets (as were others in the mission), but his ultimate fall came when he co-habited with the daughter of a chief from nearby Kaihiki, who lived with the Kendall family (Binney 2005, 2007; Cloher 2003). Kendall's analysis and study of the Maori language and cosmogony resulted in his being drawn further into the Maori world and away from that of the mission; this was accentuated by his firm alliance with Hongi. Binney's (2005) biography of Kendall provides a close analysis of his work in New Zealand and the conflict of his place between the Maori and European worlds.

The founding of the Kerikeri and Paihia stations changed the focus of the missions in the Bay of Islands, and followed the flux of the Maori

Figure 2.8. Thomas Kendall and the chiefs Hongi Hika and Waikato, 1820 (Artist James Barry. Alexander Turnbull Library, Wellington, New Zealand. G-618)

population, the focus and justification for any of the mission stations. The center of Maori population and action in the Bay of Islands moved from place to place according to local politics and *hapu* ascendancy (Sissons et al. 2001).

In the 1830s the CMS moved outward from the Bay of Islands, sending missionaries to Kaitaia (1833), Puriri, on the Hauraki Plains (1834), and a number of other stations in the Waikato and Tauranga districts from 1835, and Otaki (1839) further to the south (Elder 1932, 1934). Other missionaries followed. To note some of these, John and Anne Wilson arrived in 1833 and after a brief stay at Paihia moved to Te Puna. In 1834, they moved to the Puriri mission with the Fairburns, Morgans, and Preeces (Wilson, Anne C. n.d.; Wilson 1889; Wilson, John n.d.). Other notable missionary arrivals at this period included Colenso, Yate, Matthews, Puckey, Brown, Baker, and Chapman, to name a few. The CMS did not move into the South Island until after the arrival of Bishop Selwyn in 1842 (Stock 1899), although the Wesleyan James Watkin moved to Otago in 1840 under the auspices of whaler Johnny Jones (Tapp 2006).

Oihi: Decline and Abandonment

In 1832 the "Missionary Register" published a lithograph of Oihi, the "Church Missionary Settlement of Rangihoua, New Zealand" (Fig. 2.9). This shows an idealized pastoral English landscape. Oihi appears in the foreground, with mission houses located on flat ground, a tidy row of neat houses and a uniform central street. Rangihoua pa appears in a similar perspective on the neighboring hill, steep but unrealistically uniform, like an English town complete with hedgerows and streets.

In the distance, the landscape of Te Puna has a comparable "civilized" aspect. A version of this painted in oil colors is held in the National Library of Australia (Binney et al. 1990). The reality was quite different. From the beginning of the settlement there were complaints about the unsuitability of this location for a missionary village, due to its steepness and the difficulty of growing food here. By the time the lithograph was published, the settlement was abandoned, and the houses scarcely habitable and beyond repair (Williams, Henry n.d.b).

After only a short period of time at Oihi, Kendall was quite clear about its difficulties, writing to Basil Woodd, secretary of the CMS:

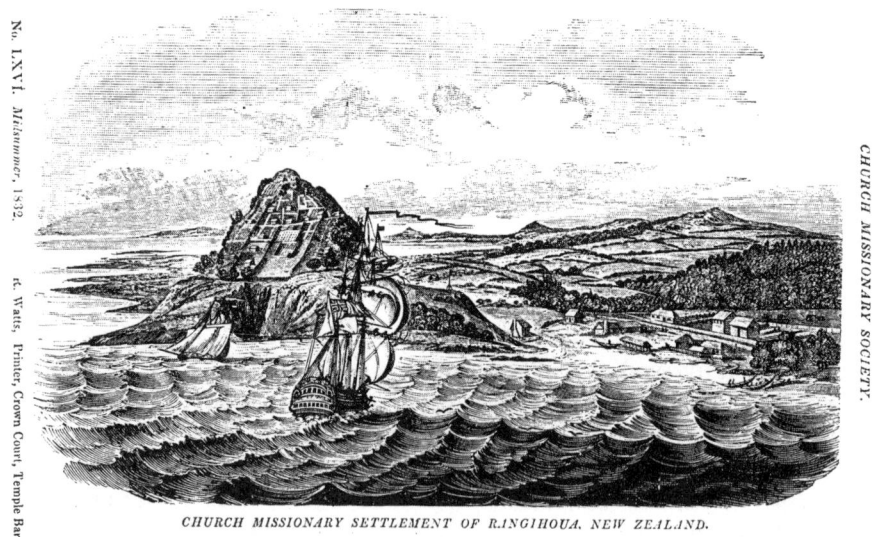

CHURCH MISSIONARY SETTLEMENT OF RANGIHOUA, NEW ZEALAND.

Figure 2.9. Oihi mission station, 1832 (CMS *Missionary Register* 1832; Alexander Turnbull Library, Wellington, New Zealand. PUBL-0031-1832-66)

> We have now resided nearly two years at this place, and to all appearances
> there is no probability of our obtaining the necessaries of life in any other
> way than at the expense of the Society. The spot on which we live is barren,
> and, as you will observe from the view, is so mountainous that it is quite
> unsuitable for the purpose of cultivation or for cattle. I objected to landing
> here at first very strongly to Mr. Marsden, because there was on the other
> side of the village and in sight of it a more even tract of land with a more
> fertile soil. (Elder 1934: 131)

The "more even tract of land" Kendall refers to was Te Puna. By
1828 the CMS committee was discussing the closure of the Oihi mission, where John and Hannah King and James and Harriet Shepherd,
along with their families were now the only missionary residents. Henry
Williams (n.d.b) wrote to Marsden in January 1829, reasoning that "a
great expense would be saved to the Society if [Oihi] were closed....It
must be rebuilt there are but very few Natives & it is situated upon a
point. Whereas we want to work towards the centre from whence light
may proceed to all around." Williams considered that Rangihoua and
Oihi were now on the margins of the CMS (a journey to Oihi from the
other mission stations required rowing 10 miles) and that King and
Shepherd should move to Kerikeri, Waimate, or Paihia.

However, King and Shepherd argued to move the station to Te Puna,
about a kilometer away from Oihi, on the western side of Rangihoua
Pa. In part, this was because Te Puna offered extensive flat and gently
sloping land suitable for both arable and pastoral agriculture. It was
also because of their attachment to place. After 15 years of living at
the Oihi mission station, King argued vehemently not to move away
from the area through his relationship to the people, the place and the
burial of his two infant sons there:

> Our two little Boys are buried in our Garden [at Oihi] and would have to be
> removed by us, or the natives would disturb them there is no doubt as we
> have known one instance of the same, this is the principle thing [I] feel of a
> private nature, we are much attached to the natives of this place especially
> to the rising generation. (King n.d.b June 22 1829)

The first missionary child born at Oihi on February 20 1815,
Thomas Holloway King, had died there three and a half years later,
of tuberculosis. Another son of John and Hannah King, Joseph, was
also buried there, aged three, in 1823. They were followed in 1831 by
the death of the infant Mary, who only lived for 10 days (Evans 1989).
The "one instance of the same" King refers to was the disinterment of
the body of the Turners' child at the Wesleyan mission at Whangaroa
when the settlement was sacked in 1827.

The debate about whether the Te Puna mission would go ahead
appears to have continued for some years, with letters written back to

the CMS secretary in England and lengthy delays in receiving replies. As late as July 1832 James Stack (n.d.), then in England, wrote to Rev. Marsh of the CMS with a long list of "Reasons for continuing Rangihoua" and "Reasons for giving up Rangihoua" (Oihi). It is likely Stack had left New Zealand for Britain some time before, when the debate was still current, as by the time he wrote his list of reasons James and Harriet Shepherd had moved to Te Puna with their family, as did the Kings in September of 1832.

At the time they moved to Te Puna, John and Hannah King had eight surviving children: Philip Hansen King (1813–1880), John Wheeler King (1816–1895), Jane Holloway King (1818–1894), William Spence King (1819–1896), Samuel Leigh King (1822–1871), James King (1825–1877), Hannah King (1827–1886), and Sarah King (1829–1889). Their last child, Elizabeth Marsden King, was born at Te Puna in 1837, the year of Samuel Marsden's final visit to the Bay of Islands prior to his death in 1838 (Berry 1981). Her name points to a reconciliation between John King and Samuel Marsden after their differences during the early years of the mission. Marsden's wife was also named Elizabeth (Elder 1932).

As the reports and letters published in the *Missionary Register* (CMS 1831: 116; Yate 1835: 171) point out, Te Puna was really a continuation of the Oihi mission, moved to a new location but still adjacent to Rangihoua Pa and serving the same population there and in the surrounding villages.

EXPANDING NETWORKS: WESLEYANS AND CATHOLICS

Wesleyans

Following Samuel Leigh's first efforts to establish a mission at Whangaroa, further Wesleyan missionaries, Nathaniel and Ann Turner and John Hobbs, arrived on board the Brampton in July 1823, on the same voyage as Henry and Marianne Williams. Whangaroa Harbor was under the control of George and his elder brother, Te Puhi, of the Ngatiuru *iwi*, responsible for the sacking of the *Boyd* in 1809, and proved a volatile location for a mission station (Owens 1974; McNab 1908, 1914; Salmond 1997; Elder 1932, 1934; DNZB 1998). James Shepherd was a somewhat peripatetic CMS missionary who lent his services to the Wesleyans in the early days of the Whangaroa station. He subsequently moved back to Oihi, and from there to Te Puna. From Te Puna he moved to Kerikeri, where he had also lived earlier, and eventually settled back on the Whangaroa harbor.

Samuel Leigh did not last long at Whangaroa. He became ill while Marsden was on his 1823 visit to New Zealand, and he and his wife returned to Port Jackson with Marsden early in 1824, where he became the first Methodist missionary in Australia (Owens 1974). With them sailed William White, hoping to find a wife in Port Jackson, a necessary requirement for a single missionary among the "heathen" in New Zealand (Middleton 2007a). The CMS considered that an English wife was essential as a civilizing influence and guardian of male morality in this outlandish environment, not only at Whangaroa but also among the CMS in the Bay of Islands. As a member of the LMS expressed it, "Never should a missionary go or remain among a Heathen People, without a wife, if she can live among them with safety" (quoted in Owens 1974: 48). Indiscretions with Maori women had taken place at Whangaroa. While White denied such accusations made against him, Turner reported that Luke Wade "has unfortunately been overcome by the flesh, was most broken hearted and went out of the meeting weeping" (quoted in Owens 1974: 49). White's reputation was further tarnished with accusations of adultery in the 1830s. White returned downcast and unsuccessful from his visit to Port Jackson, but left again for England on the same quest in 1826, returning not only with his own wife but also with a bride for John Hobbs (Owens 1974; Williment 1985). Eliza White, 15 years younger than her husband, was only 20 years old and 7 months pregnant when she arrived in New Zealand (Porter and Macdonald 1996). Eliza kept a journal providing details of her domestic life at Mangungu on the Hokianga, as well as of her visits to the Williams at Paihia where she documented her participation in a busy round of social events, a useful document to contextualize many of the day-to-day mission activities in the Bay of Islands (White n.d.; Middleton 2007a).

William and Eliza White arrived back in the Bay of Islands in January 1830 to find that Wesleydale had been sacked in the course of intertribal warfare in 1827, the same war in which Hongi Hika received his fatal wound (Cloher 2003). After fleeing to the CMS in the Bay of Islands in the midst of this war, the Wesleyan missionaries re-established themselves at Mangungu on the Hokianga, under the protection of the brothers Patuone and Nene.

On January 10th 1827, the day the Wesleydale mission was sacked, Hongi was wounded in the fighting with Ngati Pou. A musket ball passed through his right lung and out near his spine. His death appeared immanent, with repercussions for the mission at Kerikeri, where the Wesleyans had fled. The Kerikeri mission was closely allied to Hongi, under his protection and built on land purchased from him (Binney 2007). In this situation, the mission stood to be plundered if Hongi died, under the law of *utu*. At the same time, if Hongi died his enemies to the south, from Thames and Waikato and further away, would seize the opportunity to attack the Bay of Islands. At Kerikeri the missionaries loaded essential items for travel onto boats, and buried valuables, awaiting news of Hongi's death. A week after his injury they received a message from Hongi requesting food and dressings for his wound, and stating that he would recover. So the crisis abated, but arose again on Hongi's eventual death from this wound in March 1828. However, in the event, the CMS missions went untouched (Earle 1908; Elder 1932, 1934; Rogers 1961). This may be one of the points at which the balance of power between Maori and missionaries began to shift. Elder (1932: 444) considered this the case. He marked this the end of the period in the history of the mission

> during which the success of the mission depended on the favour of the chief, and the beginning of the self-reliant policy which gradually made the missionary counsellor and ambassador of peace...

Subsequent Wesleyan mission stations were set up on the Kaipara and Kawhia harbors, as well as in Taranaki (Elder 1934; Owens 1974). The Wesleyan and CMS missionaries worked closely together, supporting each other in times of difficulty or danger, with little competition over territory or areas of influence up until the 1830s. Conflict between the two began when William White, an irascible man with a hot temper, attempted to move into the CMS territory in the Waikato (Rogers 1998; Williment 1985; Owens 1974; DNZB 1998). This schism grew following the death of Marsden in 1837 and the arrival of the Anglican Bishop Selwyn in 1842 (Glen 1992; Owens 1974; Rogers 1998; Stock 1899; Williment 1985). Selwyn's "high church" practices meant that links with Wesleyans were unacceptable. These practices also alienated many of the older CMS missionaries (Stock 1899; Rogers 1998).

Mission stations existed firmly within the control of Maori, and under the exercise of Maori customary law and power. Members of the missions, such as Kendall, as well as his Wesleyan colleagues like Luke Wade, were vulnerable to the influence of this society, and able to choose to move into and live within it, as other non-mission Europeans did, forming relationships with Maori women and close alliances with their tribes and kin (for example, see Maning 1973 [1887]; Markham 1963; Tapsell n.d. [1870]). However, when missionaries chose to do so, there were consequences within the mission, as the case of Kendall demonstrated.

Pompallier and the Catholics

Catholicism came to New Zealand with the arrival of the Marist French priest Jean Baptiste Francois Pompallier in the Hokianga in January 1838 (King 1997). Before leaving France in 1836, Pompallier was chosen by the church as first "vicar apostolic" of Oceania. On the voyage to New Zealand missionaries were left at the Wallis and Futuna Islands, Pompallier reaching the Hokianga with one other priest, Louis Servant, and one brother, Michel Colombon. Pompallier celebrated the first mass in New Zealand at the home of an Irish Catholic family, located at the head of the Hokianga harbor, and established his first mission at Purakau, on the northern shores of the harbor, under the supervision of Father Servant. Servant remained at Purakau for 4 years before being posted to the island of Futuna, but in this time he developed the basis of a strong Catholic community in the area. The mission at Purakau continued until the early twentieth century (Best 2000). Pompallier moved on from the Hokianga in 1839 to found his best-known mission at Kororareka in the Bay of Islands, where the original mission printery, built in 1842 and now known as Pompallier House, is a Crown heritage property managed by the New Zealand Historic Places Trust. The Bay of Islands was not a fertile field for Catholic conversions although Hokianga and the west coast of Northland consolidated as Catholic enclaves. Pompallier continued to found a number of missions in both the North and South Islands during the 1840s, with his largest base eventually located in Auckland's St. Mary's Bay (King 1997).

While later Catholic missionaries were important, Pompallier was the most prominent among them. The arrival of Catholicism in New Zealand created a major threat for the established Protestant missions, not only for the Wesleyans who were located at Mangungu on the shores opposite Purakau, but also in the Bay of Islands, where the CMS missions had predominated for decades. In January 1840, King (n.d.b) wrote to the Secretary of the CMS that "the Roman Catholic Bishop is close upon our heels supplying any native who may be willing to receive small books or slates, the cross, beads, etc." A year later, he considered that "those few who say they belong to the Popish Bishop often hear the Gospel, are warned of the danger, and are called upon to flee to the Lamb of God..." (King in CMS n.d.b). The antagonisms between the Catholic and Protestant missionaries were deep, and were not resolved. Rogers (1998: 161), biographer of Henry Williams, states that there was "extreme antagonism between Roman Catholics and Protestants, who regarded each other as dangerous heretics." CMS initial fears of Catholicism were also related to the possibility of French annexation before the arrival of Hobson in 1840 and it was in their interests to use this threat to encourage the British to take sovereignty (Rogers 1998).

1840: ANNEXATION OF NEW ZEALAND

In 1814 the *Active*, with the full complement on board of those who were to sail for New Zealand, was detained for a week in Port Jackson by a strong gale blowing into the harbor. Three chiefs, Hongi, Ruatara, and Korokoro were on board, returning to their country after a brief visit to Port Jackson following Kendall and Hall's earlier voyage. Nicholas (1817 I: 39) describes the three of them plunged into despair, Ruatara who

> on all former occasions, was lively and communicative...appeared quite dejected, a kind of morose melancholy overspread his countenance, and it entirely lost that vivacious animation which it used to display before... His dark brow...showed us too plainly, the violence of some internal passion.

Finally Ruatara revealed the cause of his change of demeanor. A "gentleman in Sydney" had informed him that the missionaries would bring large numbers of Europeans to New Zealand to overrun the country; Maori would be either destroyed or reduced to slavery. The gentleman pointed out that Ruatara had only to look at the Aboriginals of New South Wales to see the evidence for this. Marsden and the Europeans were dismayed; they could only proceed with the protection of the chiefs, which the chiefs were now threatening to withdraw. Marsden reassured Ruatara of the motives of the mission – they were not of either "ambition or avarice," but only of "benevolent solicitude for the happiness of the New Zealanders." Marsden threatened to turn the vessel back to Port Jackson, with the desired effect that Ruatara begged him to proceed to the Bay of Islands.

Ruatara's fears may have been prophetic, but these events illustrate the dilemma that both parties were in, unable to turn back from the course they had undertaken (Owens 1985). Ruatara was committed to proceeding in support of the mission. It gave both Hongi and himself material advantages that other tribes in the Bay of Islands were desperate to acquire, as missionaries provided better access to sought-after goods (Elder 1932). At the same time, Marsden was partly shamming. He had received instructions from Governor Macquarie's secretary to explore the coast and interior with a view to its potential as a colony. When the flag flew at Oihi on the first Sabbath, Marsden

> Considered it the signal for the dawn of civilization, liberty and religion in that dark and benighted land. I never viewed the British flag with more

gratification, and I flattered myself they would never be removed till the
natives of that island enjoyed all the happiness of British subjects. (McNab
1908 I: 362)

Marsden clearly understood, however, that to Maori, *mana* was
paramount and that "they would not quietly submit to have any part
of their Country wrested from them by any other nation" (Marsden
in Owens 1985: 4). Two years later, Marsden and two others, Robert
Cartwright and the Rev. John Youl, wrote to Josiah Pratt, the CMS
secretary, in support of a scheme to establish a colony in the Bay of
Islands. Marsden still considered that

> To introduce the Arts of Civilization at New Zealand by the Establishment
> of a Small Colony is a very desirable object, and we think there would be lit-
> tle difficulty in doing this as far as the New Zealanders would be concerned
> since they are so anxious for Europeans to reside amongst them. The danger
> would be from the want of Subordination amongst the Colonists. (Marsden
> n.d.b)

This plan apparently came to nothing. Such ideas were first raised
by Governor King after his encounter with Tuki and Huru and continued to be proposed from time to time in Port Jackson, where Simeon
Lord and others attempted more than one entrepreneurial scheme
(McNab 1908; Salmond 1997). It can be seen that Marsden was aware
of such ideas, which were talked about in Port Jackson before the missionary voyage to Oihi.

As Owens (1985: 7) remarked, it was a "sad irony" for the missions
that the more influential their teachings were, the more attractive the
country appeared for settlement as fears of contact with Maori abated.
As the missions became more established, the Bay of Islands increased
in popularity as a port of call for whaling ships seeking provisions.
The numbers of European traders and sojourners increased dramatically during the 1830s and set in train a whole series of changes which
destroyed or counteracted the missionary influence, as visitors such as
von Huegel (n.d.), Marshall (1836), and Earle (1909) described. This
led to missionary concern about control of a lawless population, exacerbated in the late 1830s by land speculators from Port Jackson purchasing large areas of land in the Bay of Islands (Adams 1977; Moon 2002;
Orange 1987):

> New Zealand is now a very different place to what we once knew it Euro-
> peans are to be found scattered over almost the whole of the northern part
> of the island exerting an influence which will ere long destroy all Native
> influence. It is much to be lamented that the British Government will do
> nothing toward setting a form of Government for this distracted Country
> at a comparative trifling expense something might be done. (Clarke n.d.b
> November 15 1837)

In 1833 the British Colonial Office appointed James Busby as "British Resident," with the expectation that he would have sufficient authority to resolve problems of law and order among the unruly British settlers in the Bay of Islands. Busby established himself with his wife and children at Waitangi, not far from the mission at Paihia, from where Marianne Williams recorded her regular socializing with Busby's wife, Jane. James Busby's role as Resident was quite ineffective in controlling the settler population, although he worked with Bay of Islands chiefs to make the "Declaration of Independence" in 1835 (Adams 1977; Binney et al. 1990; Orange 1987; Walker 1990). In 1837, the CMS sent a petition to Britain requesting the reluctant government to intervene in the still unruly New Zealand. Missionaries wanted British "protection"; while annexation may have been acceptable they were strongly opposed to extensive colonization (Sinclair 1969: 63). Correspondence followed between the CMS and its evangelical allies in the British government, Lord Glenelg, the Secretary of State for the Colonies, and Sir James Stephen, the permanent Under-Secretary (CMS n.d.b Feb 12 1839; Rogers 1961, 1998; Sinclair 1969). The issue of British intervention was pushed to a head by the plans of Wakefield's New Zealand Company, which intended to bring large numbers of settlers to New Zealand. Following difficult negotiations with the Company, Glenelg decided to pursue the suggestions of Captain Hobson who was offered the position of British Consul in New Zealand in 1838. Glenelg did not intend any extended system of colonization, but to "establish a regular form of government" (Sinclair 1969: 66). Hobson was dispatched to New Zealand in August 1839, after the departure of the *Tory*, the first of the New Zealand Company's ships, with instructions to "treat with the Maoris for the recognition of the Queen's sovereign authority 'over the whole or any parts of those islands which they may be willing to place under Her Majesty's dominion'" (Sinclair 1969: 68). Sinclair considers that the British government's unwilling consideration of annexation of the whole country, not just a part of it, was precipitated by the Company's proceedings.

In the Bay of Islands, Henry Williams left Paihia for Port Nicholson (later known as Wellington) in October 1839 on the mission ship *Columbine*, accompanying Octavius Hadfield to establish a new mission station at Otaki, on the west coast north of Wellington. Williams agreed to set up this mission after repeated requests for a missionary from the chief Te Rauparaha, living on Kapiti Island, followed by a deputation from Te Rauparaha's son Wiremu Tamihana to Paihia in 1839 (CMS n.d.b). At Port Nicholson, Williams and his party found the *Tory* had been there, and "purchased the whole place" (Rogers 1998:1 41). After installing Hadfield at his new post Williams, with his Maori companions and guides from Paihia, left Otaki on December 5 to make the return journey of over 300 miles on foot overland to Tauranga, which he reached just over a month later, on January 9. After 3 days "in committee" Williams set sail for Paihia, arriving there on January 18 (Rogers 1998: 152). He then went to visit Waimate and intended to go on to his land at nearby Pakaraka, where his wife Marianne was. While he was at Waimate on the 30th January a messenger arrived to say that Hobson had arrived in the Bay of Islands and Williams was required there urgently. Williams was presented with a letter from the Bishop of Australia, urging him, and through him all the other members of the mission, to exercise their influence "among the chiefs attached to you, to induce them to make the desired surrender of sovereignty to Her Majesty" (Rogers 1998: 162). Rogers (1998: 163) considers that

> Williams required no urging of authority to play his part. For some consider-
> able time he had been advocating that New Zealand should come under the
> rule of Great Britain. The growing numbers of lawless Europeans, some of
> them escaped convicts from Australia, others sailors who had deserted their
> ships, had been a continual problem.

There was also the question of Williams' large land purchases, which he may have been anxious for the new government to ratify (Moon 2002; Moon and Fenton 2002). Whatever the motivation, Williams arrived on board the *Herald* the next day, February 1, and three days later Hobson presented him with a draft of the Treaty (drawn up by James Busby) to be translated and delivered to him at Waitangi by the next morning. On the 6th of February Hobson, Williams, and others met with Maori chiefs at Waitangi where Williams verbally explained the content of the Treaty to Maori, and encouraged them to sign it. Williams was assisted in the translation by his son Edward and fellow missionary Richard Taylor. However, his mistranslation of important concepts such as "sovereignty," and his use of neologisms such as *"kawanatanga"* and *"rangatiratanga"* in the Maori version of the Treaty of Waitangi, as well as his role in facilitating the signing of the Treaty has been the cause of much political debate and criticism ever since (McKenzie 1985; Moon 2002; Moon and Fenton 2002; Orange 1987, 1997; Rogers 1998; Sinclair 1969; Walker 1990). Williams himself was subsequently expelled from the CMS in 1850 after criticism of his extensive land purchases, but later reinstated (Carleton 1948; Rogers 1961, 1998; Thomson 1859; Williams, Marianne n.d.a).

Five years after the signing of the Treaty, Maori dissatisfaction with the outcome of this led to war between some factions of Ngapuhi and the British in the Bay of Islands, the first of several wars between Maori and the British over land and sovereignty rights (Belich 1986; Buick 1926).

It was clear from the Maori perspective "that they had not conceded substantive sovereignty" to the British (Walker 1990: 98). As John King (n.d.b October 20 1840) had remarked some months after the Treaty was signed at Waitangi:

> The natives have no Idea of being governed and the thought is repugnant to their feeling of independence and it fills them with savage anger.

Sovereignty was not a thing Maori would have easily given up, had they realized this was what they had done by signing the Treaty.

CONCLUSION (SECTION 1)

Examination of nineteenth century mission stations across a range of geographic locations demonstrates that there were two broad models, the household mission, as in New Zealand, New England, and parts of the Pacific such as Hawaii and Tahiti, and the institutional mission, as was found in Australia and North America, while a brief examination of the South African situation shows aspects of both these types. Missions across the range shared a focus on particular gender roles, with domesticity a central theme. Along with the concern for the conversion of the "heathen" to Christianity and the teaching of literacy, a common thread between household missions, institutional missions, and reform institutions was the focus on teaching girls and women the domestic skills essential for the role of good Christian wife and mother, or for the domestic servant. The cult of domesticity is centralizing, familiar thread that binds the themes of the civilizing mission across different geographical frontiers. The domestic model was the central focus of the evangelical household mission; Te Puna mission station provides a case study where the domestic front and the mission can be examined.

Across differing continents and islands and time frames, the civilizing, imperial mission's involvement with state policy varied. In all places, missions formed the penumbra of colonization, although missionaries were often initially forced to submit to local polities (Barker 2005: 88; Binney 2005). According to Johnston (2003: 19)

> Missionaries...negotiated quite complex relations with colonial administrations and settlers: in different places [and even in the same places] they were in collusion, conflict, or strategic co-operation with various colonial structures...despite the missionary societies' sometimes good intentions, the processes of evangelization inevitably assisted the subjugation and subjection of indigenous peoples and the consolidation of white institutions of colonial control.

The nature of the CMS mission in the Bay of Islands was defined by its parent body in Britain, and by the nature of the evangelist revival from which it was born. These factors impacted on the daily life of the King family at the Te Puna mission, and the archeology of the household that was its outcome. The New Zealand mission was established with little official support. It had no governmental or Church of England involvement until after 1840. While it was the outcome of Samuel Marsden's initiative, with the support of the CMS in Britain, it was really a private undertaking dependent on the fervor and commitment of its first missionary brethren, John and Hannah King, Thomas and Jane Kendall, and William and Dinah Hall. These were simple, practical men and women, chosen according to Marsden's emphasis on "the arts," or practical skills and commerce preceding the gospel and conversion. As unordained missionaries they received low salaries, and were expected to do the work of the mission while they also worked to support themselves and their families. This was an impossible task, particularly at Oihi where little food could be produced and the demands of secular life were immense, and led to the establishment of subsequent missions such as Kerikeri and Paihia in more productive places. This also led to the establishment of the Te Puna mission in a location where John and Hannah King could run their own farm in the manner that Marsden and the CMS had initially prescribed, where they were able to carry out the tasks of the mission as well. Although, as the archeology demonstrates, they lived in an economy of paucity, they were able to overcome the contradictions of the CMS instructions and to hold church services and regular school at the mission.

Although the CMS was evangelical and revivalist, it existed within the hierarchical structure of the Church of England. The focus on class and status led to divisions within the mission from the beginning, Samuel Marsden's autocratic manner contributing to this conflict. John King, an unordained missionary, and his wife, with antipodean and convict associations, were given little status within the mission (Middleton 2007a). This continued throughout their lives, and by the time of their deaths in the 1850s little had changed. By this time also, the Te Puna mission was located in a part of the Bay of Islands that had become a backwater, contributing to the isolation of the Kings and the mission. This is also demonstrated in the archeology, which gives a sense of austerity and a lack of resources.

The New Zealand mission, while an isolated outpost of the CMS, was one of many similar organizations scattered throughout the globe. In the Pacific, similar factors contributed to the successes and difficulties of these missions. They all depended on the patronage and support of powerful indigenous people like the Pomares in Tahiti, Kamehameha in Hawaii, and in New Zealand, Ruatara and Hongi Hika. The New Zealand mission differed from those in Tahiti and Hawaii in this respect as the connections between Marsden and Te Pahi and Ruatara were made well before the mission was established. In all these cases, the missions were reliant to a large extent on the local population for much of their food supplies, as well as labor for building and maintaining the missions. The distances between missions and "home" societies in England meant that there were huge delays and difficulties in communication, with replies to letters and requested supplies taking up to 2 years to be received. Missionaries in these locations found themselves caught up in local wars and internal conflicts and politics.

Missions also experienced the challenge of internal conflict and dissent. This was the case at Tahiti, especially after the arrival of the 1817 missionaries. In New Zealand, the small Oihi settlement, consisting of only three missionary families, was wracked with disagreement from its beginnings. Trade, especially trade in muskets, was an important factor in this. Although "private trade" was forbidden at Oihi, missionary families had difficulty in maintaining themselves, especially when they had inadequate material support from Marsden. Marsden participated in and contributed to the conflict at Oihi, as his letters and journals demonstrate, and he dismissed recruits in order to deal with this (Elder 1932, 1934).

All found themselves confronted with open sexuality. Single (and sometimes married) men perceived themselves as constantly tempted by the charms of local women, and occasional indiscretions and defections occurred. The married state was the preferred one for all missionaries leaving England for the unknown Pacific. This raises the question of the role of women in the missions. While they were not seen as missionaries in their own right, they did contribute not only through domesticity but also as teachers and as Christian crusaders in the public sphere (Grimshaw 1983, 1989a,b; Grimshaw and Nelson 2001; Jolly and Macintyre 1989; Middleton 2007a; Miller 1985; Wagner-Wright 1990). They all shared a similar concern about their children growing up sometimes as much within the influence of the local, indigenous culture as within the mission culture, with a limited education.

Another common factor of missions throughout the Pacific was the introduction of literacy in the indigenous language. At Oihi, as with missions on Tahiti and Hawaii, the school was seen as one of the important mission functions as literacy came hand-in-hand with ideas of civilization. It was considered important to enable people to read the scriptures and undergo conversion. This was maintained and grew from the 1830s with the arrival of new missionaries to the Bay of Islands and led to a huge demand for Bibles and published material (Lineham

1992a,b), although McKenzie (1985) questions whether Maori were really as literate at this time as missionaries considered.

With the conversion of indigenous people came the rise of transmutations and hybridized forms of Christianity on Hawaii, Tahiti, and New Zealand. In Tahiti, the Mamaia cult developed in the same way that Christianity on Hawaii had led to forms hybridized with earlier pre-Christian religious practices (Garrett 1982). In the 1830s, the CMS missionaries in northern New Zealand were dismayed to hear of the prophet Papahurihia whose religious practices incorporated aspects of Christianity, transposed into forms they considered came from Satan (Binney 1966, 1997; DNZB 1998; King n.d.b; Wilson 1965). Binney considered the appearance of the Paphurihia sect, typical of those throughout the Pacific, as a rejection of Christianity and an effort to control elements of its teaching and the new culture Maori were confronted with.

Missions in Tahiti, Hawaii, and New Zealand played a fundamental role in the eventual colonization of their countries. Garrett (1982: 38) clearly acknowledges the part the ABCFM played in the colonization of Hawaii and considered that "without them the American flag would not now be flying over Hawaii." Stock (1899), among others saw that the CMS had played a similar role in the annexation of New Zealand, and Henry Williams' part in translating the Treaty of Waitangi and hence in the process of colonization has come in for much scrutiny. The CMS was inextricably involved in the lead up to colonization 25 years after its first arrival in New Zealand, despite the ironies and contradictions this entailed for the missionaries themselves. In Tahiti, the LMS were integrally involved, along with the recently arrived Catholics, in the French annexation of this island. The Australian situation differed, with the involvement of mission societies with Aboriginal people coming decades after colonization. Unlike the situation of missionaries in New Zealand, who were at the mercy of their Maori patrons, Australian missionaries were quite independent of Aborigines, who were often virtual prisoners in missions and government institutions. However, the inclusion of government institutions with the primary aim of assimilating and educating Aboriginals in the literature and history of mission stations confuses the picture and role of the "mission" in Australia.

This section has documented these larger events of European colonization of New Zealand with the arrival of the missionaries in the Bay of Islands and the changing relationships between Maori and European from 1814 to 1840. In doing so, it has also revealed tensions and contradictions among the missionaries that constrained possibilities for the King family, for the CMS, and for Maori. The move from Oihi to Te Puna, as a result of shifts in the centrality of both the Maori and European worlds, was a move from the center to the margins. John and Hannah King's marginalized position within missionary ranks was reflected in the subsistence farm that Te Puna became. The move to Te Puna, and its outcome, will be examined in the following chapters.

Section | 2

Mission Station and Subsistence Farm | 3

INTRODUCTION

The previous chapter discussed the origins of the New Zealand mission and its first beginnings in the Bay of Islands. This contextualizes the establishment of the Te Puna mission, and introduced its central inhabitants and householders, John and Hannah King and their children. In Chap. 3, the historical context of Te Puna is introduced in more detail, and the dual role of the mission station and subsistence farm is discussed. The details of daily mission interaction with Maori at Rangihoua pa, and the interventions attempted in Maori cultural practices alongside Maori responses provide the evidence of the nature of cultural engagement in northern New Zealand. This is also demonstrated in the transition of the Te Puna landscape over the course of the nineteenth century, from Maori land to mission station and family farm, until toward the end of the century it was merged into a larger pastoral land holding (Middleton 2003).

European visitors first arrived at Te Puna in about 1805, when Te Pahi was paramount in the area and was actively provisioning ships in the Bay. The years between 1814 and 1832 saw the arrival of the first missionaries at the adjacent Oihi, the closure of this mission station, the purchase of land at Te Puna, and the relocation of the Oihi mission there. Te Puna's life as a mission station began in 1832 when John King and James Shepherd moved there with their families, and continued formally until 1848 when John King officially retired as a missionary. However, after his retirement King carried on with his role as a missionary and even after his death his adult children continued to hold school and church services in the mission house, as well as farming the land. Some of the King children remained living at Te Puna after King's death in 1854 until approximately 1874, when the mission land

A. Middleton, *Te Puna: A New Zealand Mission Station*,
DOI:10.1007/978-0-387-77622-4, © Springer Science+Business Media, LLC 2008

was sold. This saw the site of the former mission station submerged within a larger farming landscape that covered much of the Purerua Peninsula on which it is located, and its historical significance largely forgotten. The land remained within the same family ownership until the end of the twentieth century, when it was subdivided.

TE PUNA 1805–1832

Observations of European visitors to the Bay of Islands in the first decade of the nineteenth century confirm the importance of Te Puna for Maori in late prehistory, at the point of European contact, and its suitability for developing agriculture and growing new European crops, in particular potatoes. Te Puna's ascendancy at this time was tenuous, and changed with the demise of Te Pahi in 1810. Four years later, the arrival of missionaries at Oihi and the access they created to European goods for Maori ensured that the area regained its centrality and the *mana* of the *hapu* of Te Hikutu and Ngati Rehia was restored. The shift of strategic locations and ascendancy of *hapu* within the larger Ngapuhi *iwi* changed over time. Kororareka became the most notorious and most important trading center in the Bay, and was the site of battles between Maori for its control (Lee 1983). The importance of Kororareka faded after the War in the North (1845–1846) (Belich 1986; Buick 1926) and the transfer of the seat of government from nearby Okiato (the original Russell) to Auckland.

On his visit to Te Puna in 1805 the Englishman John Savage had observed that it was "the capital of this part of the country" (quoted above, Chap. 2). Te Pahi was absent from Te Puna in Port Jackson at the time of Savage's visit and his brother, Tiarrah, was "governing" in his place. Here, Savage (1973 [1807]: 60)

> never met with [potatoes] of a better quality: they keep remarkably well, and we provided a stock of them sufficient to supply the whole ship's company for several months... Though the natives are exceedingly fond of this root they eat them but sparingly, on account of their great value in procuring iron by barter from European ships that touch at this part of the coast. The utility of this metal is found to be so great, that they would suffer almost any privation, or inconvenience, for the possession of it; particularly when wrought into axes, adzes, or small hatchets: the potatoes are consequently preserved with the greatest care against the arrival of a vessel. Their mode of preserving them is upon a platform, erected upon a single post, about ten feet high.

Savage's remarks on the methods of storing potatoes on *whata* or platforms explain the low number of surface storage pits at Rangihoua, where there is one, and Papuke, where there are none. In general,

Figure 3.1. Rangihoua pa, looking toward the north-east, 1827 (Artist Augustus Earle, 1793–1838. Rex Nan Kivell Collection, National Library of Australia. NK 12/141)

there are fewer storage pits recorded in the far north than elsewhere in the North Island (Davidson 1984). This may be related to the increased use of above ground storage. Earle's watercolor of Rangihoua look-ing toward the east (Figure 3.1) illustrates a number of *whata* within Rangihoua, while Taylor's drawing of Te Puna mission station (Figure 4.12) shows a single *whata* on the ridge between the mission houses and Papuke.

Five years after Savage's visit James Finucane made similar obser-vations on his arrival in the Bay in April 1810 with Joseph Foveaux:

> This immense cluster of bays and islands is inhabited by distinct tribes each under the Government of a Chief or King, over whom Tippahee has long been acknowledged as Paramount. His principal residence is on a small for-tified island called Tippoonah, where he has a house which was constructed at Port Jackson and put together by carpenters sent from thence for that purpose. His side of the Bay, until the seizure of the Boyd, was the estab-lished rendezvous of the English vessels employed in the southern whale fishery. (Whitaker 1998: 99)

Finucane identifies, or confuses, Te Pahi Island with Te Puna (Tipoonah) itself. He confirms Savage's description of Te Puna as the "capital of this part of the country," and, at the time of the first exchanges between Maori and Europeans, the preferred anchorage in the Bay of Islands for whalers to revictual with pork, potatoes, and water. Finucane also gives some clues to the political state of the Bay. The "distinct tribes" he describes are *hapu* of the Ngapuhi *iwi*, periodically struggling for political power and control of the strategic locations within the Bay for better access to trade with Europeans (Hohepa 1999; Sissons et al. 2001).

Te Pahi's murder in 1810, for which Finucane and Foveaux were responsible, put an end to trade at Te Puna until Ruatara, Te Pahi's nephew, returned in 1812. On Samuel Marsden's first visit to New Zealand in 1814 Ruatara reported triumphantly:

> I have now introduced the cultivation of wheat in New Zealand. It will become a great country, for in two years more I shall be able to export wheat to Port Jackson in exchange for hoes, axes, spades, and tea and sugar. (Elder 1932: 70)

With these ideas in mind, Ruatara planned extensive cultivations, and to build a European style town at Te Puna. Marsden continues:

> [Ruatara] made arrangements with his people for a very extensive cultivation of the land, and formed a plan for building a new town, with regular streets, after the European mode, to be erected on a beautiful situation, which commanded a view of the harbour mouth and the adjacent country round. We, together, inspected the ground fixed on for the township and the situation of the intended church. (Elder 1932: 70)

The streets for the planned town at Te Puna were to be marked out before Marsden left Oihi for Port Jackson on 26 February 1815. The planned town never took shape, and Ruatara's wheat cultivation did not eventuate. Ruatara died several days after Marsden left, and the Oihi mission struggled to establish itself in the small valley on the other side of Rangihoua Pa.

Marsden returned to the Bay of Islands on a second visit in August 1819. In September he walked to Te Puna where he met Rakau, the father of Ruatara's wife, Rahu, as he was returning from the potato fields. Marsden

> wished to visit the Sacred Grove, which was near, where [Ruatara] died; but as I understood it was tabooed, I could not presume to enter without permission of the chief. He came, and pointed out the Tree where his daughter, Duaterra's Wife, hung herself; and showed us the spot, where both their bodies were deposited. The sacred spot was enclosed with a fence about three yards square. Here the bodies remained together till the flesh was decayed, when their bones were carefully collected and carried to their respective family sepulchres... The ground where he (Ruatara) intended the Church and European Town to stand, is now under cultivation, and divided among different families by his successors: while about half an acre is reserved, as sacred to his memory, where no shrub or tree is suffered to be cut down; and where, apparently, no foot had trod before ours, this evening, since the last funeral rites were performed for him and his faithful partner. (Elder 1932: 178)

While the location of the *wahi tapu* is identified as at P05/915 (see Chap. 4), the remains of Ruatara's "sacred grove" is no longer evident.

The nature of *wahi tapu* is such that there may be no surface evidence or physical remains (Matunga 1994).

Earlier in the same month (September 7th 1819) Marsden walked to Te Puna from Oihi with the new missionary arrivals, John Butler and Francis Hall. Here, he found the land:

> chiefly planted with sweet-potatoes, which constitute the choicest food of the Natives... The principal inhabitants of Rangheehoo have their sweet potato gardens here. We found numbers of them at work, in their respective allotments; some with spades and hoes which they had received from us; others, with wooden spades with long handles to them, the mouth made about the same size as an English spade; and such as had got neither spade nor hoe, turned up the ground with small spatulas, about three feet long. (Elder 1932: 165)

While the chief Hongi Hika appeared to be based primarily further up the Bay at Kerikeri, and had large cultivations inland at Waimate, he also had extensive gardens at Te Puna (Middleton 2007b). The missionaries continued on to visit Hongi at his seasonal village, located perhaps in the Te Puna valley or the nearby ridge leading to Papuke (see Figure 4.4). There, they

> found him in the midst of his people, who were all at work, preparing the land for planting. I observed his Head Wife [Turikatuku] at work with a spatula, and her little daughter, between four and five years old sitting on the bed which her mother was digging. (Elder 1932: 166)

Turikatuku, who was blind, was Hongi's primary wife. Her daughter, born at Okuratope on the night of Marsden's visit to this pa in 1814, was named Marsden after him. Nearly three weeks later, on September 20, Marsden walked back to Te Puna with Thomas Kendall and Francis Hall. Hongi had recently returned from a war expedition to the south. His two captive wives were living in this small village, as well as Turikatuku (Elder 1932: 177). The heads of 11 victims of this war were stuck on posts as trophies. Samuel Marsden exchanged Turikatuku's wooden *kaheru* for a metal hoe, much to her joy. On this visit they found more than 100 people here, most of them working in the fields preparing the ground for planting. Colenso (1880: 9) describes the methods used to prepare the land for planting *kumara* – men, women, chiefs, and slaves all working together under the restrictions of *tapu*, which were strictly observed:

> They worked together, naked (save a small mat or fragment of one about their loins), in a regular line or band, each armed with a long-handled narrow wooden spade (koo), and like ourselves in performing spade labour, worked backwards, keeping rank and time in all their movements, often enlivening their labour with a suitable chant or song, in the chorus of which all joined.

Samuel Marsden's observations of Te Puna in September 1819 all took place in spring during the planting season. Four years later, Te Puna was still an important area for cultivation. At harvest time in late summer, John King (n.d.a) and his family were regularly invited to Te Puna, walking over from Oihi: "I with Mrs. King and our five children went to Tipuna to feast on kumara; to our children it was a treat." Two days later, on March 16, King returned to Te Puna to preach on the Sabbath. However, his efforts were in vain, the kumara harvest proving a major distraction for his congregation: "Some natives were carrying their Potatoes on their backs to the storehouse others digging up – some eating others dancing and singing, etc…it was so much like a fair for noise and bustle that their minds could not attend to it" (King n.d.a).

TE PUNA MISSION 1832

In 1828, the CMS committee had first proposed the closure of the Oihi mission. In May of the same year, John King purchased 16 acres (although {Turton 1879} states this to be "about 10 acres") of land named "Te Puna" for the CMS, the place that Kendall had argued for from the beginning, in preference to Oihi. The boundaries of this piece of land ran

> from the foot of the hill called the Rorekahu, and from thence to Punetewao, from there it goes across to the main drain of the swamp, and follows it out to the mouth, and then along the beach to the commencement: about ten acres more or less, and trees standing and whatsoever is above or below. This is the payment we have received: 24 axes, 12 hoes, 12 spades, 15 iron pots, 24 blankets, 12 chisels, 12 plane irons, 12 prs. scissors, 12 combs, 12 knives, and 100 fish hooks. (Turton 1877–1883)

Te Puna was purchased from the chiefs Wharepoaka, Manuwiri, Waikato, Marupainga, and Pani. Turton describes a rough rectangle of land. "Rorekahu" is the steep hill just to the east of the mission, leading to Rangihoua pa. The location of Punetewao is unclear, but is likely to be at the rear of the mission site, where the valley narrows at a large swamp. The main drain of the swamp refers to either the stream itself, or a drain dug for the purpose of draining the large swamp, mentioned in later title deeds.

John and Hannah King were firmly attached to the place (Oihi, Rangihoua, and Te Puna), through the burial of their children at Oihi and the close connections that had developed between them and people from the pa, in particular Waikato and his wife (King n.d.a,b). Both King and Shepherd argued that the CMS had an obligation to maintain a mission close to the pa. At Te Puna there was flat land more suitable for growing food. James Shepherd also argued that Te Puna was a location where there was "the prospect of a generally good supply of native food for the settlement of which the other [mission] settlements have been often short" (King n.d.b). Despite complaints about the lack of Maori industriousness, missionaries were dependent on Maori for food, and Maori mostly dictated the terms of trade for this. Te Puna was important, King and Shepherd said, in order to maintain the missionaries' relationship to the large surrounding Maori population (CMS n.d.a, King n.d.b, Shepherd n.d.).

Although the land at Te Puna was purchased in 1828, the local committee was very ambivalent about proceeding with the construction of the mission there, and the committee appears to have deliberated and vacillated over the question of Te Puna until about 1830. Conflict between John King and James Shepherd contributed to this vacillation, but factions on the committee were very reluctant to proceed with the mission (Rogers 1961). While building began in 1828, disagreement between King and Shepherd may have caused the committee to halt plans for the Te Puna houses in the same year. In October 1828, Shepherd (CMS n.d.a) wrote to the committee referring to "forgiveness" between the two of them on points on which "they may have differed." "After much deliberation" the committee decided that the question of closing the Rangihoua settlement should be dismissed, and that building at Te Puna should proceed. In January 1829, Shepherd's (CMS n.d.a) report noted that building at Te Puna was continuing, and that "the natives sawed nearly 3,000 ft. of board and scantling" (framing). A long letter from George Clarke (n.d.a) to the secretary of the CMS written in February 1829 details the vacillation of the committee and the factions on either side.

Two years later, on a visit to the Bay of Islands in April 1830, Marsden went Te Puna to see the land that had been purchased, which he considered a "much more eligible situation" than Oihi (unlike 1814, when he had not complied with the suggestions of Kendall as well as King and Hall, that the mission should be sited there). Marsden found:

> there had been considerable work done in fencing, and the frame of one of the houses was up and a good cottage built, but the works had been suspended by the local committee and confirmed by a resolution of the parent committee, with an order to withdraw the missionaries to one or both of the other stations. I regret that this measure had not been more maturely considered. As far as my own opinion goes, from seeing the number of natives and their general improvement since I last saw them, I think it an important station. (Elder 1932: 482)

Marsden's opinion must have contributed to the decision of the committee (see Chap. 2 for details of the committee structure) to proceed with the mission, as work on building the two mission houses began again. At the end of 1830, Shepherd reported that "his natives during the Quarter were employed in sowing, cultivating a piece of land which had been for some time fenced in at Te Puna, and in getting shells for lime" (CMS n.d.a).

In October 1831, John King (CMS n.d.a) recorded "a principal part of my time has been taken up in the bush preparing stuff for a house at Tepuna." In the same year, the committee resolved to purchase a boat for Rangihoua (and Te Puna). Shepherd was at Matauri Bay, "getting timber for shingles and sawing plank and board" to complete his house. In 1832, John King's 15-year-old son John Wheeler King was teaching at the school, as well as putting up fencing and building at Te Puna. Later in the year, John King (CMS n.d.a) reported that he had been

> principally employed in carrying on the buildings at Tepuna, purchasing the food which the natives brought for the settlement. We have been so circumstanced that the school could not be regularly attended to. John King [junior] has been mostly at Tepuna at work. We have 15 men and boys and 9 girls.

The King family moved to their new house on 13th September 1832, and "commenced school on the 17th out of doors as we have not at present any school house," with eighteen males and eight females "under instruction" (CMS n.d.a). James and Harriet Shepherd had moved there earlier in the same year, Shepherd's (CMS n.d.a) July 1832 report to the committee only noting tersely "James Shepherd reports that during the last quarter his time was occupied in carpentry and removing to Tepuna." The Shepherds' daughter Harriet Ann Isabella was born at Te Puna in October of that year (Warth 1984). By the end of 1832 Shepherd was preparing timber to build a chapel at Te Puna. This project, mentioned several times by both King and Shepherd, does not seem to have eventuated. Shepherd's own house was used for this purpose by the time William Wade (n.d.) visited in 1837. Less than a year after moving there, Shepherd appears to have had a change of heart about Te Puna. In March 1833, he traveled with Fairburn (a missionary based at Paihia) to inspect the Hauraki region as potential mission ground, subsequently reporting this as an "important station for missionary labor." He further reported

> That the Tepuna Settlement at present wears a most discouraging aspect in consequence probably of the harmful effects of the Ships which have been in this year, the declared enmity of the principal Chiefs to the Missionary cause

and other local circumstances connected with the Station though at the same time this behaviour is respectful to our persons. (CMS n.d.a 1 July 1833)

At a special meeting in June 1833 a resolution was passed: "That Mr. Shepherd move to Kerikeri and that he take charge of the store until the completion of the new building" (CMS n.d.b). These events suggest that further conflict may have arisen between King and Shepherd, despite the "forgiveness" expressed in 1828. In the October quarterly meeting of the same year, King (CMS n.d.b) responded to Shepherd's criticisms:

> The gloom which was said to have hung over this station has I am happy to say disappeared. I cannot find that declared hostility to the gospel that was reported to exist amongst the principal chiefs of this place. Warepoaka has on all occasions done what he could to protect and assist us...

At this meeting the committee resolved "That Mr. King be allowed to erect a stable at Tepuna 11 × 15 the materials to be procured by the natives" (CMS n.d.b).

By this time the recent missionary arrivals John and Anne Wilson and their two children were installed in the house built by James Shepherd. They stayed at Te Puna until the following year, when they moved to Puriri, the new mission station on the Hauraki Plains. From Te Puna, Wilson (CMS n.d.b) reported:

> In Sept removed from the station of Paihia to Tepuna agreeably with the directions of the Com Having collected a few natives commenced our afternoon school and the cultivation of the land for their subsistence.

Mrs. Wilson began teaching the girls' school with Hannah King (see also Middleton 2007a). After the Wilsons left Te Puna the house built by Shepherd was apparently not lived in, although Edmonds, the stone mason employed by the CMS to complete the Stone Store at Kerikeri, lived there briefly, as did Henry Pilley on his first arrival in the Bay of Islands in 1834, where he was instructed to finish work on the mission house (CMS n.d.b; Pilley n.d.b).

In 1838 the Missionary Register published the first drawing of the Te Puna mission, also reproduced in the *Church Missionary Paper* (Figure 3.2).

As in the 1832 lithograph of Oihi (Figure 2.9), the mission station is represented situated within an idealized pastoral landscape. Sheep can be seen grazing on well-grassed slopes. A small boat sails on the water of Rangihoua Bay, given the appearance of a millpond, and a fisherman casts a rod from the shoreline. The mission houses look more imposing than later drawings suggest (for example, see Taylor, Figures 4.11 and 4.12). A second version of this lithograph,

TEPUNA, A CHURCH MISSIONARY STATION IN NEW ZEALAND.

Figure 3.2. "Tepuna, a Church Missionary Station in New Zealand," 1838 (*Missionary Paper* No. XCL 1838)

painted in oils, is held in the National Library of Australia, of no certain date (noted as 184-?) and the artist unidentified. CMS missionary William Wade, based at Waimate in 1837, seems the likely artist of the original drawing, perhaps a pencil sketch rather than the oil in the National Library of Australia, which may be a later version of the lithograph. His "Memorandum to accompany Drawings, April 1837," held in the Hocken Library archives (Wade n.d.) provides captions to drawings he evidently sent to the CMS. No drawings are held with the "Memorandum" in the Hocken. Wade provides a caption for a drawing of Te Puna, a place that did not agree with him:

> The house in the centre of the Drawing is occupied by Mr. King and his family. That to the left is now used as a chapel. In almost every other point of view, than the one here selected, the aspect of Tepuna is rather forbidding. Backed by barren hills, and lying open to the Bay in front, exposed to easterly gales, it possesses but few attractions in point of situation; and the neighbourhood round is almost destitute of Native Inhabitants. (Wade n.d.)

While the site of the King house was identified during fieldwork in 2002 the site of the house built by Shepherd was not located.

The Mission Work

King's first report to the Church Missionary Society from Te Puna, in December 1832, details the weekly schedule for him and his family, a routine that was followed closely in the years to come. King's reports appear in the same formula each year, with little variation apart from mention of occasional deaths at the mission from outbreaks of diseases and other extraordinary events. His second-eldest son John and his eldest daughter Jane are often mentioned teaching at the mission school. His younger children attended the school for European (missionary) children at Paihia, which began in 1827 (CMS n.d.a; Carson 1992; Fitzgerald 1995). The "English Boys' School" later moved to Waimate, where the Kings' son William was appointed to teach in 1835 at a salary of £20 (CMS n.d.b). Five years later, William was still an assistant at the school, and his salary was increased to £50. The Girls' School stayed at Paihia, run by Marianne Williams and her sister-in-law Jane Williams. Prior to the establishment of the schools for their children there was much discussion and concern about the education of the mission children and their futures in New Zealand. Consideration was given to sending them to Parramatta for their education, and in order to remove them from the "unsuitable" local influences, although this did not take place. Such concerns echo those of other missions throughout the Pacific, in particular in Hawaii, where children where dispatched back to the East Coast of the United States for the same reasons, parents and children enduring long years of separation (Zwiep 1991).

At the Te Puna mission, Sunday services were held both morning and evening, "most of which is performed in the native Language" (King n.d.b Dec. 12 1832). King also visited other villages along the coast from Te Puna. He names both Wiriwiri, the village at the eastern end of Wairoa Bay just below Papuke, and Wairoa itself, a village toward the western end of Wairoa Bay. King visited other villages along the Te Puna inlet and also walked or rode to villages on the east coast north of the Bay of Islands, traveling some 20 miles and staying overnight, and to Mataka, the high hill to the north of Rangihoua (CMS n.d.a,b; King n.d.b). During the first years at Te Puna he traveled to this part of the coast every fortnight, as he had done from Oihi; later he reports making the journey less often due to illness, perhaps the rheumatism he later complained of (King n.d.a). Through the week there was daily morning and evening prayer as well as the school:

> During the week days school commences at six O'clock in the morning the
> natives are instructed in reading and writing and in first rules of arithme-
> tic... Mrs King and Jane attends to the Girls in the afternoon on the Sab-
> baths, and... on week days school and prayers in the evenings. (King n.d.b
> 1832)

The Battle against the "Prince of Darkness"

Missionaries expressed their efforts to convert Maori from "heathenism" to Christianity as a battle between God and the devil. They
saw the "Prince of Darkness" (a favorite missionary term for the devil;
see for example Davis (n.d.)) manifested in many Maori concepts and
practices which they fought to conquer and exterminate, and saw their
own Christian practices as the signs of civilization:

> It is with much satisfaction that I have another opportunity and can
> address you in peace and quietness, tho' the Heathen rage and the people
> imagine vain things and Satan is making fresh efforts to corrupt, defame,
> and to destroy, yet his kingdom cannot stand, the work is going on and the
> N. Zealanders far as they now are must be brought nigh by the blood of
> Christ. (King n.d.b March 24 1830)

Missionaries had to submit to practices associated with the concept of
tapu, or suffer the consequences of *utu*, plundering by *taua muru*. For
example, *kumara* cultivations were considered *tapu* from the time of
planting until harvesting, and could not be walked through. Animals
were killed for infringing this *tapu*, and humans subject to punishment. Areas of the coastline where fishing nets were being made were
also considered highly *tapu*, much to the consternation of the missionaries who tried to pass such an area. While King (n.d.b) had noted in
1827 that Wharepoaka and Waikato "behaves quietly toward us and
uses their influence with others," Waikato (Figure 2.8) was not yet prepared to give up *tapu* practices when William Williams wished to pass
Rangihoua:

> Waikato, who went to England with Shunghee, is as superstitious as any of
> the Natives, and would not, on any account, neglect one of his tapus. With
> a new net there is very much ceremony; and the whole of the sea in the
> immediate neighbourhood of Rangheehoo is now sacred in consequence, and
> no canoe is allowed to pass under any pretence. Waikato would fain have
> prevented my boat from returning on the morrow; and I was only allowed to
> pass on the promise of steering as far from the net as possible. (CMS 1830:
> 470)

Such concepts connected with the seasonal round of activities leave
no archeological imprint. Areas of land under cultivation return from

tapu to *noa* after harvesting of crops or the completion of fishing nets and expeditions. Seasonal activities also confounded missionaries. At planting and harvesting times the mission schools emptied as pupils disappeared to the fields, returning when the work was completed. This seasonal cycle, fundamental to Maori society, was another factor that perplexed missionaries as they attempted to impose their own social framework on Maori.

Other practices targeted by the missionaries included burial customs such as the *tangi* and the *hahunga*, the practice of exhuming and cleaning the bones of relatives before a secondary burial (for example, see Earle 1908). *Hakari*, sometimes held in conjunction with *hahunga* were another cause for missionary concern. These were spectacular, staged feasts where food was displayed on huge pyramid-style stages sometimes 80–90 ft. high, with tiered shelves and then distributed to guests in a manner that expressed the *mana* of the host group and its chief (Binney 2007; Colenso 1880: 13; Treadwell 1999; Urry 1993; Yate 1835). Urry (1993: 32) notes that *hakari* were not single events, but formed part of a series of reciprocal feasts. Three of these structures can be seen in Binney (2007: 23, 79, 80), two of them erected in the vicinity of the Kerikeri mission.

The "last" *hahunga* was reportedly held at Waimate in 1835 (Davis n.d.; Williams 1989 [1867]). On this occasion the Kerikeri chief Rewa hosted the feast, publicly acknowledging that this was to be the last of its kind, and no return was to be made for the food distributed. William William's description of the proceedings shows the scale of these events. The food consisted of

> two thousand bushel baskets of kumara, and fifty or sixty cooked pigs, which formed a heap three hundred yards in length. ... No bones were exhibited to view on this occasion, but the different families collected their own respectively, and committed them to their final resting-place. (Williams 1989 [1867]: 216)

Williams and Davis, along with others considered the end of the practice of holding *hahunga* to be a triumph for their cause. Missionaries felt that they had achieved a victory when they were able to impose their own Christian practices and death rituals on Maori. However, Maori burial practices continue to the present with the primary burial and unveiling of the headstone a year later in a current practice that Oppenheim (1973) equates with secondary burial.

The mission work at Te Puna epitomized many of the issues missionaries considered important in their daily battle against the "Prince of Darkness." In July 1833, John Wilson (n.d.) described the tangi held on the death of the chief Toi Tapu. He found the sight "truly heathenish":

> One of the party (an old woman) who was besmeared with blood whenever her person was uncovered, presented a dreadful spectacle to a Christian eye, and strongly illustrated to my mind those passages of the Old Testament which allude to the idolatrous practice of cutting for the dead, which occasionally existed among the Jews. As the blood flowed from the wounds (the sight appeared to augment her lamentation) she wiped it off with a Mat, then made fresh incisions. – In this manner they continued to mourn for about three hours during which period their cries were truly lamentable and without hope.

John Wilson's journal for his first months at Te Puna in 1833 reflects his responses to the practices missionaries found objectionable, in a country where he considered "the author of all evil rules with an open hand":

> ... such is the unsettled state of the mind (at least of my mind) in this benighted country that it is with much difficulty I am enabled to write at all. every day brings its cares and anxieties peculiar to this land in a way which I confess I scarce calculated to meet. ... As I become more accustomed to the trials of New Zealand (God permitting) I hope to be less affected by them. (Wilson n.d.)

John King (n.d.a,b) had often paid the price for slaves from Rangihoua in the years at Oihi. John Wilson (n.d.) records "redeeming" several slaves while he was living at Te Puna, the first on October 1 1833, following a wedding the day before:

> Sept. 30th; Today two natives were married in the Settlement; the Bride by birth a Rangatira (or Lady), the Bridegroom a Slave, which circumstance that [caused] considerable disturbance.
>
> Oct. 1st. The Natives exceedingly troublesome, the wedding of yesterday having brought the Master of the Slave to the Settlement, who demands his services at the native village. The poor slave appeared much alarmed for his safety a bayonate being seen under the Chiefs mat. I entered keenly into his feelings & paid his ransom.

On this occasion, a blanket and an iron pot were paid for the slave. This transaction can be found in the "Tepuna account of trade October 1 1833," summarized in Table 5.2. Two months later John Wilson (n.d.) recorded:

> Dec. 4th. Today by redeeming a poor slave girl who has been living with us, her life was [saved] in a very remarkable manner. It appears that she was the wife of a Waimate Chief who having heard various evil reports concerning her (all of which I am persuaded were untrue) came today to receive her wages, and also to punish her, even with death were she found guilty of the accusation alleged against her. As soon as I heard he was in the vicinity of the Settlement, I went to him and at once agreed to purchase the girl (not knowing at that time the purpose of his visit).

Wilson spent the next few days keeping watch over his charge, concerned that although he had paid her "purchase price" she may still have been taken back to the *pa*, as did occur some weeks later, the woman begging for help from Wilson and John King. The next day she escaped again, and hid herself "in an underground place" in the Wilsons' house, suggesting a cellar in this as well as the Kings' house. Wilson kept vigil outside the house, and eventually her pursuers left her in peace following the intervention of Wharepoaka on her behalf. The Te Puna "Account of Trade" for January 1 1834 records one axe and 1 lb of tobacco as part payment for a slave (CMS n.d.a). However, having paid the price of the slave, missionaries evidently expected continued loyalty and service. On his visit to Te Puna in 1834, William Barrett Marshall reported an instance of "native ingratitude" Mrs. Wilson recounted to him. A redeemed slave, most likely the one John Wilson wrote about in December, having lived with the missionaries for some time after the above events, and was married in the mission "when to the astonishment and grief of her employers, her husband and herself eloped, and returned to live among the natives...and have not since been heard of" (Marshall 1836: 19).

By the time of the Wilsons' arrival at Te Puna, John and Hannah King were old hands in the missionary world. The kind of events that shocked John Wilson may have become everyday occurrences that they were used to dealing with. In 1836, John King reflected on the changes of the past 20 years:

> the first eight or nine years the natives were so insulting threatening to kill & eat us, our wives & children & burn our houses etc etc ... that little could be done but to exist & that with difficulty at some seasons, when I compare these times with the present I say great things has been done, a great change has been effected & a great work is going on... (King n.d.b September 9 1836)

As Wilson's journal demonstrates, missionaries intervened in the social fabric of Maori lives. Missionaries understood that they were under the protection and patronage of particular chiefs. At the same time, they refused to sanction the Maori social structure which included the taking of slaves in warfare. The (Christian) wedding of a chiefly woman and a slave showed a complete disregard for status, and brought an indignant response. At other times the rank of Maori of high status was disregarded and those of lower rank, especially slaves, exulted by the missions, at the risk of violating *tapu*. Christianity may also have offered slaves, who had lost *mana* through enslavement, a way out of bondage and a society in which they no longer had any status. Ideological conflict occurred when Maori women of chiefly lineage worked as domestic servants in mission households. At the same time, the CMS missions brought with them their own concepts of rank and status from their homeland, and attempted to replicate this in the Bay of Islands (Middleton 2007a). Missionaries like Henry and Marianne Williams maintained their own English upper-class status, the household "demarcated by restrictions from the yard to bedroom inner sanctum," Maori their "social and spiritual underlings" (Gillespie 1996: 143). Other mission families such as the Kings and the Fairburns were considered their social inferiors.

The Mission Children

The CMS brought about further intervention in the social fabric of Maori life through its strategy of taking children to live at the missions, a central policy of missionaries across both the "household" and "institutional" mission. As George Clarke (n.d.b) explained, "they will be separated from their parents, consequently from their evil habits, they will see...more of the Advantages of Civilized life." At the same time, from the reading of the archival material it appears that Maori parents gave their children to the missions almost as *whangai*, a traditional form of adoption in which links to the birth parents were maintained while the family to which the child was given had day-to-day responsibility for its care and wellbeing (Ballara 1998; Salmond 1991b; Webster 1973). As Bender (1967) has pointed out, one of the chief roles of the household, along with the completion of domestic tasks and economic co-operation, is the socialization of children, a primary role for the "household mission." The New Zealand situation differed from that in Australia, for example, where children were sometimes forcibly removed from their families, having no further contact with them, and held in missions and government reserves.

Ewhora, the daughter of Ruatara and granddaughter of Rakau, chief of Rangihoua, was the first child left with the Kings at Oihi, brought there by her grandmother, "desiring...us to nurse the child to learn to read to sew to clean the House to do everything like White People" (King n.d.c). Two of Wharepoaka's daughters were brought up in the King household. In 1834, after the death of his eldest daughter Witirua, Wharepoaka brought a second daughter to the care of the Kings (CMS n.d.b). After her death, Witirua was buried in the burial ground on the summit of Rangihoua pa, in a coffin and with Christian ritual, no doubt a triumph for John King and his efforts to transform Maori ways:

> Was informed that Witirua died on the fourth, Mrs King went with me to see the corpse, her father said, you have brought her up, she belongs to you, it is for you to say how she shall be buried.

> I & my son made a coffin & on the seventh buried her at Rangihoua along-
> side her Aunt's grave & paled it in – Witirua was the daughter of Warepoak
> the chief of this place died on the fourth & was buried on the seventh – she
> lived with us nearly ten years, she could read & write & sew etc – she under-
> stood & could speak the English language very well she was not a strong
> healthy Girl, she was troubled with a disorder that is common to Newzea-
> landers, something like that which is called the kingieire [?] & often proves
> fatal, she was a trusty Girl in the house, & made herself useful – Being
> poorly she went to see her father, & continuing unwell, & drawing near her
> end he did not like to move her, we supplied her with such food etc as she
> needed, she died at the Village in the midst of her relations & friends, they
> disputed with her father about burying her, wishing to set the body up in
> a box according to the custom of N.Z. – looking upon burying in the ground
> a chief or his Children as very degrading – however, they agreed that we
> should decide the matter, therefore it took place as above stated. (King n.d.a
> June 1833).

The numbers of Maori, male and female living at the mission are recorded in every quarterly report to the committee. In 1834, 12 males and 12 females were living at the mission, an average number reported during the 1830s. Six years later in 1840 King notes five men, five girls, and four children present (CMS n.d.b). King, however, tends only to name those members of the household when they died, while Wharepoaka and Waikato are mentioned regularly because of their close relationship with the Kings, and their chiefly roles at the pa.

In 1846 King noted the death of Meriana Kahurere, the sister of Ruatara. She was baptized in 1840, and lived at the mission for the months before her death (CMS n.d.b).

"Reduced in number through disease and death, war and bloodshed"

In 1830 Shepherd estimated

> The number of natives living in the neighbourhood those who are constantly
> visiting the Settlement for the purpose of bartering with us being in number
> not less than 500 together with considerable bodies which live on the North-
> ern Coast. (in Clarke n.d.b)

George Clarke (n.d.b) confirmed Shepherd's estimate, with a further 1,000 people located on the coast north to Whangaroa, in the villages King and Shepherd visited from Rangihoua and subsequently Te Puna. On a visit to Rangihoua in 1830, Marsden estimated that the pa itself had a population of at least 200 (Elder 1932). Several years later, the numbers had fallen. In June 1834, King reported that there were 200 Maori associated with the Te Puna station, and more again on the coastal settlements. In the same year, Davis (n.d.) lamented

> There are not more than two thirds of the natives in this part of the Island
> that were to be found here ten years ago!!! At Rangihoua, in the specified
> time, I believe they are diminished more than half – other tribes in the Bay
> have suffered in the same way, while one tribe here has been annihilated.

Only 7 years after moving to Te Puna, King was lamenting the loss of
population in the area:

> Once we were settled in the midst of a populace people, but now they are
> much reduced in number through disease and death, war & bloodshed, many
> young men go to sea and never return, others removing to different parts of
> N.Z. among their relations, many children die through disease derived from
> their parents – some few are destroyed, so I conclude that only about one
> third are left in this place, those families are living at a distance from each
> other so that it takes much time to pay each small party a visit. (King n.d.b
> March 1839)

As King points out, the population at Rangihoua and Te Puna
decreased not only because of the number of deaths due to European
diseases, but also because of the movement of *hapu* within the Bay of
Islands. At the beginning of the nineteenth century Rangihoua and Te
Puna were possibly the paramount location in the Bay of Islands, the
"capital of this part of the country" as John Savage (see Chap. 2) had
described, under the control of Te Pahi. Thirty years later this was no
longer the case. The advent of the missions, inter-*hapu* rivalry for the
control of trade and the effects of increasing numbers of European settlers produced a dramatically altered picture.

From the beginning at Oihi, missionaries were aware of the toll
of European diseases on the Maori population, Ruatara himself dying
from what was likely to have been a western illness. Only 6 months
after Oihi was established, King reported to the CMS that a number of
people were very ill, with some dying, Maori blaming the Christian God
and missionary prayers for this (King n.d.a). In the early 1830s, George
Clarke (n.d.b September 13 1833) noted that the missions were witness
to "appalling depopulation among the poor Heathen around us," while
the large mission families continued to thrive. He blamed the decrease
in the Maori population on "their system," that is, the practices of
Satan, which he thought would lead to extinction in a few years. Clarke
was evidently blind to the effects of the epidemics of European diseases
which he as well as other missionaries reported sweeping through the
Bay of Islands. Writing to the secretaries in 1838 he stated that there
"was much disease which cannot be traced to European origin, nor yet
to change of diet or want of clothing," but could only be attributed to
"Godly vengeance" for barbarities committed (Clarke n.d.a). In 1828,
whooping cough affected almost every child in the missions. Many
Maori were also dying, "not only destitute of the many temporal com-

forts we enjoy, but altogether strangers to the promises which support and comfort the Christian" (Clarke n.d.b November 22 1828). Both the Shepherd and the Clarke families lost a child to this illness and John King (CMS n.d.a) reported to the committee that the school could not be held at this time, because of the effects of whooping cough on his own family as well as on the Maori population.

Davis considered that "pulmonary consumption" was responsible for the largest number of deaths. Influenza was another European disease responsible for the decline of the Maori population in the Bay of Islands (Davis n.d.). At the first committee meeting in 1848, King reported that "most of the Natives have been suffering from influenza," along with his own family, and that 20–30 of the sick were supplied with food and medicine from the mission (CMS n.d.b). The previous year the mission had supplied food and medicine to about the same number of people suffering from whooping cough.

A Decade of Progress?

After nearly 10 years at Te Puna, John King's reports followed the same formula. His weekly routine reads the same as a decade before, and much the same as the last years of the mission at Oihi:

> Public Service at the Station has been regularly held, and the Natives visited in the afternoons, at Warengaere, Kaiki, Tangitu, and the Tonu: divine Service has been attended to by myself and the Christian Natives. A number of Natives come twice a week to Tepuna to read the Scriptures and receive instruction, they are making some progress in the knowledge of Christianity. Ten natives have been baptised during the past half year, which make a total of forty three. Twenty three have been admitted to the Lord's Supper.
> —
> A number of the Natives at Tohoranui, Takou, Waiaua, Matauri and the Ngaere, whom I frequently visit, have been baptised. In the morning sow they seed and in the evening withhold not thy hand. God giveth the increase. My son John has attended to the men and boys on sabbath afternoons, or visited others at a distance. Mrs. King and one daughter attends to the females. 5 Men and Boys 5 Girls in the Settlement. (King (CMS n.d.b April 21 1841))

By 1844 King states that there were 100 converts in the vicinity of Te Puna, more than double the number he quoted in 1841 (CMS n.d.b). This reflects the higher number of converts the CMS reported in the Bay of Islands from the 1830s (Binney 1969, 1970; McKenzie 1985). But by this time King was also complaining of Maori turning away from the mission teachings, to their "former ways" (King n.d.b).

Missionaries reported wide success in literacy from the 1830s, along with their increased success in conversions (Lineham 1992a,b).

"Books" first appear on the Te Puna quarterly returns of trade to the committee in December 1830 (CMS n.d.a). From this time on they appear regularly in station accounts and can be found in the Te Puna Account of Trade (see Table 5.2). In 1833 (Table 5.2), King records "Catechisms," "L. Books" and "P. [prayer?] Books." These may have been the results of the first CMS efforts at printing their own translations in the Bay of Islands.

Printing returns from Colenso to the committee for June 30 1841 show the range of his work and the quantities of books he printed. These books were then issued to all the mission stations. At the last meeting in 1841 the committee authorized the production of 5,000 copies of William Williams' recently completed Dictionary and Grammar of the New Zealand Language, with fair copies to be dispatched to the CMS (presumably in London) for publication (CMS n.d.b).

In 1833 William Yate estimated that 500 Maori in the vicinity of the Bay of Islands could read and write. A year later, the Englishman Markham suggested there were "not less than ten thousand people that can read, write and do sums in the Northern end of the Island" (quoted in McKenzie 1985: 27), doubtless an exaggeration. From the time of Colenso's arrival and his first publications, the CMS reported something of a clamor for books, with many Maori making long journeys to procure the desired items and exchanging once-valuable iron tools for their copy of the Bible (Lineham 1992a; McKenzie 1985). McKenzie (1985), however, contests that this quest for the written word was evidence in itself of literacy, in a society where oral traditions stood firm. He points out that the Bible was given totemic, ritual power by Maori, while Jenkins (quoted in May 2003: 18) suggests that Maori "believed that the missionaries were actually in touch with God, were really able to talk to God through the power of the printed word... Thus Maori society was persuaded to believe in the necessity of print literacy." The "printed word" also had other material applications, paper being used as ear decorations and to roll cartridges (McKenzie 1985; Colenso 1888; Carleton 1948). McKenzie's point can be demonstrated by the illiteracy of Wharepoaka and Waikato. Although John King (n.d.b) reported in April 1829 that Wharepoaka "has undertaken to learn to read and write and attends the school regular," he and Waikato were only able to sign the 1835 Declaration of Independence with a mark (McKenzie 1986: 38). This debate about literacy has important implications for understanding the processes that took place during the signing of the Treaty of Waitangi (McKenzie 1985; Moon 2002, Moon and Fenton 2002; Orange 1987).

The mission teachings and schools also fostered the rise of resistance, and as elsewhere in the Pacific and Australia syncretic forms of religious beliefs and practices appeared (for example, in Australia see Swain and Rose 1988; Taylor 1988). In 1833, missionaries were alarmed to find further evidence of the workings of the "Prince of Darkness" appearing in the form of a syncretic religion known as Papahurihia, the first of the hybrid, visionary Maori religious movements. Papahurihia was both the name of the religion and its leader, a young chief of the Hikutu *iwi* from Rangihoua and Te Puna, a former school pupil of John King who was "particularly hostile" to the mission and its influence (Binney 1966, 1997: 155). Papahurihia, also known as Te Atua Wera (the fiery god), believed that the missionaries were murderers who had brought about the high numbers of Maori deaths since the beginnings of the mission through *makutu*, or witchcraft, and told his followers that their heaven had "nothing but books to eat" (Binney 1997: 155; Wilson 1965). John King reported the rituals involved in this form of worship in December 1834. The Papahurihia

> Have appointed saturday for their sabbath telling us we are under a mis-
> take, for saturday is the ancient sabbath and that the Apostles turned mon-
> day into a sabbath for us they hoist a flag on a pole, pay little or no respect
> to the day, but at night a few assemble together (as the workers of darkness
> chooses darkness) their priest performs his foolish ceremonies and mixes
> portions of the holy scriptures which they have learned with their old super-
> stitions, which causes much dispute & inquiry among themselves. (King
> n.d.b December 3 1834)

Waikato, the long-time supporter of the mission, was a leader of the new faith, which was centered at Rangihoua. Papahurihia moved to the Hokianga some time in 1834, where the Wesleyans reported his activities there. Father Servant, who arrived at Purakau with Pompallier in 1838 to establish the first Catholic mission, described Te Atua Wera as a chief of Te Puna and recorded the beliefs of the faith, and the spirit of the god "who appears from time to time at night and who makes himself heard by whistling" (in Wilson 1965: 479). Believers were promised a heaven where "everything is found in plenty, flour, sugar, guns, ships; there too murder and sensual pleasure."

Three years later King considered that the Papahurihia practices were dwindling. He wrote to the CMS in April 1837

> The delusion among the natives which my other Letter referred has partly
> ceased, hoisting their flag on a pole on saturday as their sabbath and their
> public meeting at night are laid aside, but sin is still their element, they
> have not turned to the Lord. (King n.d.b April 7 1837)

It seems that from this time, Papahurihia was no longer a significant threat to the CMS missions. Papahurihia himself became a Wesleyan convert to Christianity (Binney 1997: 163). At about the same time as Papahurihia took up with the Wesleyans, Waikato of Rangihoua:

> collected all the people of this place and told them that he would leave off his old bad ways, and for the future he should observe the sabbath and attend the Missionaries and Native Teachers should visit him at his residence as often as they could to instruct him in the Truths of the Gospel. (King n.d.b January 2 1840)

Four years later the chief, his wife, and family were baptized:

> 'Waikato' a very bigoted, superstitious Heathen possessed of a very turbulent and avaricious disposition hasty in his decision and resolute in the execution thereof – Years ago when Warepoaka his brother in law came to divine service on Sabbath days, Waikato generally found some work to do, to annoy, & oppose him; he now says that he opposed the gospel a long time … he resigned himself to the call of his Maker & Redeemer. … The Rev. H. Williams baptized Waikato "Josiah Pratt" and Hira his wife "Jane Marsden" and his eldest son Toko "Mortlock", his three younger children are also baptized. (King n.d.b January 18 1844)

In 1838, John King (n.d.b) reported the death of "our old friend Wharepoaka." Wharepoaka had also evidently converted to Christianity. King states that he had "attended divine service on sabbath days constantly for some years until he was taken ill and not able to come." Wharepoaka, ill with consumption, moved to the mission where the Kings took care of him and his health appeared to improve. However, an outbreak of influenza affected the whole mission, and Wharepoaka did not survive it. After Wharepoaka's death his son came to live at the mission.

During the 1840s King's (n.d.b) reports begin to complain of "attention to old laws." Maori were once again "under the powerful influence of their old destroying system" and practicing

> many of their old customs – plundering their neighbours for trifling offences – taking their dead up again, making a feast and collecting their friends and performing their superstitious rites – At other public feasts they chat over their grievances, consult together what is to be done, about going to war, etc, etc. (King n.d.b August 5 1847).

While the "last" *hahunga* was held in 1835, King's report makes it clear that such customary practices had merely gone to ground for a short time. Their reappearance may have been stimulated by Maori grievances following the signing of the Treaty of Waitangi. These concerns led to Hone Heke's three assaults on the British flag flying at Kororareka, and the consequent "War in the North," also known as "Heke's war" which broke out during 1845 (Buick 1926; Belich 1986). In September 1845, King (n.d.b) was

At a loss to account for this extraordinary outbreaking of the natives, as the Governor took the largest interest in their welfare. many of them say there is no cause for it, they have been told in a tantalizing manner [by] ill disposed Americans and Europeans that their country was taken and themselves made slaves and that the flagstaff was the true signal.

According to King, most Maori of Rangihoua and Te Puna

Have kept at home and keep up the true form of religion altho sadly gone back to many of their old ways in practice, Hohaia Waikato has used all his influence to keep these people from joining Heke's party.

This war ended following the last battle at Ruapekapeka, in which the British ironically attacked the pa on a Sunday while Maori were at prayers outside their defenses, an occasion the British labeled a victory after earlier heavy losses in the area. King noted that Heke was not "humbled" by events at Ruapekapeka. The war against the British gave the divergent *hapu* of wider Ngapuhi another opportunity to settle old scores as Tamati Waka Nene fought with the British against his old enemies.

In his report of June 1850, King notes the death of "an aged chief... who was among the first who welcomed us...on the shore in 1814." King (n.d.b) also complains:

The Natives are in want of Prayer Books and Psalters. Medecine wanted for Family and Natives. The house in bad repair as reported last meeting but I received no answer.

MISSION AND FARM

The Te Puna mission functioned as both a mission station and a subsistence farm. King and Shepherd had argued for the Te Puna mission on the basis of the suitability of the valley for growing food, as compared with the steep hills at Oihi. From the beginning of the mission the two roles went hand in hand. After the retirement of John King from the mission itself, Te Puna still continued to function as a mission in a sense, with the old associations with people from the pa maintained, regular services being held, and occasional visits to villages along the coast, as before. This dual role continued even after King's death, as his sons and daughters carried on with the weekly routines "strictly attended to" (Davis n.d.) and the Rev. Richard Davis traveling to the mission to administer communion and carry out baptisms (discussed further below). The demise of the mission truly occurred only after the last of the King children moved away from Te Puna at about the time the land was sold to their cousin, John Tollis Hansen. The former mission then became merged within the larger Hansen pastoral holding, its function as a farm ascendant until the end of the twentieth century.

The work of the Old Land Claims Commissioner was significant in the transition of Te Puna from Maori land to mission station and subsistence settler farm. In 1840, when Hobson proclaimed British sovereignty over New Zealand, the question of prior purchases of Maori land by Europeans had to be addressed. No further private purchases of Maori land by Europeans were permitted after the Treaty of Waitangi was signed, the government retaining the only right of purchase until this was abolished by Hobson's successor in 1844 (King 2003). After Hobson's government was set up, two Commissioners were established to investigate the validity of all land purchases from Maori prior to this time. Purchases by missionaries formed a large part of this investigation, and John King was finally (under the slow processes of the Commissioner) awarded a claim totaling nearly 20,000 acres, a claim of 11,770 acres further north as well as 710 acres backing onto the CMS blocks at Te Puna and Oihi (Lee 1993; Thomson 1859). King's land was subdivided among his children after his death.

Old Land Claim 21 (Figure 3.3) provides an overview of the Crown Grants at Te Puna and Rangihoua, with Old Land Claim 40 (the Waikapu block, purchased by the CMS in 1832), Old Land Claim 57 (the Te Puna mission station itself), and part of OLC 126 layered within it (see detail enlargement, Figure 3.3). In OLC 21, dated 1857, John King's purchase of 710 acres has been subdivided among eight of his nine children, Philip Hansen King's name not appearing there.

From its first beginnings Te Puna appears to have been considered a "farming establishment" as much as a mission station. In May 1833, while he was visiting the Bay of Islands, the Wesleyan missionary Joseph Orton sailed from Paihia to Te Puna. Orton did not appear impressed with the missionary operations:

> This may be [a] suitable situation for a Mission Station and these brethren stationed here may be excellent Missionaries which I doubt not for a moment but I could discern no traces of Missionary operations beyond that of erecting houses, cultivating land, rearing stock with all the et cetras of a farming establishment. This station has been occupied as such nearly twenty years and there does not appear to have been much accomplished. They are but now preparing materials for the erection of a Chapel. (Orton n.d.)

Orton (who mistakenly thought Te Puna had been occupied "nearly 20 years," or perhaps conflated this with the Oihi mission) considered that the lack of "progress" at Te Puna was partly due to the number of British ships that "frequently lie at anchor in an adjacent roadstead," from where there was much exchange between Maori women and the seamen of the vessels, as von Huegel and Marshall described on their visit in the following year, 1834 (see Chap. 5).

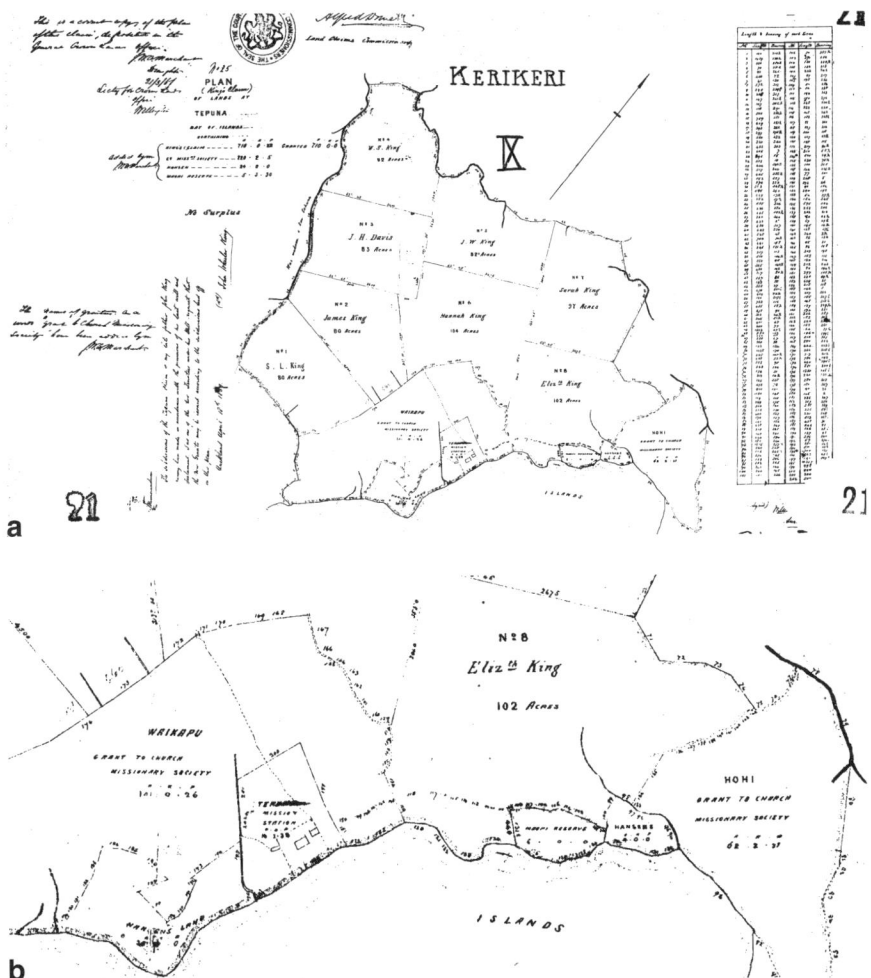

Figure 3.3. (a) Old Land Claim 21 and (b) detail enlargement (Land Information New Zealand)

Three years later in November 1836 Daniel Wheeler (1840: 97) made similar comments after a visit to Te Puna:

> The morning proved rough and stormy, and the cold very piercing: the wind being contrary, it was more than two hours and a half before we reached our destination. Here we saw John King, one of the first missionaries that trod the shores of New Zealand, but now so far advanced in years, as to be considered at liberty from the general work. He has a family of ten children; the two oldest sons are cultivating land on their own account. The natives now

surviving are so few and widely scattered, that Tepuna is now scarcely considered one of the stations. Our visit did not seem to amount to much more
than just seeing the family, by whom we were kindly received and entertained. This family appear to have taken up their residence here for life.
At one time, a considerable congregation used to assemble, but the whole
is now laid waste, and the natives, owing to war and other circumstances,
seem swept off the soil. By the wreck of the establishment now remaining, it
is obvious that this station at one period must have been an important one.
We returned on board by six P.M.

Wheeler's comment that Te Puna "was scarcely considered one of the
stations" is telling, as the minutes of the committee meetings along
with King's reports and journals do not give this impression. King was
aged 49 at the time of Wheeler's visit, and did not retire until 1848,
although even then he continued to write reports to the CMS and to
hold services. Wheeler and Orton's comments confirm the household
and subsistence family farm nature of the mission.

Examination of the correspondence and minutes of the CMS committee meetings provides more detailed information about the demise
of Te Puna as a mission station and John King's retirement. In 1845,
King wrote to the committee, noting his claims before the Old Land
Claims Commissioner, and requesting that the CMS transfer its land
at Te Puna (the mission block of 16 acres as well as the adjoining land in
the Waikapu block) to his children, land that they had "cultivated and
fenced in and otherwise improved by much labor and expense" (CMS
n.d.b October 17 1845). In the same letter, King notes that "it is now
considered here are not a sufficient number of natives about Tepuna to
justify the Committee in continuing it a mission station after my labors
cease." The committee resolved that King's suggestion be recommended
to the "Parent committee" as "Tepuna is not likely to be required as a
Mission Station after [King's] decease, and is in itself of no real value."
The CMS in Britain agreed with the local committee in granting the
Waikapu land to King's children, as the Old Land Claims maps show,
while the CMS retained the 16-acre block on which the mission house
was built. This was the piece of land the CMS trustees sold to John
Tollis Hansen in 1874. At the same time Hansen also purchased all the
surrounding land from King's children.

While King points out that his children had cultivated the CMS land
at Te Puna (and Oihi) he supplies few details about the day-to-day farming, although his claims to the Commissioner state that he ran cattle
and sheep on 150 acres neighboring Te Puna and Oihi (King n.d.e). His
journals written at Oihi were peppered with references to his attempts
to grow wheat, often thwarted by disease, pests, and unsuitable land.
By the 1830s King's sons may have taken over much of this work, as his
claims to the Commissioner state. The archeological evidence discussed

in Chap. 4, along with the drawings by Taylor and Wade, provide some picture of farming at the mission station. While Wade's pastoral land-scape is clearly an idealized depiction, the landscape was grazed, as his picture shows, with cattle or sheep on the hillside. Crops such as wheat may have been grown on the extensive ploughed land, and seed for pasture may have been sown in order to supply more feed for sheep, cows, and horses. At Waimate, the "pioneer New Zealand farm" (Hargreaves 1962: 39), preparing the land for cropping and pasture was a difficult task. Fern and scrub were cut down, wooden roots removed with a hoe or grubber, and stones removed. Then the land could be ploughed, but the thick fern root, once a staple of the Maori diet, often choked or broke the ploughshares. Two or more ploughings were required to clear the land of fern roots before seed could be sown. While the Te Puna land was regularly cultivated by Maori before the mission moved there, plough-ing would have been carried out for the same reasons as at Waimate, to sow crops and grass seed for pasture. Farming practices at Te Puna may have followed those Richard Davis developed at Waimate. This was a mixed farm, with livestock and crops, emulating methods common in Great Britain. Other aspects of farming may also have been similar to Waimate, where fencing was wooden post and rail. While cattle ran wild, unfenced, in the early mission days, it is likely some at least were fenced in at Te Puna, as in 1834 von Huegel (n.d.) noted "a number of cows being driven up to the house for milking." Keeping cattle was not always an easy task. In 1839, Richard Taylor (n.d.) reported the death of one of the mission residents:

> Mr. King had a lad killed two months ago by a bull which ran wild whilst endeavouring to shoot it, the animal ran his horn through the poor lad's neck and from loss of blood died in a few minutes.

Horses were kept, for riding as well as perhaps for ploughing, although bullocks often pulled the plough in the Bay of Islands. As the committee minutes (CMS n.d.a) note in 1833, King built a stable at the mission, and in his journal King (n.d.b) occasionally records riding his horse to the more distant villages he visited. In January 1834, he reported to the committee that he was recovering from a fall after being thrown by his horse a month earlier (CMS n.d.b). The flock of sheep at Te Puna may have been merino, as they were at Oihi during the 1820s, supplied from Samuel Marsden's farm near Parramatta (Hargreaves 1962). William Spence King reported that as a child he watched his father shearing sheep at Oihi in 1824. The wool clip of 11 bags was sent to Sydney where it was sold for 2s 6d per lb (*Weekly News* 1896).

Although this wool clip was sold in Sydney, there is no record of later income from such farming initiatives. The King family's efforts

at Te Puna are likely to have produced a subsistence economy, supplementing the basic flour, tea, sugar, and salt that was supplied from
the CMS store. Surplus produce was likely to be exchanged for goods.
In his claim to the Old Land Claims commissioner King records paying for 3,000 acres he purchased in 1835 at Tohoranui, about 10 miles
from Tepuna with three sheep "bred in the country," among other
goods (King n.d.e). After 1840 the economy of the CMS changed as it
held accounts with the New Zealand Banking Company at Kororareka
(CMS n.d.b). After the CMS store at Kerikeri was transferred to the
private ownership of the Kemp family in 1843, King's methods of paying for goods changed. He paid for items by cheque and cash, and in
March 1847 brought three pigs to the store to exchange for some of his
goods (Kemp, Richard n.d.).

King's sons also used produce to pay for goods from the store. The
later store records note that Philip King paid for some of his account
in wool, 138 lb of this being worth £5-3-6 at the store in 1845 (Kemp,
Richard n.d.). By this time, Philip King was farming independently on
his own land at Waiaua, north of the Bay of Islands.

Another of Wheeler's observations, "the family appear to have
taken up their residence here for life" is also telling, and of course it
was correct. While some CMS missionaries made the return journey
to Britain, or Port Jackson, John and Hannah King and their children were in New Zealand to stay. On a visit to Te Puna in November
1844 Cotton (n.d.) considered Te Puna "quite mythic ground, Mr. King
having held on steadily there during all the turbulent times – He has
never been outside the heads [of the harbor] for this past 25 years."
As King's arguments to the CMS in 1828 demonstrated, he felt a close
connection with Oihi, Rangihoua, and Te Puna. He argued vehemently
to remain in the area where two (and later others) of his children were
buried and where he had established a strong relationship to the people of Rangihoua and the surrounding villages. King considered that
his children also had this connection, and that the land was their
only potential source of livelihood. He expressed these connections
about place and their relationship to Maori to the Old Land Claims
Commissioner at Kororareka 10th February 1842, in defense of his
claims at Tohoranui:

> The Missionaries were instructed some years ago by the Church Missionary
> Society, that an allowance would be granted by the Society to each Child on
> arriving at the age of 15 for the purpose of establishing them in the Country,
> and at that age we received a sum of 50 pounds for each from the Society for
> that purpose, and as the only possible means of procuring for these young per
> sons born in this Country, were by enabling them to cultivate the soil, and rear
> Cattle, we necessarily purchased Land for them, all my Deeds state that the

> Land is given to myself and Children and the Natives have always considered
> them as virtually belonging to the Tribe they were born amongst. (King n.d.e)

King's account of his children as "virtually belonging to the Tribe" recalls
Henry Williams' concern about the location of his mission for the same
reasons, the "missionary [becoming] one with the tribe with which he is
connected" (Gillespie 1996: 124). Ten years later, after Hannah King's
death, John King expressed the same feelings to the committee when he
made a further request for his children to remain in the mission house
after his death:

> I now feel more the exposed situation of my family, who have instructed the
> natives in various ways and set a good example before them. A great deal
> of mutual friendship and good will is manifested among them and no doubt
> would continue, could the society admit of an exception and make some
> arrangement to allow my family the house and premises after my decease
> instead of their being obliged to leave this place, and the natives with whom
> they have been brought up. (John King n.d.a May 10 1852)

No doubt King's consideration of his children "belonging" to the tribe
had its limitations, and any behavior considered "going native" (Gibbons
2002) would have been severely sanctioned. This relationship could only
be condoned within the realms of mission jurisdiction. But cultural
engagement was not a one-way process; missionaries such as King were
themselves transformed by long-term interaction with Maori. They were
no longer English, but became Pakeha, through the colonial processes
Silliman (2005: 59) has described as "entanglement."

JOHN AND HANNAH KING: RETIREMENT AND DEATH

In 1848, a letter from King refers to his retirement at this time.
He writes at length about his retirement allowance, "begging that our
support be not reduced" (CMS n.d.b December 21 1848). In response,
the committee records

> On the retiring of Mr. King from the duties of the Mission the Committee
> feel desirous to place on record their full and perfect satisfaction in the faith-
> ful discharge of his Mission duties according to the best of his ability during
> a period of Thirty Four years

Resolved

> That the affectionate regard of this Committee be expressed to Mr. King and
> their desire that his declining years may be in peace. The Committee sympa-
> thize with Mr. King in his present separation from the Mission Duties. They
> would have been happy to have seen that he had been allowed to terminate

> his days in the Mission work having been the First of their number to tread
> these shores in 1814. (CMS n.d.b January 14 1848)

Having had no reply to his first request that "their support be not
reduced" John King pursued this with a second letter in December
1849, noting "our expenses have not been lessened during the past
year, we have been liable to losses, and incidental expenses as hereto-
fore. We have helped others, and now need help and support as well as
Christian sympathy" (CMS n.d.b December 20 1849). The chairman,
Henry Williams, noted in response "The Committee regrets they have
no power to meet Mr. King's wishes. They can but sympathize with him
and record his application." King's pleas about his retirement allowance add again to the argument that the household economy was a
frugal one, and the farming enterprise a subsistence operation, with
little opportunity for luxury goods.

Despite his retirement from "active service," King continued to
write regular reports to the CMS about his activities at Te Puna. He
records the same kind of routine as in previous years. Services were
held on Sundays, with occasional visits to villages along the coast:

> A few natives came also on week days to read the scriptures ... others came
> to be catechized ... evening prayer with those at the station has been contin-
> ued, they have also been catechized, and instructed in reading — there has
> been much sickness among the natives, and several deaths
>
> Psalters and Prayer Books are much wanted for the use of the natives, and
> Medicine. (King n.d.a July 1 1851)

In this letter King notes that Mrs. King "has been very unwell the last
six months." In the next report, at the end of December 1851, King
reports his wife's death at the end of November, at the age of 60 after
37 years in the Bay of Islands. The following May in a long letter to "the
Secretaries" of the CMS in Britain John King extolled Hannah King's
virtues and described her death and funeral service, led by Henry
Williams. Maori from the mission dug her grave at Oihi, close to the
graves of her three children, and carried her coffin there. "Josiah Pratt
Waikato and his wife with other chiefs and natives were present" (King
n.d.a May 10 1852) as were a number of mission families and other
Europeans. As King's letter points out, Hannah King was also active in
the missionary role, and a teacher in the mission:

> She has been to me a faithful friend, and a willing helper in the work, and
> a comfort and support to her family ... and thus ended one of your first
> female teachers in the mission ... At our first arrival Mrs. King took a few
> girls in, taught them needle and household work, they were likewise taught
> a catechism, the Lord's prayer, to read and write etc etc - When well grown
> they left for different purposes, some of which were among many others of a

> most trying and mortifying discouragement to female teachers. … The sick
> and afflicted, the wounded and lame shared in her sympathy she visited
> them at their villages to dress their wounds, and administered medicine,
> and often proved useful among the natives, and Europeans too. … She con-
> stantly attended to her public and private duties. (King n.d.a)

As was the case with most missionary women, Hannah King carried
out "public" as well as "private" duties.

On December 1853 King penned his last report to the secretaries.
He had

> commenced my fortieth year in the Bay of Islands and now report that suffer-
> ing much from Rheumatism and weakness I have not been able to hold divine
> service with the Natives, and with my family on sabbath days as usual; there-
> fore my sons have held regular services with them on sabbath days. Archdeacon
> H. Williams has administered the Lord's Supper to my family and to a few
> natives, and baptized four adults, two men and two women. (King n.d.a).

King died on May 6th 1854 and was buried in the family graveyard
at Oihi. In his letter of May 1852 to the secretary reporting his wife's
death, John King looked back on his nearly 40 years in the Bay of
Islands. When they arrived, the missionaries

> Had no interpreter was months without seeing a vessel … there was no
> other settlement to run to in time of danger, no ships to fly to, no escape
> – now it may be said what hath God wrought? the testament and prayer
> book is translated, thousands can read, and do join in the public worship of
> the sabbath throughout the Island – war is kept down, most of the slaves are
> liberated who had been taken in war, many ships visit the ports, large towns
> are established by Europeans, the country is filled with European property,
> the natives have horses, cows, sheep, ploughs, carts & drays, wheat & mills,
> boats & vessels, much more might be mentioned, I saw the small beginning,
> and have been spared to see and to know something of the wonderful change
> (King n.d.a; Elder 1934: 60).

In the year following King's death, 1855, the Rev. Richard Davis, recently
widowed for the second time, married John and Hannah King's eldest daughter Jane Holloway King, the eldest daughter King regularly
recorded teaching the girls' school with her mother. After King's death,
Davis's journals and reports provide some insight into life at Te Puna,
where he and his wife made "quarterly" visits and Davis held church
services and gave communion until his death in 1863 (Coleman 1865).
On a visit in 1856 Davis reported that the

> Sunday duties are as strictly attended to by Mr. John [Wheeler] King as
> they were during the lifetime of his father, and Miss King assists him in his
> Sunday School. The sick are attended to also as heretofore. But from death
> and the extreme poverty of the Country adjacent, there are but few people
> living in the immediate neighbourhood. (Davis n.d.)

In October 1856 Davis reported that three adults and a child had been baptized there, "and the Holy Sacrament administered to seventeen natives and six Europeans" (Coleman 1865: 383). In May 1859, he reported a surprising 51 communicants. But once again, in 1863 a decrease in numbers at the mission was reported: "At Tepuna our number has been reduced by death and removal" (Davis n.d.). Waikato, the chief who had sailed to London with Hongi and Kendall in 1820, was now an old man. Much of the "removal" occurred in 1863 because Waikato had freed his slaves, who returned to their own tribal territory, among them some of the mission's "best communicants." Elsewhere in the country, missionaries reported that slaves were freed after the Treaty of Waitangi was signed. Davis reported of Waikato "He is much attached to Mr. King's family and they are attached to him."

In 1859 he counted 60 communicants there. Davis recorded that John and Hannah King's children continued the mission work: "the Congregation of Tepuna is well attended to by Mr. J.W. King and his sisters; they also have two valuable Maori teachers among them"... "Here Mr. J.W. King and his sisters attend to the Natives and carry on the Missionary work" (Davis n.d.).

After John King's death in 1854 his children continued to live in the mission house on the mission land, as he had requested, until the 1870s. In March 1874, John Tollis Hansen, son of Thomas Hansen, Hannah King's brother, purchased the 16 acres of CMS land on which the mission house stood, for £48, as well as the land King's children owned, extending his land holdings at Te Puna and Wairoa Bay (LINZ n.d.). The mission land, along with the land John King purchased from Maori in the 1830s (inherited by his children) then became incorporated into larger land holdings.

For most of the twentieth century the mission past of Te Puna was submerged in the economic farm unit, and overwhelmed by the better-known past of the Oihi mission, identified and memorialized by the Marsden Cross located there and the reserve status of the mission land. The significant "mythic" history of Te Puna was forgotten, the site of the mission erased from the landscape.

CONCLUSION

Missionaries saw the fight for Maori converts as a battle between Christianity and Satan, believing that Satan "ruled" Maori social customs that they disapproved of. In this way, missionaries were the "advance party of cultural invasion" (Walker 1990: 85), believing implicitly in their own superiority and seeing the loss of Maori customary practices as a victory for Christianity and "civilization," as John King described in his letter to the secretary in 1852. The mission was inextricably linked with the arrival of European sojourners and settlers, and with the processes of annexation and colonization. In the same way, it also became linked with the process of alienation of Maori land, as missionaries purchased their own land holdings and began the process of clearing, ploughing, and farming the land, anticipating the work of later colonists.

The weekly routine of the Te Puna mission and its relationship with Maori from Rangihoua pa encapsulate the kind of activities that other CMS missions in the Bay of Islands and elsewhere carried out. This routine relied heavily on the participation and contribution of the missionary wife, as teacher and housewife providing an example of the Christian home and family (Gillespie 1996; Middleton 2007a; Porter 1992). This involved the missionary wife having both a public and a private role in the mission, as John King so precisely expressed it in his eulogy for his wife Hannah. This role of the missionary wife was typical throughout the CMS and other evangelical missions of the nineteenth century (Grimshaw 1983; Grimshaw and Sherlock 2005; Johnston 2005; Jolly 1991, 1993; Zwiep 1991).

The archeology of the Te Puna mission house is simultaneously the archeology of the household, the farm, the mission, and of the interaction of Maori and Europeans in this part of the Bay. The question is, to what extent are the historically known aspects of Te Puna reflected in the material record. Absences may be as telling as the material preserved. The historical information is full and voluminous but it does not tell the only story, and may not tell some of the most significant stories of all.

The Archeological Investigations

4

INTRODUCTION

The name "Te Puna" was used historically in several different ways, and the places Oihi, Te Puna, and Rangihoua may be confused (Heap 1964; Lee 1983). Savage (1973) used the term "Tippoona" in 1805 to refer to the settlement on Te Pahi Island and the adjacent mainland at the northern end of Wairoa Bay leading to Papuke. Marsden (Elder 1932), in the 1815 deed of sale for land at Oihi, used the same term to refer to the bay where Rangihoua, Oihi, and Te Puna are located, known today as Rangihoua Bay (Figure 4.1).

In this general sense, other historical and archival material sometimes refers to Oihi and Rangihoua as "Te Puna". Marsden (Elder 1932, 1934) and other missionaries such as King (n.d.a,b) also use "Te Puna" to refer to the specific valley important as a cultivation area for Rangihoua Pa, where Ruatara's *wahi tapu* was located, and the eventual location of the Te Puna mission. In this work, the terms Te Puna, Oihi, and Rangihoua are used to refer to these specific locations within Rangihoua Bay.

The site of Te Puna mission station is situated within a complex archeological landscape that includes the Oihi mission station, Rangihoua pa as well as a number of smaller pa, and the whole coastal strip of Rangihoua and Wairoa Bays and Te Pahi Island. The mission station, identified on figures as archeological site number P05/24, numbered according to the New Zealand Archaeological Association's site recording system (Walton 1999), should be considered in this context, as an integral part of the wider archeological landscape (Middleton 2003). Te Puna (sometimes "Tippoona" in the historical literature) was an important anchorage in the early nineteenth century, the source of a good supply of potatoes. The Bay of Islands provides a number of safe anchorages, depending on the prevailing winds, allowing vessels to move

A. Middleton, *Te Puna: A New Zealand Mission Station*,
DOI:10.1007/978-0-387-77622-4, © Springer Science+Business Media, LLC 2008

Figure 4.1. Aerial photo, Rangihoua and Wairoa Bays, 1950

from the northern bays to the southern, according to the weather. In 1810, James Finucane stated "All the navies of Europe could lie here, not only in perfect security but in absolute concealment from each other" (Whitaker 1998: 98).

Te Puna provides evidence of a landscape altered from its indigenous past by the first phases of European settlement. This can be seen in features associated with ploughing and European house sites situated within a cadastral landscape. Land deeds of the first transactions between Maori and missionaries, acting on their own behalf as well as the CMS, began the process of changing land tenure and use (Lee 1993; Mutu 1999; Wyatt 1991). Maori land tenure was traditionally based on descent from a common ancestor or *take*, transmitting the notion of the growth of roots connected to the earth (Salmond 1991b). Descent groups could be reformed or reconstituted at different levels, as *whanau*, *hapu*, and *iwi*, or as Lundsgaarde (1974) expressed it, "land rights waxed and waned as an integral part of other social and demographic processes."

By the beginning of the twentieth century this had changed and Te Puna was part of a large pastoral landholding, owned by one descendant of the Hansen family (Martin 1990). In the midst of this landscape and as part of events enacted here, "sites of memory" (Nora 1989) were created, places sacred to both Pakeha and Maori.

NEW ZEALAND IN PREHISTORY

The Polynesians who settled New Zealand arrived from a Polynesian "homeland" or "Hawaiiki" about 700 years ago (Higham and Jones 2005; Walter et al. 2006). Although the islands forming this homeland are not known, the area is in the region of the southern Cook Islands, Austral Islands and Society Islands in eastern Polynesia; these were the places "where the fundamental structures of Maori society developed" (Walter et al. 2006: 275). These early Polynesians brought with them aspects of East Polynesian culture and social structures that evolved over time within New Zealand to become Maori, distinctive from any other Polynesian culture.

The material culture of the New Zealand Maori developed from an early period identified as "archaic," distinguished by artifacts such as large quadrangular adzes and ornate personal ornaments. By the time of European contact, these forms had changed. Nephrite tools were in more common use, ornaments were also made from nephrite, and adzes were smaller and more rounded in section (Duff 1956; Golson 1959; Walter et al. 2006: 278). A change in settlement structures also took place along with the change in material culture. From about the beginning of the sixteenth century Maori began the construction of *pa*, or large fortifications on defended positions such as hilltops, headlands, and ridges. These fortifications contained features such as terraces for house structures and pits for *kumara* storage, and were enclosed by ditches and palisaded banks. While this type of monumental construction, still highly visible in the landscape today, predominates in the north of the North Island, *pa* can be found extending into the upper South Island, but are not found in southern most parts of the country.

At the time of first human settlement, New Zealand's fauna was characterized by the presence of big game, in particular the moa (*Dinornithiformes*), a large flightless bird that was present throughout both main islands, although more prevalent in the south, where the economy was based around fishing, hunting, and gathering. By the sixteenth century this bird was extinct, and numbers of seals, once plentiful around the coast, had been severely depleted from southern coasts and extirpated from northern areas (Smith 2005a). By contrast, in the north the economy had a horticultural focus. Maori brought five cultivars from Eastern Polynesia (Leach 1984; Davidson 1984). The *kumara* or sweet potato (*Ipomoea batatas*) formed a staple of the diet for northern Maori, as did taro (*Colocasia esculenta*) and yam (*Dioscorea alata*). *Kumara* was planted in spring, harvested in autumn and stored over winter, either in roofed pits or on *whata*, platforms supported by posts. The *hue*, or gourd (*Lagenaria siceraria*), was grown for food and for storing liquid while the paper mulberry (*Broussonetia papyrifera*) was a delicate plant, used to produce small amounts of *tapa* cloth. This plant was last seen growing in the Bay of Islands at mid-nineteenth century, but is now no longer cultivated. While prolific birdlife and fish formed important sources of food, there was no animal life in pre-European New Zealand apart from the introduced *kiore* (*rattus exulans*, the Pacific rat) and the *kuri* (*Canis familiaris*, the Polynesian dog). These last two were also eaten. The *kumara* was grown as far south as the top of the South Island; beyond that, the climate was too cold for horticulture, and crops were not grown there until the European introduction of the white potato in the late eighteenth century. However, throughout the country the rhizome of the uncultivated fern or *aruhe* (*Pteridium esculentum*) was also a staple food item and other uncultivated plants formed a seasonal food source.

Anderson and Smith (in Walter et al. 2006: 280) have characterized New Zealand prehistoric settlement as a "transient village" type. This involved "residence in base settlements (varying from small hamlets to fortifications) with regular travel to exploit resources, some of which were seasonal, or for social reasons" (Walter et al. 2006: 281). Undefended villages (*kainga*) consisted of a cluster of small houses, occupied by a number of extended family members, known as a *hapu* or subtribe (Ballara 1998). War, seasonal hunting expeditions, and social events may have brought a number of *hapu* together, with a coalescence into the larger *iwi* or tribe providing access to a wide range of resources and also intensifying social life through exchange and the commonality of achieving communal tasks (Allen 1996: 670; Phillips 2000a,b). Walter et al (2006: 281) note that New Zealand's archeological record shows "marked regional and chronological consistency in sedentism and mobility" across both the northern horticultural region as well as the south. They argue that the "transient village concept" applies to the northern horticultural zone as well as the south and persists throughout the whole prehistoric sequence. This settlement model is comparative with, and probably derives from, that found in early East Polynesian villages, where a range of resources was exploited from a home base. This was the type of settlement that New Zealand's first European visitors described.

ARCHEOLOGICAL SITES: ARCHAIC THROUGH TO LATE PREHISTORY

Sites surrounding Te Puna mission point to a rich archeological landscape, and indicate occupation in the area dating up to about 600 years ago (Best 2003b). Figure 4.2 and Table 4.1 demonstrate this archeological context. While this indicates the density of archeological sites surrounding the mission station itself, a similar number of recorded sites, not indicated, (both prehistoric and historic) continue along the coastline both to the east and west, and along the Mangonui Inlet.

Te Puna is situated in a valley below the steep slopes leading from Rangihoua Pa which lies to the east of the mission (Figures 4.1, 4.3, and 4.4). To the west, a gentle slope leads up to the ridge and promontory separating Rangihoua Bay from Wairoa Bay. Papuke pa (P05/25) is located on the point of this ridge. A stream runs through the valley into the center of Rangihoua Bay, running from a broad swamp at the north of the valley and also draining a much smaller swamp lying in a depression in front (south) of the site of the mission house, close to the beach. The curved ridge behind this swamp, where both the mission houses were once situated, is a Pleistocene beach ridge, c. 120,000

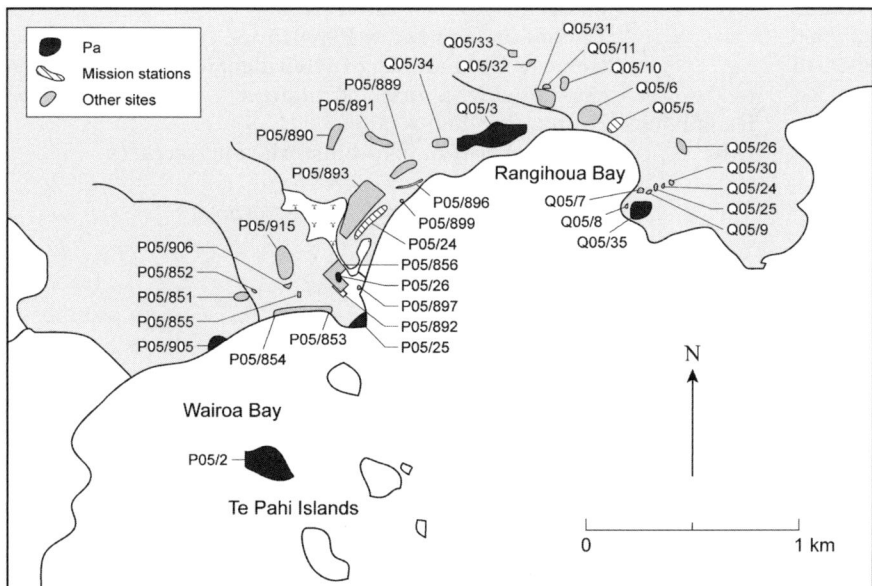

Figure 4.2. Rangihoua Bay and Wairoa Bay archeological sites

Table 4.1. Site record numbers, name, and description

S.R. No.	Name	Description
P05/2	Te Pahi Island	Pa associated with the chief Te Pahi
P05/24	Te Puna	Site of the mission station
P05/25	Papuke	Headland pa between Rangihoua and Wairoa Bays
P05/26		First recorded as "ridge pa," now difficult to identify
P05/851		Horticultural features (prehistoric)
P05/852		Horticultural features (prehistoric)
P05/853		Midden and hangi continuous in shoreline to 854
P05/854		Midden and hangi continuous in shoreline to 853
P05/855		Grave of John Tollis Hansen and Maria Ann Hansen
P05/856		Agricultural features – ploughing "lands"
P05/889		Terraces on the eastern ridge above the mission
P05/890		Terraces down a spur, 300 µ back from P05/889
P05/891		Terraces on ridge between P05/889 and P05/890
P05/892		Site of T. Hansen house and Norfolk Pine planted by T. Hansen
P05/893		Agricultural features – ploughing "lands"
P05/896		Historic pathway from Te Puna to Oihi
P05/897		Hangi exposed in eroding bank
P05/898		Horticultural features (prehistoric)
P05/899		Two sawpits on the shoreline, likely to date from the building of the Te Puna mission house
P05/905		Pa to the west of Wairoa stream
P05/906		Terrace on spur below P05/915
P05/915		Home of Hannah King Letheridge; waahi tapu associated with death of Ruatara
Q05/3	Rangihoua	Hilltop Pa
Q05/5	Oihi	Recorded as drains (prehistoric) and terraces (historic)
Q05/6		Horticultural features (Prehistoric?)
Q05/7		Terraces and pits
Q05/8		Terraces
Q05/9		Headland terrace
Q05/10		Ridge terraces
Q05/11		Terraced knoll
Q05/24		Pit
Q05/25		Terrace
Q05/26		Ridge terraces
Q05/30		Terraces and pits
Q05/32		Terraced knoll
Q05/33		Terrace
Q05/34	Rangihoua	Terraces outside the main earthworks, location of Earle's 1827 painting (Figure 4.X)
Q05/35		Headland pa

Figure 4.3. Rangihoua pa (Q05/3, foreground) and Oihi Mission Station (Q05/5, upper left), 2004. Horticultural features run down the slopes (Photo Kevin Jones, Department of Conservation, Wellington, New Zealand)

years in age, dating to the Last Interglacial (Horrocks et al. 2007). The smaller swamp contains a number of drains, presumably features associated with prehistoric gardening.

Analysis of pollen remains and diatoms (fossilized algae) in two continuous sediment cores taken from each of these swamps revealed aspects of the early environment in the valley and changes leading up to human presence approximately 500 years ago (Horrocks et al. 2007). Human presence is indicated in the small swamp core at a depth of 108 cm, by a consistent presence of charcoal, and possibly earlier

Figure 4.4. View over Te Puna looking west to Wairoa Bay, with Te Pahi Island at upper left, Papuke at extreme left, 2002

at a depth of 148 cm, with pollen and spores from "disturbance indicators." These "disturbance indicators" consist of vegetation such as bracken fern (*Pteridium*), or *aruhe*, the root of which formed a staple of the Maori diet (Colenso 1880; Davis n.d; Leach 2001, 2003), *tutu* (*Coriaria*) and tussock (*Poaceae*). Appearing at the same level were "agricultural microartifacts," starch grains and xylem cells of the introduced Polynesian plants *taro* (*Colocasia esculenta*), *kumara* (*Ipomoea batatas*), and phytoliths of paper mulberry (*Broussonetia papyrifera*). The other Polynesian introduced food staples, the yam and gourd (Leach 1984; Hargreaves 1963), are not indicated. A date prior to 500 B.P. could be given to this human disturbance as a radiocarbon date of 492 ± 42 B.P. was obtained from material at a depth of 90 cm in the same core. The upper 69 cm of the core consists of coarse gravel, with modern soil in the top section. Horrocks notes that this gravel, from Pleistocene dunes is most likely to have been redeposited in the swamp through human activity, giving better drainage to agricultural soils.

This explanation is consistent with the drains still evident in the swamp and the horticultural microartifacts. Horrocks has noted, in particular *taro*, which was grown on the flat and sometimes in wetland conditions (Barber 1989; Colenso 1880; Leach 1984). Modified soils with added gravel, along with sand and charcoal, are a common feature of Maori gardening (Colenso 1880; Hargreaves 1963; Law 1968; Leach 1984). In the uppermost sections of both cores the arrival of Europeans is marked by the appearance of exotic pine (*Pinus*).

Pre-European Horticulture

Further evidence of pre-European horticulture can be found in a number of archeological features found across this landscape, areas of channels or drains running down slopes in parallel or converging lines (Table 4.1). Terminology for these features varies with the literature. They are variously described as drains, channels, boundary markers, ditches, or depressions. Barber (1989) prefers the term "ditch systems," as used in the New Zealand Archaeological Association's site recording handbook (Walton 1999). The problem with the use of any particular term is that it preempts an interpretation of function, as this is uncertain, and has been the subject of discussion for a number of decades (Barber 1989; Kennedy 1969; Leach 1984). Two series of these ditches (P05/851 and P05/852) can be found on the slopes above the Wairoa stream, dendritic in pattern at the top of the slope and converging into the swampy area beside the stream. A number of these features can be extrapolated from the 1950 aerial photo (Figure 4.1), as well as the similar ploughing "lands," discussed in a later section of this chapter (Figure 4.7). Similar features are recorded at Rangihoua (Q05/3), Oihi (Q05/5), and just to the north of Oihi (Q05/6) (Figure 4.3), also running downhill into a small swampy stream. The site of the Oihi mission, Q05/5, is recorded as a horticultural site (rather than historical) due to the large number of cultivation drains or channels that run down the slope. These features can be clearly seen, predating the European occupation, running down a slope later terraced for the construction of the missionary houses, toward the beach (Spencer 1983). Some of these systems may have continued in use into the contact period. Superimposed on these earlier features are those associated with the mission.

Hangi and Midden

Large areas of midden and *hangi* (cooking ovens) have been noted in the past along the shoreline of Rangihoua and Wairoa Bays, continuing to the further stream at the western end of Wairoa Bay, providing evidence of prehistoric occupation of the area.

Sites P05/853 and 854 mark the eastern and western extent respectively of a line of midden and *hangi* that extended nearly continuously along Wairoa Bay, from the rocky point close to Papuke (P05/25), west to the stream mouth at P05/854. While the sites recorded are evident in the stratigraphy on the shoreline, similar subsurface archeological evidence was once likely to continue on the terrace above, along with possible structural evidence of habitation. However, much of this archeology may have been modified or destroyed by recent development (Best 2003b). Shell midden from these two sites has been radiocarbon dated, P05/853 giving a date of 712 years ±39 B.P., while shell from P05/854 was significantly later at 513 years ± 38 B.P. This evidence, along with further radiocarbon dates from Best (2003b) confirms the occupation of this terrace in prehistoric as well as into historic times. The historic occupation is likely to be associated with Te Pahi and his eponymous island located just off shore (Middleton 2003, 2005a). Similar features were noted at Rangihoua Bay during Lawn's survey in 1972, with *hangi* stones, midden and postholes recorded as part of the Te Puna mission site (P05/24). These features are no longer visible, destroyed by erosion and cattle damage. Further midden and *hangi* (P05/897) are still evident at the western end of Rangihoua Bay toward Papuke. A human patella was recovered from this area in 2002. Midden is also evident on the terraces (P05/889) above the Te Puna mission.

Sea mammal bone found in Wairoa Bay provides evidence of early occupation. Further evidence of settlement dating to the fourteenth century or earlier was found during a small excavation by Best (2003b) in November 2002. The investigation was situated on the terrace at the east end of the bay, close to Papuke. The earliest feature contained snapper remains, along with the leg of a small *moa* (*Pachyornis mappini*), a dog pelvis with cut marks, and some shellfish. Radiocarbon samples of wood (kanuka and pohutukawa) and shell (dog cockle) from this feature dated to the fourteenth century. Best (2003b: 39) notes:

> Cut marks on the dogbone are from a stone tool, and suggest that one of the flakes found in the deposit may have been used to either butcher the animal or remove the meat from the bone. Tool manufacture was also carried out, with a longbone segment scored across with a stone flake then snapped, the unsuccessful end result then discarded into a burning fire. The feature could well represent just one meal and the activities that were carried on around it, that took place some 600 years ago.

Three other radiocarbon samples (shell and short-lived wood species) from Best's features one, three, and four gave dates slightly later, overlapping and continuing through to the twentieth century.

Horrocks (in Best 2003b) examined material from Best's excavation at Wairoa Bay and found *taro* microfossils in the early deposit and *kumara* starch grains in later material. Pollen remains indicated an absence (or low values) of tall forest trees and high values of bracken fern (*Pteridium*) along with *puwha* (*Sonchus*), *tutu* (*Coriaria*), fern

(*Pteris*), and hornworts (*Anthrocerotae*), inconspicuous plants that colonize freshly exposed soils. The presence of fern and the other "disturbed-environment colonizers" indicated that anthropogenic forest clearing had already happened or was taking place at the time that the features Best investigated were formed (Horrocks in Best 2003b: 28). Pollen remains from two tall trees (rimu and matai) along with charcoal from the same feature, which included kauri, point to remnants of forest in the area at the time.

The presence of bracken fern (*Pteridium*) here and in the small swamp at Te Puna confirms the observations of missionaries living in the Bay in the early nineteenth century as well as other European visitors. Nicholas (1817 I: 190), companion of Marsden on the 1814 voyage, reported that fern, covering "the greatest part of the land" was the staple item of diet of the Maori. The botanist Cunningham (n.d.) who spent several months in the Bay of Islands in 1826 observed that all the hills were covered with fern root. While Cunningham considered that this was a "dire resort" for Maori when other crops failed, the missionary Richard Davis (n.d. November 1826) believed, as did William Colenso, that the indigenous New Zealanders were always well supplied with food, and ate fern root, which did not need to be cultivated "from choice and not necessity." Colenso (1880: 22) provides details of the proper preparation of fern root, noting that "The old Maoris thought highly of it, and always liked it, even preferring it in the summer with fresh fish." Leach (2001, 2003) reviews the differing explanations of Colenso, Cunningham, and Davis for the role of fernroot in the Maori diet, a fibrous, tough food that Europeans generally disliked. Explanations ranged from the "seasonal stop-gap," a staple food item during spring and early summer when the last season's harvest was exhausted and the next was still immature, to "rations for people under stress," such as siege provisions, and "default staple where cultivation of crops was difficult or impossible," for example in the South Island south of Banks Peninsula, where the climate did not allow the cultivation of *kumara* (Leach 2001: 34–35). Leach also notes that fernroot was a good food to carry when traveling, and was used by European explorers. It was light, easily prepared and replenished en route, and was only finally replaced for this purpose by flour. But as Colenso and Davis pointed out, this was a food also enjoyed for its own sake, outside any of the explanations or rationalizations required by Europeans.

Colenso (1880) remarks that in earlier times (that is, before the middle of the nineteenth century) paper mulberry (*Broussonetia papyrifera*), known as *aute* by the Maori, microfossils of which were found in the small swamp at Te Puna, was commonly grown, although at the time of his writing, none remained. It was common at the time of Cook's visit, when he saw it growing in plantations in the Bay of Islands (Beaglehole 1955: 217). It was worn in the hair and through the ear as a decoration, as shown in the drawing of Te Uri o Kanae (Figure 2.6) and also used to make ornamental paper kites. Its cultivation in New Zealand only produced plants of a small size, not large enough to produce clothing as in other parts of Polynesia. In 1835 Colenso saw one small tree of *aute* growing in the Bay of Islands, at the head of the Kawakawa River, in an old plantation. This died soon after.

Late Prehistory: A Defended Coastline

Defended *pa* are the predominant archeological feature in the contemporary landscape of Rangihoua and Wairoa bays. The coastline is dominated by a number of *pa* located on the headlands, with terraces and defended terrace sites scattered between these. Fortified sites such as these are found throughout northern New Zealand, associated with warfare and the intensification of agriculture from about the sixteenth to the late eighteenth centuries (Davidson 1984; Schmidt 1996).

Rangihoua (Q05/3), located on the highest point in Rangihoua Bay, appears to be the most preeminent of these sites (Figures 2.4 and 3.1). It is the *pa* in the northern Bay of Islands most-commonly referred to in missionary and other historical literature, and occupies a larger area than any of the other *pa* in Rangihoua and Wairoa Bays. Defended by a single ditch on the western side and a series of three ditches on the east (Spencer 1983), it was further fortified in the past by palisading (Earle 1909; Marshall 1836). Numerous terraces, both within and outside the defences would have supported houses, storage structures, and activity areas. Other terraces extend outward from the main *pa* toward the east, beyond Oihi, and toward the west, including a series which lead down the spurs away from Rangihoua toward the Te Puna valley (P05/889, 890, 891). The terraces of P05/889 run down a spur from the hill named in Turton (1879; see Chap. 3) as "Rorekahu," connecting the *pa* with the valley that was important for cultivation. The terraces of P05/890 and P05/891 extend along a ridge to the north and east above the valley. The terraces on all of these sites may have been used for house structures associated with cultivation at Te Puna.

The eastern end of Rangihoua Bay is defended by site Q05/35, a headland cut off by a defensive ditch and bank, with a series of terraces on the seaward side of this. The headland at the western end of the bay, Papuke (P05/25), has similar defenses. This *pa* is cut off from the ridge behind it by a deep defensive ditch and high bank, with steep cliffs leading to the sea on the south. There are several terraces within the defenses. A ridge *pa*, P05/26, was recorded in 1972 behind Papuke, leading to the Te Puna valley. Although this appears to have largely eroded away, one terrace is still evident, with midden exposed in the topsoil. Richard Taylor's drawing of the mission (Figure 4.12) has a *whata* (or storage platform) close to the same place.

Papuke divides Rangihoua Bay from Wairoa Bay, to the west. Just offshore at Wairoa Bay stands the heavily terraced *pa* of Te Pahi Island (P05/2), commanding the western and southern approaches to Te Puna (Figure 4.4). It stands among four islands known collectively as the "Te Pahi Islands." While other evidence is ambiguous, the archeology of this island suggests it is the likely location of Te Pahi's house, given to him by Governor King in 1806 and erected by the carpenter of the *Lady Nelson*, and attacked by whalers in 1810. The defensive earthworks and terraces of Te Pahi Island (also known as Turtle Island for its shape) can be clearly seen from the mainland and the sea and suggest that it was the most occupied of the group, fortified to withstand attack. Missionary journals (Elder 1932, 1934; Kendall n.d.b) note that the island remained uninhabited after the attack because it was highly *tapu*. Passing Te Puna from the sea, Marsden noted his implicit belief in Te Pahi's innocence in the *Boyd* affair, and sadly remarked

> I never passed Tippahee's Island without a sigh. It is now desolate, without an inhabitant, and has been ever so since his death. The ruins of his little cottage, built by the kindness of the late Governor King, still remains. (Elder 1932: 87–8)

Te Pahi Island was gazetted as a Native Reserve in 1981 "for the purpose of a place of scenic interest" (New Zealand Gazette No. 29 1981: 728).

Evidence for contemporaneous occupation of the mainland at Wairoa Bay can be found in a number of sources. To quote again from Savage (1973 [1807]: 22)

> The capital of this part of the country, which is situated partly on the main land, and partly on a small island, is called Tippoonah, and consists in the whole of about an hundred dwellings. On the main the dwellings of the natives are surrounded each by a little patch of cultivated ground; but the island is appropriated to the residence of a chieftain and his court, where no cultivation is carried on.

Savage's observations confirm Te Puna, stretching from the island to the long terrace at Wairoa Bay and over the Papuke headland, as initially the most important location in the Bay of Islands and the north for trade between Maori and European (Middleton 2003). A further map drawn by the French on a visit in 1824 names Te Pahi Island, but not Te Puna (Middleton 2005a: 165; Spencer 1983). The location of these islands close to the long (natural) terrace at Wairoa Bay, along with the 1820 map and historical reports of Te Pahi's village on the mainland, associated with the island, suggests that the historic midden at Wairoa Bay is likely to have been associated with Te Pahi's mainland village

and occupation at this time. Occupation of Wairoa Bay continued into
the era of the mission. John King's (n.d.a,b) journals note regular visits
to preach at Wiriwiri, a village located at the eastern end of the bay
close to Papuke and sites P05/853 and P05/854, as well as Wairoa, a
village toward the western end of Wairoa Bay.

A knoll further inland overlooking the Te Puna valley, Rangihoua
Bay, and Wairoa Bay as well as the Bay of Islands harbor is recorded
as site P05/915. This has been the location of European occupation in
the nineteenth and twentieth centuries, with a farmhouse and associated buildings there. This knoll is also likely to have been intensively
occupied in prehistory given its prominent outlook and position. While
any surface features on the knoll itself are no longer apparent due to
recent building and landscaping, a terrace can be found on the slope
toward Wairoa Bay (P05/906), likely to have been associated with
further terracing and habitation on the knoll above it. From a close
reading of the landscape, the archival material, and historical literature, this prominence presents itself as the site of Ruatara's planned
town at Te Puna and the location of the *wahi tapu* associated with his
death (Elder 1932), discussed in more detail in the next section. This is
confirmed by T. M. Hocken's caption to a photograph of Te Puna dated
c. 1905 (Middleton 2005a: 169; the 1906 photograph in Figure 4.5 is
taken from just below this knoll). Part of Hocken's caption reads

Figure 4.5. Te Puna, 1906 (Hocken Library, Dunedin, New Zealand. S04–009b)

> On the top of the slope, *Ruatara* in his love for all English proposed to lay out
> a town with streets etc. *a la Sydney*. He was moved here in his last illness
> and there died in *1815*.

These sites collectively point to a long, continual prehistoric occupation along Wairoa Bay and Rangihoua Bay, with a local population returning to the area to exploit resources and carry out seasonal horticulture in the manner Walter et al. (2006) have described.

TE PUNA 1905 AND 1906

A photograph taken in 1906 (Figure 4.5) shows the Te Puna valley at this time and demonstrates some of the historic and prehistoric features discussed above. This image can be compared with Figure 4.6, a photograph taken from a similar point in 2002.

The site of the King mission house is just beyond the trees in the center of the valley. In the 2002 photo, archeological investigations can be seen in progress on the site of the King house. In the 1906 photograph relevant features are identified by letter. Many of these features are also visible in the 2002 photograph. The hill named "Rorekahu" stands at the back of Te Puna valley. The white cottage (B) visible in both the historic images in the foreground of the mission station site was built in the late nineteenth century, but burnt down in 1933 (Skudder personal

Figure 4.6. Te Puna from a similar aspect, 2002

communication 2002). The remains of the house are still evident today, with concrete front door steps and chimney base standing just outside the old garden. The gabled roof (A) just visible through the trees to the right of the cottage may be the eastern-most of the outbuildings associated with the mission, although it is not the mission house itself. This structure had a different roofline (see Figures 4.12 and 4.13) and was likely to have been demolished before the date of this photograph (Middleton 2005a). The tree (pohutukawa or puriri) just to the left of the white cottage is still standing at the rear of the garden in the 2002 photograph. The second mission house, built by James Shepherd, is no longer standing. The exact location of this house has not been identified, although as Figures 4.12 and 4.13 show, it was further to the east on the same ridge above the small swamp. Other buildings visible in Figure 4.5 include a small shed near the flax along the shoreline (G) and another small shed or other building on the slope of the ridge leading to the small swamp (F), similar to a structure shown in one of Taylor's 1839 drawings (not illustrated; see Middleton 2005a: 197). Other archeological features connected with the mission station include two sawpits and a pathway. The sawpits (P05/899), used to cut timber for the mission houses, are located on the shoreline not far from the house site. These are two pits approximately 10 μ long dug out at right angles to the beach, over which logs were cut using pit saws. While they are now filled in, the outline of the original indentations remains. In the 1906 image, a roofed structure is visible over the sawpits (E). Sawpits were often covered over, no doubt to provide shelter for the sawyers who spent long periods of time working there. The pathway (P05/896) running from the mission station over the hill to Rangihoua and Oihi (Figure 4.6) is noted as that used in early mission days to walk between Oihi and Te Puna (Mountain pers. comm. September 2002). It can be seen in both the 1906 (C) and 2002 photographs cutting diagonally across the hill behind the mission site, below the terraces of P05/896, as well as the Old Land Claim maps (Figure 3.3). These terraces are also evident in both the historic (D) and contemporary landscape. In both the 1906 and 2002 photographs, Oihi can be seen just beyond the point in the middle distance. In the 2002 image, some of the terraces where the missionary houses were built are still evident. In the 1906 image a house (H) can be seen, still standing at Oihi, in an enlargement of the image.

AGRICULTURE: PLOUGHING

Throughout Te Puna and the slope leading to Papuke, to the west, the landscape is covered with a series of ridges and furrows similar to those noted above, associated with prehistoric/protohistoric Maori horticulture and agriculture. However, these are lands, artifacts of the horse-drawn plough, regular in size and quite parallel. Close examination of the 1950 aerial photograph of Te Puna (Figure 4.1) reveals the extent of these still apparent at that date. Figure 4.7 shows these features, as well as the similar ditches or channels, extrapolated and mapped from the 1950 aerial photograph. A large number of these are still visible on the ground. The most evident is a discrete series to the north of the mission site (P05/893). Another series (P05/856) is evident to the west of the stream, and continues up the slope to the large Norfolk pine (P05/892), almost continuous over this hill. P05/893, situated about 50 m behind the mission house, is a series of 13 lands,

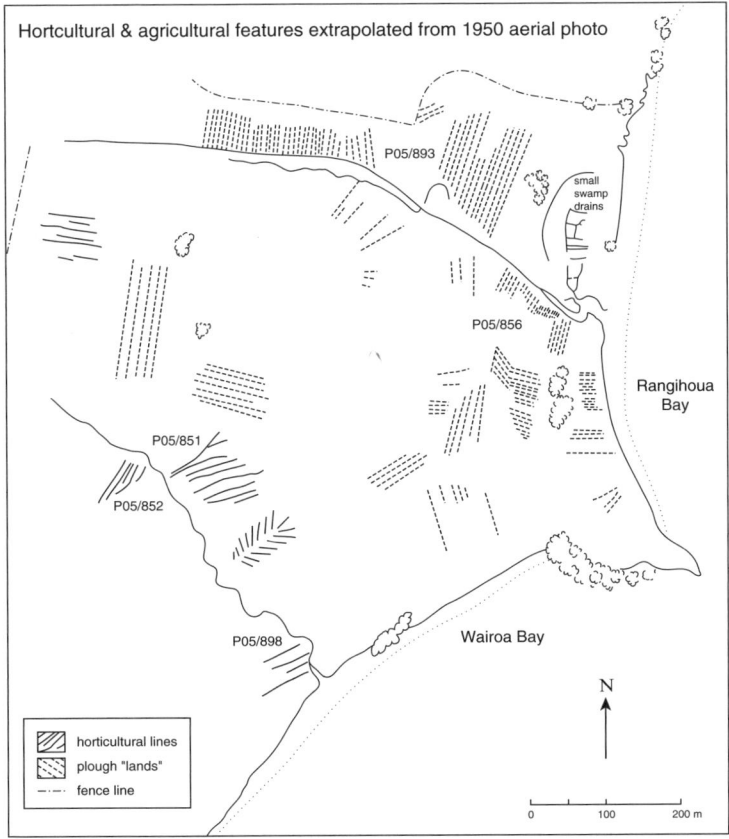

Figure 4.7. Horticultural and agricultural features extrapolated from 1950 aerial photo (Figure 4.1)

parallel depressions about 10 m apart, about 0.3 m in depth, 1–2 m wide and up to approximately 100 m in length, separated by low mounded "ridges."

Similar agricultural landscapes have been documented in Australia (Connah 1993; Twidale 1971, 1972; Twidale et al. 1971) and in Britain (Orwin and Orwin 1938), resulting from the use of implements and machines developed in the early years of the industrial revolution. In Australia lands vary in width between 2 and 18 m and are generally 50–65 m long (Twidale 1971). In some areas the lands are visible from the air, and in aerial photographs, with "many sets of furrows, some faint, some remarkably clear, and some aligned at obtuse angles to each other because of cross-ploughing," while on the ground little evidence remains (Twidale 1972: 52). Twidale (1971: 219) explains that lands resulted from the British practice of ploughing a deep central furrow by running the plough in opposite directions; "Thereafter the ploughman returned on either side of the top throwing soil toward, and filling in the double furrow, and then as the runs continued on alternate sides of the top, making a broad ridge known as a land." This was a lengthy procedure which involved working over the same strip of land a number of times in order to ensure the area beneath the initial two ridges was ploughed. "If a ploughman merely traversed in opposite directions throwing soil toward a central ridge, he simply threw soil over an unploughed strip" (Twidale et al. 1971: 498). Ploughing was always carried out across the contours of slopes, as is seen at Te Puna at P05/856 (Figure 4.7). This was safer than working along the contour of a hill, which created problems with controlling the plough and the direction the soil fell. Ploughing with the single share plough was carried out in the nineteenth century for cereal cultivation, in particular wheat. In Australia it continued to be used up until the middle of the twentieth century, and it is likely that the same could be said of New Zealand (Walton 1982).

Although the ploughing lands at Te Puna cannot be clearly identified as features dating from the missionary occupation, as ploughing could have continued on into the twentieth century, these are an artifact of methods associated with early European agriculture and settlement, and the use of the type of plough John Butler first to put to use in New Zealand soil at Kerikeri in 1820 (Barton 1927). Lands remain if the area is allowed to revert to pasture after the abandonment of cereal cultivation, while the use of later cultivation methods tends to destroy the pattern of ridges and furrows (Twidale 1972).

Connah (1993: 91) points out that lands are "remarkable archaeological evidence for the strength of a tradition and the persistence of cultural practices. The man behind the plough imprinted onto the South Australian landscape a pattern that he had learnt in his homeland." These features remain in the landscape as artifacts of early European agriculture and pastoralism, along with the items of material culture recovered from the Te Puna mission investigation, such as scythes, reaping hooks, and spades (see Chap. 5).

The Te Puna landscape is scattered with markers from both Maori and European occupation. These are visible in features like the ploughing lands, Norfolk pines, and early house sites (Figure 4.4). Other less evident marking places, such as Ruatara's *wahi tapu*, also remain reflecting the power of the chiefly individual over the landscape.

STRUCTURAL FEATURES OF THE MISSION HOUSE

A field survey conducted in early summer 2002 identified the likely location of the mission house, marked by a depression in the ground in the area shown on Old Land Claim maps (Figure 3.3) as the mission house. Several months later a team from the University of Auckland returned to investigate the site. A 20 m base line running east–west, along the edge of the depression was laid out, intersected by a north–south line running from squares E to M (Figure 4.8). A total area of approximately 93 m2 was excavated. In the text, references to the

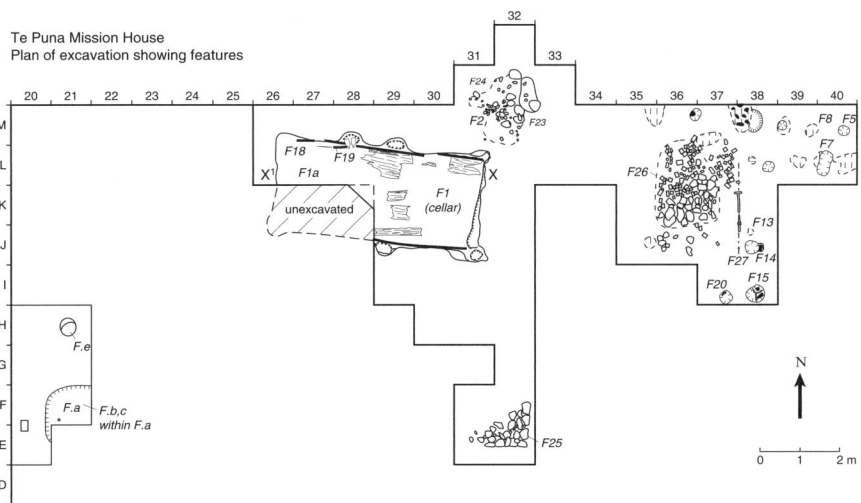

Figure 4.8. Plan of excavation showing relevant features, Te Puna Mission House investigation

orientation of the excavation and the cellar walls are made according to this baseline orientation. Magnetic north is actually located at a point between the north and the east baselines.

The largest structural feature uncovered was a cellar, designated Feature 1, approximately 3 m × 5 m × 1.5 m deep, likely to have been situated under the main body of the house (Figures 4.8 and 4.9). The southwest quarter was not excavated, but was left in situ when the cellar was back filled. Structural features in the cellar included four round postholes approximately 50 cm in diameter along the northern wall, with complete bottles recovered from the bases of these postholes. Two similar postholes were located on the opposing south wall, with two more postholes likely in the unexcavated quarter of the cellar. The timbers, likely to have consisted of whole tree trunks, had been removed from these features. Further horizontal recesses in the clay of the eastern cellar wall are likely to have been for shelf supports. A glass trade bead was found in one of these recesses.

Some 3–4 m out from the southeast corner of the cellar, a flat triangular stone feature (Feature 25; Figure 4.8) with mortar (lime cement) in situ indicated the likely location of this corner of the house itself. Out from the opposing northeast cellar corner more stones and mortar indicated a possible second corner of the building (Feature 2). Features 23 and 24, adjacent to Feature 2, shallow scoops filled with mortar and stone, may have been part of this corner structure. Attempts to

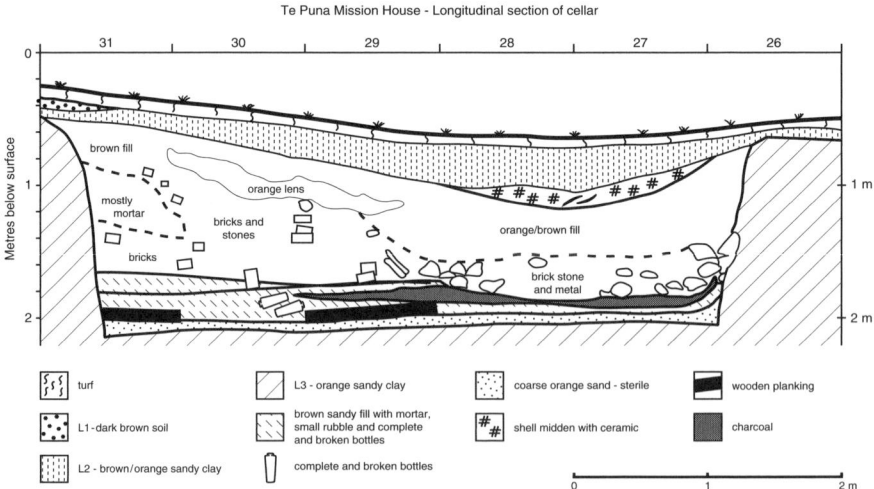

Figure 4.9. Profile of cellar, looking toward the south, Te Puna Mission House investigation (see Figure 4.8 for location of cross section)

locate similar structural features at the south and northwest corners, in order to prove that features 23 and 24 were part of a rectangular house plan, were unsuccessful due to time constraints. It is also possible some features may have been destroyed at the time of, or after, demolition. Squares E to H, 20 and 21, in the western area were excavated in an effort to locate a third corner of the house (Figure 4.8). While there was a large depression in 21 G–F (Feature A), and a series of possible postholes along with a small fire scoop (Features B–E), no definite structural features were identified.

Approximately 7 m from the east baulk of the cellar, a series of postholes pointed to the likely location of an outbuilding associated with the house (Features 5, 7, 8, 11, 14, 15; Figures 4.8 and 4.10). Just to the west of these postholes, between the postholes and toward the east wall of the house, a cobbled path, and above (or postdating, stratigraphically) part of that, a flat stone feature indicated the possible location of an entrance into the eastern lean-to of the house (Figure 4.11). In the same area, at the edge of this cobbled surface, a number of metal artifacts were found in layers one and two in a line between squares 37 and 38, from squares M to J (feature 27), indicating that they may have been left lying against a wall or wooden fence. These artifacts included a large hinge, a pickaxe, an axe, a metal bar, and pieces of a cast iron cooking pot (Figure 4.8).

The structural features consisting of a main building and lean-tos at both the east and west sides, with a further out-house to the east are in keeping with drawings of the house from the 1830s and 1840s (Figures 4.11 and 4.12).

Attempts to locate the chimney indicated in drawings (not illustrated) on the southwest wall of the western lean-to were not successful, perhaps because the chimney may have been entirely flattened at the time the house was demolished, with most of the bricks being pushed into the cellar.

According to Fergus Clunie (pers. comm. March 2002) the flat stone corner (feature 25) is consistent with early CMS building methods used at the Kerikeri Mission House. A similar feature can be seen beneath a building at the Te Papa mission station in Tauranga in Figure 5.8. Floor joists or beams were often placed directly onto these foundation features instead of onto posts. At the same time, small postholes relate to the outbuildings and lean-to on the eastern edge of the site. Some of these postholes were filled with broken metal artifacts (such as flat irons and pieces of broken goashore pots) in a method that Challis (1993) suggests was used to shore up timber posts at the Bedggood blacksmith building, associated with the Waimate mission house, at a time before concrete was available.

Figure 4.10. Excavation area showing relevant features, Te Puna Mission House investigation

The Cellar Fill and Floor

Figure 4.9 represents a profile of the cellar stratigraphy. This was drawn early in the investigation, prior to the excavation of the cellar fill, looking toward the south. Above the cellar fill, Feature 1a, located in L 27 and 28, consisted of shell midden and broken ceramics including

Figure 4.11. Te Puna Mission Station, looking toward the west, 1839 (Artist Richard Taylor, 1805–1873. Alexander Turnbull Library, Wellington, New Zealand. E-296-q-071–1)

Figure 4.12. Te Puna Mission Station, looking toward the east, c. 1839–1841 (Artist Richard Taylor, 1805–1873. Alexander Turnbull Library, Wellington, New Zealand. E-296-q-160–1)

an Asiatic Pheasant ashet (large serving plate). This feature in the upper layers continued into the unexcavated quarter of the cellar. Fill in the main body of the cellar indicated demolition of the remains of the house. The body of the cellar was filled with a mix of bricks, mortar, wood, stone, and artifacts of all material including metal, glass, broken ceramic material, shell, and faunal remains. Beneath this fill artifacts found in situ on the wooden floor included complete bottles, buttons, wrought nails, and iron tools, as well as fragments of broken cast iron cooking pots. The presence of charcoal and burnt material along the western edge suggested a fire, perhaps as part of the demolition process. Within the cellar along the northern baulk there was a rectangular area of pebbles (Feature 18) at about 75 cm from the surface in M27, which merged into Feature 19, a large lens of charcoal below the cellar fill in L28. Broad wooden planking was found in situ lining the floor of the cellar and at the base of the walls (Figures 4.8 and 4.9). Figure 4.10 illustrates the Layer 3 surface of the investigation with relevant features numbered.

THE MISSION HOUSE STRUCTURE

Drawings and Documentary Material

CMS missionary Richard Taylor, who arrived in New Zealand in 1839, visited Te Puna first on September 25 1839 and again in January 1841 (Taylor n.d.). He continued to visit the mission from time to time, usually when traveling north between Kaitaia or Whangaroa and the Bay of Islands, until 1843 when he was posted south to Wanganui. Taylor penciled three drawings of the mission on these visits, two of these illustrated here (Figures 4.11 and 4.12). These drawings, along with one done by Hutton (illustrated in Middleton 2005a: 199) provide the best visual record of the Kings' house. The more idealized, westernized view published in the Church Missionary Paper and Missionary Register in 1838 (Figure 3.2, "Mission Station, Te Puna"), probably drawn by William Wade, is not so useful in considering the structure of the building. Taylor (n.d. Vol. 2:153 25 September 1839) considered that the house was "situated in a romantic spot," unlike William Wade, quoted in Chap. 3, who evidently disliked the place.

Drawings by both Taylor and Hutton, looking toward the northeast, show what appears to be a vertical boarded, or board-and-baton building, roofed with wooden shingles. Two windows either side of the front door face out toward the bay, with two dormer windows in the hipped roof suggesting attic bedrooms. The lean-to shown on the western side of the main building has the same vertical lines drawn on it, with a chimney in the south corner identifying this lean-to as the most likely location of the kitchen. A fence runs along the east, close to the house, and along the south, fencing in the garden that looks rather wild and unkempt. In Figures 4.11 and 4.12 lean-tos at both the eastern and western sides of the main building can be seen. Beyond the eastern lean-to is an outbuilding close to the house, and beyond that again another low shed or outbuilding. Taylor's 1839 drawing, Figure 4.11, looking toward the west, shows the eastern side of the house in more detail. The second mission house, built by James Shepherd, is situated further along the old beach ridge toward the west, while on the ridge in the distance the gabled roof of Thomas Hansen's house can just be seen. Taylor's second drawing, (Figure 4.12) undated but most likely drawn either on his visit in 1839 or subsequently in 1841, gives a view of the mission station from the headland, Papuke. Two figures in European clothing sit on the bank; while on the ridge back from them the *whata* (storage platform) can be seen. The second mission house has a chimney on the west and a third building is located behind the house itself. Between this house and the Kings' is the garden. This drawing shows the outline of the fencing running in front of the Kings' house to the edge of the swamp, indicating that perhaps this was an area enclosed to contain animals. While the fencing is no longer present in the 1906 photograph (Figure 4.5), the fence line running through the swamp is suggested by a line of flax running in the same direction.

Both the mission houses evidently had cellars. While Anne and John Wilson were stationed at Te Puna John Wilson tried to help one of their servants, a young woman that men from the pa had captured to take back as the third wife of a chief. Wilson noted:

> Today the girl escaped from her captor and returned to our house, where she concealed herself in an underground place. The chief and his party appeared shortly afterwards. He was a man of middle age, rather short, broad set, strong, and active. He came at once to me and furiously demanded the woman. I replied, 'You must find her,' and as I was afraid that he would enter the house, I fastened all the doors and then sat outside in the verandah, he and his men sometimes sitting near me or walking before me. Late at night they withdrew. (Wilson, John n.d.)

Comparative Structures: Other CMS Houses

The journal of Thomas Surfleet Kendall (n.d.), son of Thomas Kendall, gives some insight into missionary building methods used in the 1820s and likely to still have been in use 10 years later. Thomas Kendall junior kept his journal from 1822 to 1824, while he was building

Kendall's church at "Bethel," about 4 miles from Rangihoua, near
Kaihiki in the Te Puna inlet, and at Oihi and Matauwhi Bay near
Kororareka. Kendall junior appears to have been working on the family home at Oihi in 1822, although his father was soon to be dismissed
from the CMS (Elder 1932, 1934; Binney 2005). The house at Oihi had
"waterspouts" along the eaves and three water troughs on the roof.
Kendall (n.d.) notes:

> October 16 & 17 Employed in making & finishing the kitchen window frames
> 11 feet by 3 1/2 feet, also putting up the same & repairing part of the front
> of the house.
> 19. The Rev. Thos Kendall employed from the commencement of this month
> in superintending 4 native sawyers, & sharpening pitsaws, and assisting me
> in carpenters work. Used 75 Squares of Glass.
> 21st. Employed in casing 2 windows for the study & parlour. The Rev. Thos
> Kendall is under the necessity of sharpening the pitsaws himself, there
> being no other men in the settlement willing to do it.
> November 25th During the last quarter of a year the Native sawyers under
> the superintendence of the Revd Thos Kendall have sawn about four thou-
> sand feet of boards. The Revd Thos Kendall's dwelling house is now in a good
> state of repair, having cover'd the roof with new boards in front and painted
> them, repair'd the passage between the house & the school house & done
> such things as were needful to be done.

Kendall also describes repairing the sitting room chimney (indicating
that this house had more than one), making moldings for and building an "observatory," building a rabbit coop, digging drains behind
the house and paving the "roads" (paths) between some of the houses
with slabs of wood. Rooms in the house were lined with planed boards.
It is interesting to note that in February of the following year (1823)
Kendall's building activities ended abruptly and he was employed
from the 8th until the 25th in making packing cases with the assistance of the carpenter of the *Asp*. On the 26th the household moved
with all their belongings, in seven whaleboats to Pomare's residence
at Matauwhi Bay, near Kororareka, where once again Kendall junior
began his usual employment of sawing and planning boards in order
to build another house for the family. This upheaval, explained by
Kendall's conflict with other Oihi missionaries including King, over his
adultery with the daughter of the chief Hauraki, was followed by his
expulsion from the CMS at the end of 1823. These events are discussed
in detail in Binney's (2005) biography of Kendall.

William Hall's (n.d.) diary for 1816–1825 is also a useful source
for contextual material. Hall, joiner and carpenter, was a busy man in
the early years of the Oihi settlement, constructing houses, a schoolhouse, two boats, a barn and a chapel among other smaller structures
for all the settlement's inhabitants. Houses were surrounded with gated

pailing fences 8 ft. high in an effort to keep the settlement secure from *taua muru*, plundering parties, who occasionally tried to exact *utu* from missionaries for cultural offences, sometimes made unawares. His journal continually refers to the quantities of timber and plank sawn by Maori sawyers who appear to have been constantly at work at the Oihi saw pit. Timber was sourced from the "timber grounds" on the south side of the Bay of Islands, and logs rafted back to Rangihoua Bay. Sawn timber was not only used for building houses at Oihi, and later Kerikeri, but also to fill the hold of the *Active* and other ships, to be sold on return voyages to Port Jackson. Hall made furniture – tables, cupboards, boxes, as well as joinery for windows for the houses, built chimneys with bricks and stone, and mentions making a brick oven. When discussing many of the buildings, including the schoolhouse, he mentions lofts (as does Kendall, above) suggesting that this may have been a useful means of economizing on building resources by using the roof space. Hall also notes work carried out by the blacksmith at Oihi. He made "trade," metal items that were used to pay Maori for their work at the mission, such as adzes and axes (Middleton 2007d). On the arrival of a blacksmith from a ship in the Bay, Hall (n.d. September 4 1820) set up a forge and "set him to work to make nails and other Iron work, for the benefit of the Settlement."

THE INVESTIGATION: FEATURES AND ARTIFACTS RELATING TO THE STRUCTURE

Features uncovered during the archeological investigation relate clearly to a structure located over the area of the cellar and corners located in the southeast and northeast (Figure 4.8). Features to the east of this, that is postholes and the cobbled path, identify further structures beyond the main part of the house, the eastern lean-to and outbuilding. The area covered by these features suggests a house of approximately 110 m2 for the ground floor of the main building and two lean-tos, with the eastern outbuilding approximately 13 m². Drawings of the building point to an upper storey, or loft, as mentioned above, with attic windows. Metal items recovered from the investigation included building fixtures as well as sheet metal and fasteners such as nails, spikes, and screws. Tools found related to both building as well as agriculture. A large proportion of the fill of the cellar consisted of bricks, no doubt from the demolished chimney which can be seen in drawings of the King house, located at the western end of the building. A number of large stones also formed the fill, possibly hearthstones or used as part of the chimney structure.

Structural Artifacts

Adams (2002) argues that nails can provide the key to dating historic sites, especially where there is no documentary evidence available, and calls for regional nail chronologies such as that developed by Wells (2000), with the consideration of local and regional variations caused by factors such as importation and transportation. In Australia, Varman (1980) had earlier developed a similar chronology. This is relevant in the case of the mission house, where no documentary records exist of the date of its abandonment or demolition and the presence of both wrought and cut nails, including numbers and proportions, may indicate the period at which house maintenance ended (Middleton 2005c).

In the Bay of Islands, long-term restoration and investigation work on heritage sites such as that carried out by Best (1995, 1997, 2003a), Challis (1993, 1994) and Fergus Clunie, curator of the Kerikeri Stone Store and Mission House, has yielded some of this specific local information about nail chronology. In this region of New Zealand, the CMS imported British-manufactured wrought nails from Port Jackson until the early 1840s, when the cut nail started to become more popular. Both wrought and cut nails have been found at the Kerikeri Mission House and Stone Store, used in building contexts dating to about 1860. From the 1870s onward the wire nail became increasingly popular, while the use of cut nails such as brads continued for the nailing of floors and other areas where a tight fastener was required (Clunie pers. comm. September 2002). As noted above, Hall's journal records that wrought nails were hand-forged at Oihi, and this may have continued at many of the settlements, as it was a simple matter to set up a small forge. Quantities of iron accounted for at the CMS store suggest that it was likely that this metal was reworked at mission settlements (Challis 1993, 1994; Middleton 2007d).

Analysis of the nails recovered from the investigation and their location within the excavation areas demonstrated that wrought nails and spikes were the most commonly used in the mission house structure, with mostly wrought nails recovered from the cellar floor (Middleton 2005a–c). This is consistent with the type of nail (wrought) being used by the CMS at the time the house was built, according to CMS records kept at the Kerikeri mission house and the type of nails recovered from comparative structures such as the Kerikeri Mission House. It is also consistent with the historical research that demonstrates that this was an early nineteenth century structure.

Copper and zinc sheeting recovered is likely to have provided areas of waterproofing (possibly around the chimney and windows), spouting or a water tank, as noted above (Kendall, Thomas Surfleet n.d.). The largest quantity of sheet copper, 1.651 kg, was found below the turf and in layers one and two in the eastern squares of the excavation (K/L/M/36–40), and around the stone southeast corner foundation feature (F. 25).

Other building fixtures recovered included seven hinges of varying sizes. The mission store issued a variety of hinges in the early 1830s: butt hinges, box hinges, and T hinges (Appendix F). The appearance of the single complete hinge suggests that this may be the T hinge, while the other hinge fragments are of the same form with the horizontal arm missing. Other metal items consist of tools relating to both building and agricultural work. The pickaxe recovered from the surface (feature 27), spades found on the cellar floor and in the fill, as well as axes were the kind of tools required to excavate the cellar and prepare wood for building. They could also be used for agriculture and are discussed further in Chap. 5.

Most of the whole bricks and fragments retrieved from the site were thin, between 10 and 11 cm wide, only 4–6 cm deep, and 21–22 cm in length, resembling the dimensions of Sydney-made bricks (Simon Best personal communication 25/06/2003; Middleton 2005a,b). One of the incomplete bricks has a clay pipe fragment in the matrix, perhaps a signature left by its maker, or merely ceramic debris dropped in. The clays used for these bricks vary from a deep red with dark flecks to an orange. Some of the dark red bricks are under-fired and very crumbly. While the bricks recovered from the Te Puna mission were used in the building itself, the variation in the size and the matrix of these bricks suggests that they may have originated from a number of different sources, including Port Jackson. Bricks were made at Oihi in 1816 by the convict laborer/brickmaker Tully Matthews (Hall n.d.). In the same year, Hall (n.d.) also notes receiving bricks from the tryworks of the *Catherine*. Other missionaries record brick laying and chimney building as an important and somewhat frustrating task carried out by men who had not always perfected these practical skills (Rogers 1961; Wilson n.d.).

Window glass is also useful for confirming dates of archeological sites (Orser et al. 1987; Roenke 1978). A total weight of 1,392 g of window glass was recovered from the Te Puna cellar and surrounding squares. A large proportion of this, 1,357 g, was very thin glass varying from 0.86 to 1.24 mm in thickness, with several fragments slightly thicker at around 1.50 mm. This is comparable with window glass from the Kerikeri Mission House, where thickness varied from 1 to 1.5 mm (Best 1995). Only 35 g (eight fragments) of modern window glass measuring around 2 mm (1.7–2.12 mm) in thickness was recovered at Te Puna. Much of the thinner glass has a patina, making it appear somewhat opalescent in color due to the deterioration of the surface. This is glass produced by either the crown or cylinder methods, used in the 1800s to produce flat window glass (Noel Hume 1969; Lorrain 1968). As a result of these techniques, particularly the crown method, early nineteenth century window glass varies in thickness, and could only be used to form small panes, of the kind shown in drawings of the King house. Thomas Kendall, quoted above, noted that he used 75 squares of glass while he was building at Oihi.

THE ARCHIVES: GOODS RECEIVED

Archival records from the CMS store at Kerikeri are introduced in more detail in Chap. 5, where they can be referred to in the context of the majority of the artifacts recovered from the investigation. A complete list of all articles held in the CMS store at Kerikeri for the year from April 1831 to March 1832 can be found in Appendix 1, along with a record of those supplied to John King. They are referred to here outside that context in order to produce a more complete record of materials used in the mission building.

However, it is useful to examine them here in the context of the mission house structure in order produce a more detailed picture of the materials that the CMS was importing to use in its buildings, and to compare this archival source with artifacts recovered from the mission site. A more complete consideration of the relationship between goods supplied to missions from the CMS Kerikeri store, artifacts recovered from the investigation, and trading relationships can be found in "Mission Station as Trading Post" (Middleton 2007d).

Records from the CMS store (CMS n.d.f; Middleton 2005a, 2007d) note that 6,000 bricks were delivered to the Kerikeri store from Port Jackson by the schooner *Active* in 1830, with a further 1,200 arriving on the same boat in September 1831, these noted as destined for Rangihoua and the School and valued at £15–0-0. Which school is not noted; Rangihoua is likely to refer to Te Puna, where King was busy building at this time, "Rangihoua" and "Te Puna" often being used in a generic or interchangeable sense to refer to these locations in Rangihoua Bay. Wright also brought hearthstones from New South Wales, 14 in 1830 and 11 in 1831 (CMS n.d.f), which may account for the large stones in the cellar fill. While King (and Shepherd) may have used the 1,200 New South Wales bricks in construction of their chimneys, it is likely that the crumbly, under-fired dark red bricks are of local manufacture. Henry Williams, manufacturing bricks at Paihia for a new kitchen chimney in 1827, complained that his products were "so tender as scarcely to bear handling" (Rogers 1961: 78). Bricks originally made at Oihi by Tully Matthews and William Hall in the earlier days of the mission may have been taken from there to Te Puna while King and Shepherd were building their houses. There is no mention in King's journals of bricks being made on-site at Te Puna, but the CMS store did include both bricks and brick moulds in its list of goods in 1831 (CMS n.d.e).

Other goods that may have been used in the construction of the house from Wright's August 1830 shipment are iron bark shingles, although these do not appear in the outward accounts for John King at this time, and James Shepherd made shingles from local timber at Matauri Bay (see Chap. 3). The store accounts note that Wright supplied 9,970 large iron bark (Australian) shingles at a cost of £17–8-0 and 10,000 small at £6–8-0. The store also supplied sash weights, lines and pulleys for window openings (CMS n.d.e; Appendix).

On October 4 1831 John King's (CMS n.d.f) account from the store included many goods required for building:

To King for Settlement at Rangihoua

3 dozen Pit saw files	3 Gil lamp oil
12 Plane irons	18 Hoes
15 Rugs	18 Blankets
56 lb White lead	6 Gil paint oil
2 qts Turpentine	2 Hammers
5 lb Saltpetre	2 Plasterers brushes
2 Tennon Screws	3 Hatchets
100 lb Shingle nails	200 Fish hooks
4 Woodstock locks	3 dozen gimlets
224 lb Iron	12 lb Whitening
50 yard Duck	4 Broad axes
6 pr Tce hinges	12 Saw files
6 Red shirts	3 [??] Pots
2 Bags salt 426 lb	17 lb Arrowroot

"100 lb Shingle Nails" indicates that the roof was shingled. Ingredients for white house paint consist of white lead, turpentine, paint oil, and perhaps whitening. Pit saw files relate to sharpening saws used in the sawpits, the activity Kendall junior noted his father spent so much time at. Gimlets, locks, hinges, plane irons, plasterers' brushes, axes, files, and not least, hammers, were all important requirements for house building.

In the following year, accounts for the first "quarter" (January to March) indicate that John King was still using a lot of building materials. The list includes six "felling" axes and six small axes, 9 lb of brads (nails for flooring and lining), 296 lb of nails (type unspecified), 22 gimlets, six shaving boxes (the use of these is not clear), 11 sheets of copper

(55 lb), 2 lb of copper nails, 24 panes of window glass, 10 door locks, 10 pairs of butt hinges, one gross of screws, chisels, more paint ingredients, and another 12 plane irons (CMS n.d.f; see Appendix). Some of these goods (axes, nails, copper, window glass, etc.) acquired by John King to build the mission house became part of the archeological record after the abandonment and demolition of the house, and were among the artifacts recovered during the investigation.

CONCLUSION

The use of archival material and documentary evidence including drawings and photographs alongside the archeological record reconstructs a picture of the King mission house – the materials, the structure, and the process of building it over 4 years. Locally available timbers such as kauri, kahikatea, totara, matai, and puriri predominate in the structure and it is most likely that Maori labor was used to build it. The archeological evidence also revealed the cellar, an important feature of the structure not indicated in the documentary material.

The archeological record is helpful in pointing to a likely date for the demolition of the house. Documentary sources give a date of 1828 for the commencement of building and 1832 for its completion (CMS n.d.b; King n.d.a,b). The archeological evidence for dating the building provided by the nails from the Te Puna cellar is congruent with this, indicating that the mission house was built using mostly wrought nails. This is the kind of nail issued by the Kerikeri store up until the late 1830s or early 1840s, and used at the Kerikeri Mission House and Stone Store and other mission buildings in the Bay at this time. The small number of cut nails and the larger number of either wrought or cut (unidentified) nails from the site is consistent with the occupation of the house by the King family over the 40 or so years following completion of the building. As only two of the cut nails were found on the floor of the cellar and the rest within layers one and two of the stratigraphy, wrought nails may have been mainly used for the construction of the building and the cut nails for later repairs or additions.

However, while there is archival evidence for the building of the house, no documentary evidence has yet been found for the demolition of the mission house. Following the death of Hannah King in 1851 and John King in 1854 their children remained living in the mission house on the 16 acres owned by the CMS at Te Puna, until it was sold in 1874 (LINZ n.d.; Martin 1990). The chronological evidence provided by the nails sheds some light on a likely end date for the occupation of the mission house. The use of wrought and cut nails is consistent with construction in the 1830s and ongoing repairs and occupation up until approximately 1870, when wire nails became increasingly popular in New Zealand and in the Bay of Islands. The small number of wire nails excavated, only 14, provenanced to the upper layers of the stratigraphy indicates that the site was abandoned before wire nails were used consistently from the early 1870s onward.

The window glass points to the use of crown glass manufactured in the early nineteenth century by a different method from modern glass and confirms the dating evidence provided by the nail assemblage.

The contents of the cellar and other excavated material are consistent with the archival information relating to the house construction and the period of time it was inhabited. Built out of untreated timber, it lasted for a period of approximately 40 years before it was abandoned and eventually demolished, with its standing structure then being pushed into the cellar and some of this burnt.

The following chapter examines the interior of the mission house and domestic life in more detail, demonstrating the domestic nature of the CMS's household missions in New Zealand. This provides insight into the economy and material culture of an isolated rural household in the Bay of Islands in the first half of the nineteenth century. While this was a family household that included children from nearby Rangihoua pa, school was held there, as were regular church services. The surrounding land was worked as a small subsistence farm unit, evidently by John and Hannah King's sons, who also developed other land holdings at a distance from Te Puna itself. The mission station also functioned as a trading post, John King bartering goods in exchange for food and labor. Despite its isolation, Te Puna and its inhabitants, both Maori and Pakeha, were part of the globalizing economy of the CMS in New Zealand, Australia, and Britain, as it formed the advance guard of colonization in New Zealand.

Domesticity and Daily Life | 5

INTRODUCTION

The data of archaeology consist of the discarded materials of everyday life. The wider events of colonialism and globalization are reflected in these materials as goods produced in Britain, such as glass and ceramics, were scattered throughout widely separated parts of the globe, from Europe to South Africa, Australia, and New Zealand (Brooks 1999, 2003; Klose and Malan 2000; Lawrence 2003; Malan and Klose 2003). This chapter demonstrates the nature of the CMS mission in New Zealand, the small scale of its operations, its dependence on the local, indigenous economy, and the model of the family and domesticity that lay at its core. Included in the baggage of missionary arrivals in New Zealand were attitudes relating to class as well as gender, carried with them from Georgian Britain. Within the small community, evidence can be found of efforts to replicate and maintain the class structure of their homeland (Middleton 2007a). This included an ideology of respectability, in which material culture played an important part. The same kind of efforts to produce a respectable domesticity can be seen in far-flung outposts of the British Empire, from South Africa to the gold mines of Victoria, Australia, to the isolated Bay of Islands missions, as well as urban missions within New York City (Fitts 1999, 2001; Lawrence 1999, 2000, 2003; McClintock 1995).

The dynamics of domesticity and the details of daily life have often been considered as part of the private realm controlled by women, subjugated to the more important public realm of the male and hence held in little regard. Household archaeology has itself been undervalued for this association with the domestic role of women (Spencer-Wood 1999, 2004). In stereotypical large-scale reconstructions of the past, women, children, and households may have been devalued or absent or subsumed within male biased categories. Women have often been

A. Middleton, *Te Puna: A New Zealand Mission Station*,
DOI:10.1007/978-0-387-77622-4, © Springer Science+Business Media, LLC 2008

presented within a simplistic male/female, dominant/subordinate, or public/private structuralist dichotomy, while in historical archaeology households have often "been identified only by the male head" (Spencer-Wood 1999: 163; Brandon and Barile 2004). This is a temptation in the case of the King household, where CMS records continually refer to "Mr. John King," and Hannah King is rarely referred to in the written record (Middleton 2007a). Spencer-Wood suggests an inclusive both/ and approach, where the household is examined from an integrated perspective.

In fact, the details of domesticity at Te Puna provide important insights into the way of life in this isolated mission house in the economy of early colonial New Zealand. These details demonstrate the daily practice of the cult of domesticity, the essential colonizing and controlling feature of the mission station (McClintock 1995: 35). Although the mission house was the home of the King family, it was a broader household with an alternative structure (Beaudry 1999) as it housed a small number of Maori, usually boys and girls from Rangihoua Pa, some of whom lived in the household for a number of years and were considered part of the family, and it also functioned as a trading center.

The mission economy is reconstructed from several different sources: the recovered artifacts, other artifacts held in the collections of the NZHPT, mostly donated by the King family; published and unpublished written material as well as accounts from the Kerikeri mission store (Middleton 2005a). The presence of Maori is documented throughout all these sources. While Maori provided the focal point for the establishment of the mission in 1814, by the 1840s this focus began to change.

As part of this process, the role of material culture in the transformation of the Bay of Islands economy is examined. This goes hand-in-hand with the palimpsest of archaeological features visible at Te Puna and the transformation of this landscape. The central theme of the evangelical missionary quest was the transformation of the indigenous society (in a state of savagery) through conversion to Christianity and the imposition of the benefits of civilization. Marsden wanted to "excite a spirit of trade" as part of this process. To achieve these ends, missionaries in New Zealand had to maintain strict standards of propriety, appearance, and behavior, the fundamental aspects of the cult of domesticity, despite the fact that (and because) they were living in the midst of a very different Maori society, with quite different standards. Material culture – the goods of European civilization – formed an essential part of the process of colonization, representing Georgian (and later Victorian) values and the means of maintaining them, as well as the means of transforming the landscape with the tools of the pastoralist economy. At the same time, CMS missionaries themselves, being placed in an entirely foreign environment, were transformed in this process. Some, such as Kendall suffered the ultimate downfall, expelled from the CMS for such misdeeds (Elder 1932, 1934; Binney 2005). Others, who attempted to maintain strict CMS discipline and standards, were still forced to bow to Maori superiority in the early days of the CMS missions. They had to defer to *tapu*, rigidly enforced by Maori (Hohepa 1999; Middleton 2003). They were controlled by the Maori economy, and found themselves going without food because Maori preferred to sell their pork and potatoes for the goods offered by the visiting ships. Conversion was a two-way struggle in the early days of the mission.

Dietler (1998) has examined trade, consumption, and cultural entanglement between indigenous people and colonials in the context of Etruscan, Greek, and Roman colonization of indigenous societies in southern France. Dietler argues the case for native agency and alterations in patterns of native production, exchange and social relations, bringing about changes in both indigenous and colonial cultures in processes that can be applied to analysis of later events of colonization in the modern world. In New Zealand, through the process of cultural entanglement of Maori and European, mission families became Pakeha, embedded in the cultural landscape of New Zealand. While John King may not have expressed his identity as "Pakeha" in the 1840s, in his letters to the Old Land Claims Commissioner he was explicit about his and his children's attachment to place and their association with Maori. John King, and his children who had been born in New Zealand, were no longer entirely English, as they struggled to adapt to the realities of their New Zealand existence.

KERIKERI MISSION STORE RECORDS

The Kerikeri mission store accounts, consisting of several different kinds of documents (CMS n.d.d, CMS n.d.e, CMS n.d.f), are an important archival source used in this chapter to reconstruct the material culture and economy of the Te Puna mission. They allow a broader interpretation of the archaeological remains and a more precise examination of domestic life, along with the documentary record of journals and reports. These accounts document the flow of goods into the mission store at Kerikeri and their movement from the store on to mission stations, which effectively functioned as trading posts, from where they were exchanged for Maori goods, such as pigs and potatoes, and services, such as labor (Middleton 2007d).

Inward goods arrived onboard ships, of course, the only possible source of European goods at the time. Henry Williams evidently paid for these goods in cash (Rogers 1961), although in earlier years, it seems likely that Samuel Marsden played an important role in controlling the mission finances and paying for goods from Parramatta. The Appendix provides a complete list of all the items available from the store for the year from April 1831 to March 1832, inward goods received (that appear in the CMS stores) from Captain Wright of the *Active*, from Sydney, NSW on August 4, 1830 (CMS n.d.f), items supplied to John King for the same period and those that are represented in the Te Puna archaeological assemblage.

Table 5.1 summarizes the information from this Appendix and includes goods that appear in King's *Account of Trade* return to the CMS committee for the period from July 1 to October 1, 1833, summarised in Table 5.2 (CMS n.d.a).

Figure 5.1 is a reproduction of the first page of the "General account of stores issued" for January 10 to March 22, 1832, an example of the accounts from which the data in columns 1 and 2 of Table 5.1 was drawn. Names of missionaries (the male head of the household) to whom the goods for the various settlements were supplied (Te Puna, Kerikeri, Paihia, Waimate) are listed in the first vertical column, as well as for an "Expedition to Tauranga," while along the horizontal

Table 5.1 Categories of goods in CMS store

Listed in store inventory	Supplied to John King	In Te Puna return 1833	Represented in assemblage
Food and dry goods	X		
Tobacco, pipes	X	X	
Fishhooks	X	X	X
Kitchen/dining equipment	X	X	X
Bedding	X	X	
Toiletries	X	X	
Household/other	X	X	X
Reading and writing	X	X	X
Clothing and haberdashery	X	X	X
Fabric	X	X	
Building materials	X	X	X
Building tools	X	X	X
Agricultural (tools)	X	X	X

Table 5.2 Summary of Te Puna account of trade from July 1 to October 1, 1833

Item	On hand	For pigs	For food	Redeem slave	Mission use	Shepherd expenses	King expenses	In exc.
Sundries								
Tobacco	13 lb		2			5	6	
Pipes	6						6	X
Fishhooks	100						20	X
Household								
Kitchen/dining								
Iron spoons								X
Knives	13							X
Iron pots	13	2		1			1	X
Lighting					1	6		
Lamps	9						1	X
Bedding								
Blankets	10	6	1	1				
Toiletries								
Razors	7					1	1	
Soap	4							
Horn and bone combs	13		3			6		
Miscellaneous								
Scissors	12							
Reading and Writing								
Books	12				2		1	
Scriptures	6				2			
Catechism	19					2	2	

Table 5.2 (continued)

Item	On hand	For pigs	For food	Redeem slave	Mission use	Shepherd expenses	King expenses	In exc.
L books	20				1		1	
P books	6				5			
Clothing								
Men's wear								
Belts	7							X?
Cotton shirts	24						3	
Cotton trousers	16						3	
Blue jackets	7							
Scotch caps	10						1	
Fabric								
Parramatta Cloth	9							
Haberdashery								
Handkerchiefs	15		1				1	
Agriculture								
Axes	15				1		1	X
Adzes	10					2		
Hoes	12	4			2	4		X
Spades	7		2		3			X
Horse gear								
Bridles								X?
Miscellaneous								
Shaving Boxes	8	1					1	

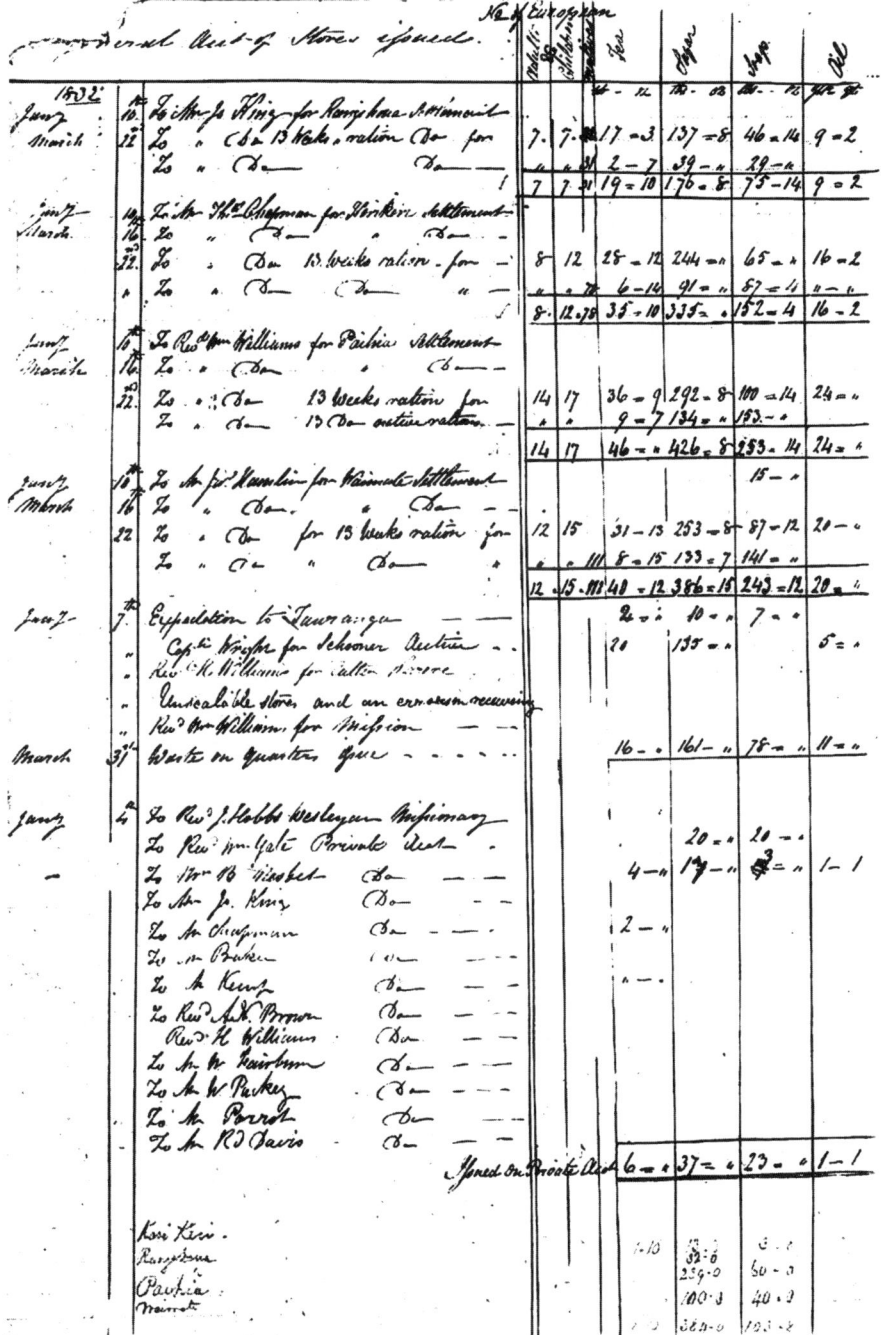

Fig. 5.1 General account of stores issued, Kerikeri Mission Store, Jan to March 1832 (CMS n.d.e)

columns at the top of the page goods are listed, with the first three columns sometimes noting the numbers of European adults and children and "Natives" at each station. In this quarter, there are seven adults and seven children (the King and Shepherd families) listed at the mission, with Maori (likely to include those provisioned at Rangihoua pa) numbered at 31. Food regularly distributed consisted of tea, sugar, salt, and flour, as well as arrowroot and salt, large quantities of this and saltpetre (Potassium nitrate) being required for preserving meat such as pork. Mission families used "fine" flour, while "seconds" was given to Maori. Soap and lamp oil was also supplied quarterly. Figure 5.2 lists store goods supplied to John King, January 10, 1832 (from the Journal, Te Kiddee Kiddee Store, CMS n.d.f), a list that is duplicated in the "General account of stores issued" (CMS n.d.e).

Quarterly returns, or accounts, were copied into the minutes of each CMS committee meeting. King lists the goods received from the Kerikeri store that he has "on hand" at the beginning and end of each quarter, with quantities of items used also listed. John King's *Account of Trade* for the quarter from July 1 to October 1, 1833 (Table 5.2) demonstrates the goods that were present at the Te Puna mission for trade and mission use during this period. The mission had received, and presumably consumed, the regular supplies of flour, sugar, tea, and occasional supplies of wheat and rice, and these were not included in the return. Two iron pots, six blankets, four hoes, and one shaving box (exact function unknown) were exchanged for pigs, along with another blanket, more hoes, a handkerchief, combs, and 2 lbs of tobacco for other food such as potatoes. An irregular expense was the cost of redeeming a slave, for one iron pot and one blanket, an event that is discussed in Chap. 3. Other goods were used "for the settlement," and for the two families. Items for King's own use included the six tobacco pipes he had at the beginning of the quarter, while he and Shepherd both appear to have used nearly all the tobacco. It is possible that these two columns also included items used for personal trade. King's final two columns of his accounts, not reproduced here, include total expenditure of goods and what remains "on hand" on October 1, numbers that can be reconciled with those on hand at the beginning of the quarter. A rather large amount of men's clothing remained in the mission supplies, but only 9 yards of cloth, mostly used for sewing women's clothing, as gowns were not usually available ready made at this time.

Goods brought in on the *Active* by Captain Wright that went to the CMS included a larger range than those that appeared in the Kerikeri store. Other goods listed in the store journal supplied by Wright (CMS n.d.f) include a printing press (likely to be the one imported in this year by William Yate), a church bell, three cases containing spinning

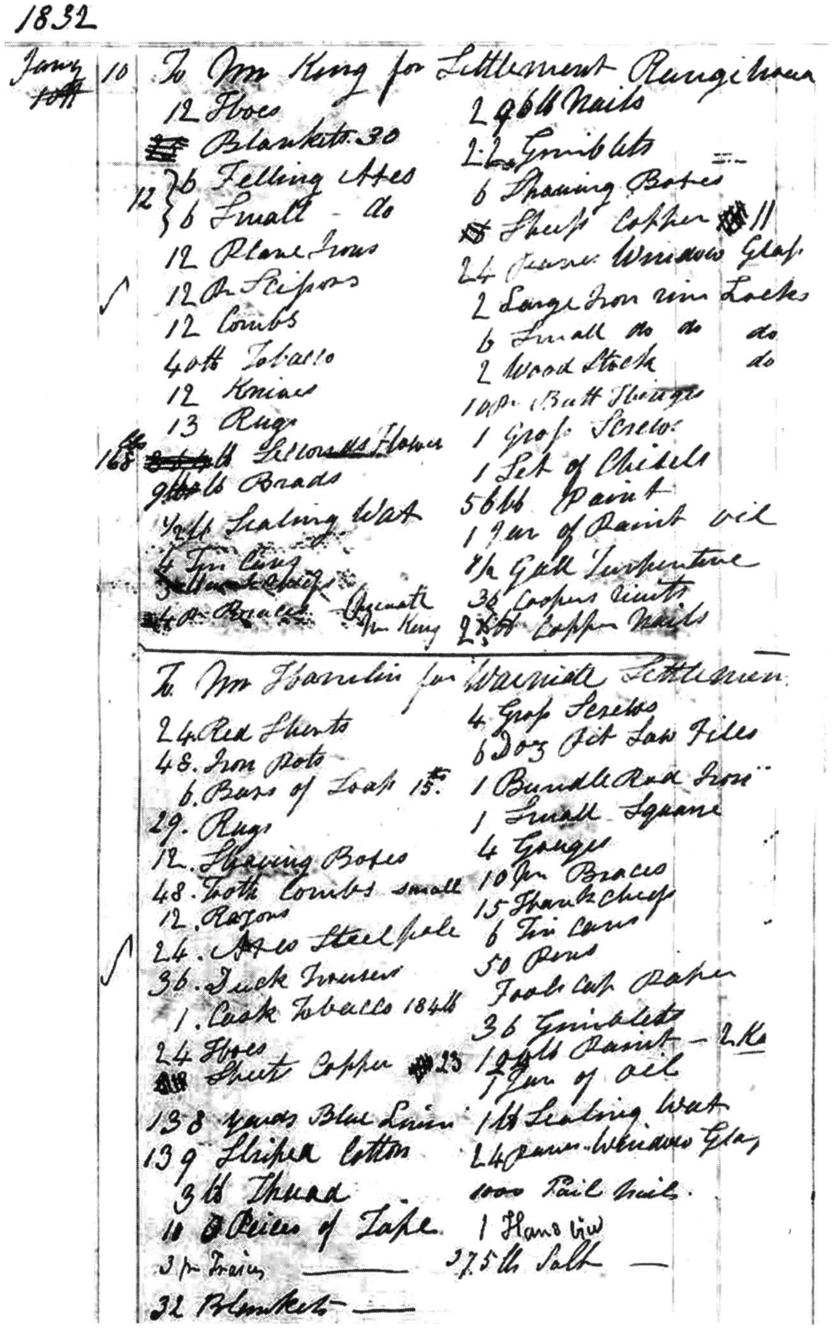

1832

Jany 10 To Mr King for Settlement Rangihoua

12 Hoes
Blankets 30
12 { 6 Felling Axes / 6 Small do
12 Plane Irons
12 Pr Scissors
12 Combs
40lb Tobacco
12 Knives
13 Rugs
168 lb Settlers Flour
9 lb Brads
½ lb Sealing Wax
6 Tin Cans
3 Handkerchiefs
4 Pr Braces — Account Mr King

2 96 lb Nails
22 Gimblets
6 Shaving Boxes
Sheets Copper 11
24 Panes Window Glass
2 Large Iron rim Locks
6 Small do do do
2 Wood Stock do
10 Pr Butt Hinges
1 Gross Screws
1 Set of Chisels
56 lb Paint
1 Jar of Paint oil
½ Gall Turpentine
36 Coopers rivets
2 lb Copper Nails

To Mr Hamlin for Waimate Settlement

24 Red Shirts
48 Iron Pots
6 Bars of Soap 15 lb
29 Rugs
12 Shaving Boxes
48 Tooth Combs small
12 Razors
24 Axes Steel pole
36 Duck Trousers
1 Cask Tobacco 184 lb
24 Hoes
Sheets Copper 23
138 yards Blue Linen
139 Striped Cotton
3 lb Thread
11 Pieces of Tape
3 pr Traces
32 Blankets

4 Gross Screws
6 Doz Pit Saw Files
1 Bundle Rod Iron
1 Small Square
4 Gauges
10 pr Braces
15 Handkerchiefs
6 Tin Cans
50 Pens
Foolscap Paper
36 Gimblets
10 lb Paint — 2 Ka
1 Jar of Oil
1 lb Sealing Wax
24 panes Window Glass
Rail Nails
1 Hand Saw
275 lb Salt

Fig. 5.2 CMS goods supplied to John King, Kerikeri Mission Store, January 10, 1832 (CMS n.d.e) apparatus, and a quantity of wooden shingles. Wright also sold 87 "Soldiers Old Great Coats" to the CMS. These may have been a regular item, although they do not appear in the "General account of stores issued" in 1831–1832. Earlier in the year that Wright's goods arrived, 1830, John King received 26 Soldiers belts and 8 Soldiers coats, "for the settlement at Rangihoua" (CMS n.d.d). Other goods such as ceramics do not appear in the accounts for the 1831–1832 year, but are represented in the archaeological record. As is discussed below (under Ceramics), William Yate ordered a large quantity of ceramics on the missionaries' private account in 1832, suggesting that China was an item missionaries had to supply themselves, while the mission store supplied pewter tableware. Other goods again appear in the archaeological record of the mission house but do not appear as part of the legitimate CMS economy. Alcohol and alcohol bottles, as well as guns, gunflints, and gunpowder may all have formed a part of a "black" economy. However, the single word "powder" does appear once in the account lists, and it is possible that it represents gunpowder (Appendix). Wright supplied one "case of medicines" to the store. Although this item appears in the store accounts, John King did not received any for this time period considered, and no pharmaceutical bottles were evident in the archaeological record.

The accounts provide a record of all the items distributed to the mission families from the CMS store, from the early 1820s until 1843, when the Stone Store was sold to Richard Kemp, son of the missionary James Kemp, who had previously kept the CMS store accounts. Accounts for the years from approximately 1828–1832 formed the main focus, this being the period when the two houses at Te Puna were being built, although data for some earlier and later years were also consulted and quarterly "Accounts of Trade" appear in the minutes of CMS committee meetings for a wider time period (CMS n.d.a, n.d.b). As can be seen in Fig. 5.2 and the Appendix, building supplies and tools formed a significant part of goods supplied to John King at this time.

DOMESTICITY: INSIDE THE MISSION HOUSE

There are few references to, or descriptions of the interior of the mission house. John King's journals, letters, and reports remain resolutely fixed on the details of his mission work, his regular journeys to nearby villages, and the numbers of those attending services. As noted earlier, these documents were written for the secretary and committee of the CMS, and portions of them were published annually in the Missionary Register. King gives very little information about the domestic affairs of the mission. Hannah King did not apparently keep a journal or write any letters that still exist. Few of the CMS women left archival documents behind after their deaths, or appear to have had time to write them. The better-known of those who did are sisters-in-law Marianne and Jane Williams, wives of brothers Henry and William Williams, who provide many details of their domestic lives, Marianne from Paihia in the Bay of Islands and Jane from both Paihia and later the Gisborne area (Fitzgerald 2004; Gillespie 1996; Williams, Henry n.d.a; Williams, Marianne n.d.a, n.d.b; Williams, Jane n.d.). Eliza White, who arrived in the Bay of Islands in 1830 as the wife of Wesleyan missionary William White also kept a journal in which she discusses details of her life at the Wesleyan mission in the Hokianga and her visits to the Williams at Paihia (White n.d.). Anne Wilson, who lived for almost a year at Te Puna with her husband John and their two children, kept a journal and wrote a number of still-extant letters from the time of her arrival in New Zealand until her early death from breast cancer at the age of thirty-seven (Wilson, Anne C. n.d.). While Anne Wilson was remarkably silent during that first year at Te Puna, the journals and letters of these women provide a context for life at the Te Puna mission, where everyday life would have involved similar tasks and materials. The daily life created by these documents can be put together with artifacts recovered from the investigation as well as the goods issued from the CMS Store (Appendix), to produce a more complete picture of everyday life at the Te Puna mission. These issues are further explored in Middleton (2007a), along with the social dynamics of missionary life in the Bay of Islands, dominated by the prestigious Williams family.

Although John King's journals and reports do note Hannah's role in the mission, the presence of women at the Te Puna mission house, and the daily routine of domestic life is indicated with more immediacy by domestic artefacts associated with female activities.

Outside Observers: Visitors to the Mission

On Sunday March 9, 1834, the *Alligator* sailed into the Bay of Islands. The captain had intended to use Cook's old anchorage (on the opposite side of the Bay), but was prevented by the wind, and seeing

> three three-masters in a bay to the right ... made thither with a light wind. It was the little bay of Tipuna. We saw sailors on the ships ... and soon a boat with two natives came alongside the *Alligator*. We were not far short of the anchorage when the wind fell to a flat calm; we just managed to make the bay and to anchor in what is certainly as good an anchorage as is to be found among the many excellent choices along this coast and especially in the Bay of Islands. (Von Huegel n.d.)

The German Baron Karl von Huegel, a traveller on board the *Alligator*, kept a journal during his stay in the Bay of Islands, as did his fellow-passenger William Barrett Marshall (1836). The ship was anchored below Oihi, in "a sandy little bay with a few hundred feet of beach." Von Huegel noted that "Between this beach and the mission settlement [Te Puna] is higher ground and a pa; the settlement has its own beach, but it lies open to the sea, and the breakers rarely allow of landing there." Soon after landing, von Huegel walked to the mission with the ship's Captain Lambert. Von Huegel proceeds:

> As we went down the slope towards the settlement we saw two Europeans, and being informed by the New Zealanders that these were the missionaries I ran down the hill without thinking exactly why, but no doubt to give my legs some proper exercise after the voyage rather than for any other reason; but I regretted it for a time when, having rushed up to the group, I was received stiffly and coldly. They were Mr. King, the oldest and first missionary in New Zealand and head of the Tipuna mission; Mr. Williams, a former naval lieutenant and now head of the Paihia mission; and Mr. Wilson, a young man newly arrived. After initial greetings the former asked if Captain Lambert did not remember him, and when the captain denied it, recalled to his memory 'your old middy', now married and for several years past a missionary.

"The former" von Huegel refers to is actually the latter, John Wilson, previously Lambert's midshipman. Von Huegel follows with a criticism of the work of the mission, and of Wilson, whose vocation he considers "but a misunderstood figment of the imagination," for bringing his wife to live a "lonely, difficult and profitless life among savage hordes". Von Huegel (n.d.) described his visit:

> The settlement of Tipuna is unpretentious: the wooden mission house consists of several rooms all on a single floor, it stands in a neglected little garden, and behind this are a dozen or more acres of land, the property of the mission, most of it swamp requiring drainage. In the parlour lit with a few candles the conversation kept dying away; a cup of tea would have been welcome after so many days without milk, but neither tea nor fresh butter appeared, although in the course of a stroll, which I took directly on arrival in the company of a well-mannered young person, I had seen a number of cows being driven up to the house for milking. It was Sunday, and in the adjoining room was assembled the spiritual congregation of Tipuna, consisting of five or six girls singing psalms. I was glad when Captain Lambert, who had been visiting Mr. Wilson, returned; I found it sultry in the parlour, as if a deathly spiritless ennui had established its headquarters there.

On this visit Acting-Lieutenant Woore painted Rangihoua, from the beach below Oihi (Middleton 2005a: Fig. 5.4).

The day after von Huegel's visit to the mission, William Barrett Marshall and Woore rowed across to Te Puna, where they found King, Wilson and Henry Williams on the point of setting out to visit the ship.

Te Puna Account of Trade.

Received —																						
On hand Jan. 1, 1836	6	.	9	19	6	.	11	28	16	8	.	1	46	.	3	2	7	23	1	12	5	.	.	.
Since received . .	12	200	12	.	12	6	.	12	.	.	2	.	.	12	.	.	.	24	23	.	.	.	12	12	216
Total rec.d	18	200	21	19	18	6	11	40	16	8	2	4	46	12	3	2	31	46	1	12	6	13	12	216
Expended —																						
For Pigs . .									.	.								20					
Native food .	4	.	4	1			.	1	.	.		8	.	.	1	16	12	7	.	.	1	.	.
At King's expenditure	1	.	2	8	8	1	1	.	.		.	1	10	4	2	.	4	2	.	1	.	1	1	.
Furniture		100	2	.	.	.	.	.	2	.	.	.	22	.	.	2	9	.	7	.	.	.	.	72
Unsaleable							18	14	.	.										5	.	.
Total Exp.	5	100	8	8	9	1	1	15	16	2	.	.	40	4	3	2	23	34	1	1	5	2	1	72
On hand July 1, 1836	13	100	13	11	9	5	10	25	.	6	2	4	6	8	.	.	8	12	.	11	.	11	11	144

(Signed) John King.

Fig. 5.3 Te Puna account of trade, January 1 to July 1, 1836 (CMS n.d.b)

NIGHT SCENE IN NEW-ZEALAND.

Fig. 5.4 James Kemp, itinerant missionary, 1837 (CMS *Missionary Register* 1837)

King took them on a tour of the pa, and they returned back to Te Puna "round the foot of the hill, by a narrow footpath, on either side of which the Toi-Toi, or high grass of the country, grew in great abundance" (Marshall 1836: 13). Marshall notes that this plant was used as an abortifacient. At the home of John and Anne Wilson, Marshall received better hospitality than had von Huegel the day before:

> At the table of Mr. Wilson, I partook for the first time, of the kumera, or sweet potatoe of this country, a pleasant enough vegetable, the flavour of which is a mixed one, resembling that of the common potato and the parsnip. And here it is but just to mention the kindness of the two missionaries, King and Wilson. It had been told them that the sick men on board stood greatly in need of a little vegetable diet, upon which they procured from the natives what they did not possess themselves, namely, six baskets of potatoes at a reasonable price, and added as gifts from their own gardens a quantity of onions, all the pumpkins they had, and a liberal supply of cabbages. (Marshall 1836: 18)

These two visitors to the mission give some insight into daily life here, as well as the social relations between missionaries and those on board ships, often railed against in the missionary literature. Von Huegel was embarrassed by his high-spirited canter down the hillside and the following cold reception from John King and Henry Williams, and felt further rebuffed by the lack of hospitality at the King household. The conflict between missionaries and the shipping is further illustrated by the persistent Von Huegel's subsequent visit to Henry and Marianne Williams at Paihia when the *Alligator* was later anchored there. Von Huegel (n.d.) complained again: "it seemed that the missionaries feared we would regard them as high-livers if they offered us any hospitality whatever, and on this occasion too we were offered nothing, which is quite contrary to the English custom" and objected to Henry Williams' "stiff formality". The artist Augustus Earle (1909: 136) also complained of a similar cold reception and lack of hospitality from the missionaries at Oihi on Christmas Day, 1827. On returning to the ship, von Huegel noted that there were 114 Maori women on board. The next morning, the day the ship was to leave Paihia, the women "wound their blanket and presents up round their heads and were jumping off the frigate into the water, delighting the crew with a final revelation of their charms before starting on the mile swim to the shore." On arrival at the Te Puna anchorage, von Huegel had also described a large number of women visiting the ship, noting "most of these girls ... had established good relations with the sailors in the first half-hour." It is not surprising that the Kings and Williams displayed some coolness toward him. In contrast, Marshall's warmer welcome may be explained by his effusive praise for the work of the missionaries, and his criticism on arrival of women from Rangihoua in canoes, "exhibiting but too plainly, by the gross indelicacy of their gestures, how low a standard governed their morals" (Marshall 1836: 3).

Von Huegel noted after his visit to the mission house that it had a parlor and another room where girls were singing psalms. As at this time John and Hannah King had three daughters, Jane Holloway King, born in 1818, Hannah, born in 1827, and Sarah, born in 1829, the "girls" were likely to be the Kings' daughters as well as Maori women or girls who were part of the household. Their last child, Elizabeth Marsden King, was born in 1837. Marshall noted on this visit that there were ten Maori girls and ten men and boys living at the settlement.

Although it was apparently daylight, the parlor was dark enough to require the light of "a few candles." Although von Huegel states the mission house was a single storied building, he may have only been in the parlor and not noted a staircase to the rooms suggested by the attic windows in Figs. 4.11 and 4.12 and other drawings (Middleton 2005a), or not included the attic rooms as another floor. In 1834, the house would have had eight King children resident (three daughters and five sons), and John and Hannah King, as well as a number of Maori household members, a large population to fit into a dwelling of approximately 110 m2 (Middleton 2005a). Access to the cellar may have been constructed in a manner similar to that originally beneath the Waimate Mission house, a trap door and ladder. The stone lined Waimate mission house cellar, still intact beneath the house floor, is of similar proportions to the one at Te Puna. Although the principal function of the cellar was for storage, it may also have had a dual function, providing a possible hiding place in the threat of attack, as Wilson's journal (above) describes. The attack on the Wesleyan mission at Whangaroa in 1827 made the CMS missionaries aware of their own vulnerability.

Although William Hall (n.d.) had made a kitchen table for the Kings in December 1816, not all the furniture in the house was colonial. Furniture in the collections of the NZHPT at Waimate Mission House, donated by the King family, provides further information about the appearance of the interior of the house. An elegant secretaire bookcase, purchased from John Butler when he left the CMS in 1823, may have been part of the parlor furnishings. Two chairs, one of these reputedly the one in which the pregnant 22-year-old Hannah King was lowered from the side of the *Active*, may have been in the dining room or the parlor, along with an extending dining table of a dark wood-like mahogany.

Easdale (1991) reports that the Halls and the Kings had four-poster beds at the Oihi mission, and if this was the case it is likely that

John and Hannah King still had this style of bed at Te Puna. CMS missionaries commonly used such beds in the early years of the nineteenth century. Both the Kerikeri and Waimate Mission Houses display beds like these, previously used by missionary occupants, and women's journals document the time spent in washing, starching, and ironing bed hangings (Williams, J. n.d.; Williams, M. n.d.b). Marianne Williams (n.d.b) was very concerned about a bed for Bishop Selwyn to stay in, in the days leading up to his arrival at Paihia in July 1844, noting in June "Mariana Tahapai to wash my white bed hangings for the Bishop," followed the next day with "dried off the bed hangings, which had been starched before the fire," and again some days later "Made the Bishops bed and was all over the house to find fault and put in order."

Marshall (1836: 15–16) described the mission settlement enclosed by "high and strong stockades," because of the "insecurity in which the missionaries must once have lived." Although this evokes the 8-ft high paling fences that Hall built around the houses at Oihi, Taylor and Hutton's drawings do not give this impression. Although the houses are fenced, the fence appears much lower than a "stockade", and the front of the Kings' house is open to the surrounding field, indicating that by the time the Te Puna mission houses were built, the Kings and Shepherds felt more secure with their neighbors at Rangihoua Pa, unlike earlier years at Oihi.

THE MAORI PRESENCE

In 1830, John King argued that the CMS had a responsibility to Maori at Rangihoua pa, a relationship that had begun with the founding of Oihi in 1814 that would be broken if this mission was not resited at Te Puna. One of his justifications for the Te Puna mission was the importance of the population at the pa; the mission only remained because of the pa. His journal documents the continuing mission activities at the mission house, such as the school and church services, along with noting the number of people from Rangihoua who lived as part of the household, as did visitors such as Marshall (1836; see earlier).

Lithic artifacts recovered from the site before and during the investigation also demonstrate the presence of Maori at the mission. These artifacts consisted of a broken adze, recovered from the mission garden, and a number of obsidian flakes. The largest of these, 9-cm long, was found in layer one in the eastern area of the excavation, in association with a broken willow patterned plate. Other smaller obsidian flakes were found in layer one of the excavation, in the same vicinity as the large flake, and more small obsidian flakes were picked up from the surface of the terraces on the hill above the site of the mission house. One other flake is chert. A broken gunflint was also recovered. This can be compared with Best's (2002: 72) investigation of the site of Rewa's Pa at Kororareka, where a total of nine gunflints were recovered, eight of these of English origin and the ninth French. At Rewa's pa, the pa of a fighting chief, a number of gunflints could be expected to be found. The single gunflint from Te Puna indicates the presence of guns, perhaps more likely used as part of the domestic economy.

READING AND WRITING

The school formed an important aspect of mission life at Te Puna, and was often the focus of King's reports to the CMS in Britain. Artifacts connected with teaching reading and writing found during the investigation confirm these activities. These artifacts are closely allied with the discussion of literacy, and the Maori quest for books (Chap. 2).

In October 1829, the Kerikeri store supplied John King with two dozen writing slates and 105 slate pencils (CMS n.d.d). Between 1830 and 1832 accounts regularly note "Native books", printing paper (not used at Te Puna), pens and quills, sealing wax, ink powder, blotting paper, brown paper, foolscap paper, letter paper, slates and slate pencils, and black lead pencils (Appendix; CMS n.d.e, CMS n.d.f). Fragments of flat and pencil slate were recovered from the investigation, and one of the flat fragments with a small hole drilled through it. These fragments were found throughout the area of the excavation, from the squares in the western area to the eastern squares, but were recovered mostly from the upper layers and surface. Only two pencil fragments were found within the cellar, from the floor and below the rubble. This suggests that teaching activities took place at the eastern end of the house, in the lean-to at this side of the building.

A pen nib and several other items of a similar shape, not identified, as well as a lead pencil stylus also relate to these activities, and may have been used by John King in his report and journal writing. The Stone Store displays a large number of similar slate pencils and boards, important items for all the mission schools.

Other items recovered from the mission house site can be indirectly associated with schooling and rewarding children from the pa for attendance. Although fishhooks were likely to have been used for their intended practice of fishing (though this activity is not mentioned in journals), they also feature in large quantities in goods supplied from the Kerikeri store and kept "on hand" for trade at the Te Puna mission. They appear early on in the mission literature as items given to children to encourage attendance at school and church services. For example, on a Sunday in October 1823 John King noted that

> The natives in general tell me that if I will pay them – they will sit still on the sabbath or come to receive instruction – some food or fishhooks they ask. – (King n.d.a)

John King had 1,200 fishhooks "on hand & received" on October 1, 1826 when he was still living at Oihi (Middleton 2005a; Fig. 2.8; CMS n.d.a). In the last quarter of 1826, he used 600 of these to pay for general work and 100 to the school. Eight years later the numbers he used for trade purposes appears to have dwindled. He had 100 on hand in July 1833 (Table 5.2) and 200 in January 1836 (Fig. 5.3). He used 50 of these on his own account in 1833 (CMS n.d.a), and 100 for sundries in 1836 (Fig. 5.3). A single large J-shaped fishhook, 10-cm long was the only item of this kind found in the investigation.

Glass trade beads were also used to reward attendance at school and church services. Four of these were found in the environs of the cellar, discussed later.

Work and Industrial Occupations

A number of artifacts in the collections of the NZHPT at Waimate Mission House relate to John King's initial employment by the CMS as shoemaker and "twine spinner" (rope maker). Other artifacts recovered from the investigation relate to King's long-term involvement with the secular occupation of clearing land and growing food, tools that could also be used for building and animal husbandry.

It appears that King gave up shoemaking in 1822. The store accounts record in December of this year:

> Rec'd of Mr King
> 20 lbs of sole and 13 lbs of Upper Leather which he have returned into the Store having declined making shoes. (CMS n.d.d)

In the following year, quoted above (Chap. 2) Samuel Marsden wrote to King complaining about his refusal to make shoes. Whether King continued to make rope is uncertain. While he constructed a ropewalk at Oihi (Elder 1932; Hall n.d.; King n.d.b Sept. 19, 1825), his journal makes little reference to this occupation after the first years at Oihi, when he wrote to the CMS, repeatedly requesting equipment to carry this out. The twine spinner King used to spin rope, along with bobbins, and a sample of unspun fiber (probably flax) are displayed at the Waimate Mission House. King does not appear to have manufactured enough rope for it to be exported, as Marsden's first expectations may have been. This employment seems to have disappeared over the course of the move to Te Puna, where the landscape gives evidence that pastoralism predominated.

Although no artifacts relating to animal husbandry were found in the investigation, apart from several metal buckles that may have been used on horse gear, we know from the archival and documentary sources that cows and horses were kept at Te Puna. Food remains (discussed later in faunal material) also confirm that cattle were kept for food. Von Huegel reported seeing cows about to be milked on his visit in 1834. Five years later, on one of his visits in September 1839, Richard Taylor (n.d.) reported that a bull had killed one of John King's Maori workers which ran wild while he was trying to shoot it. John King (n.d.a, n.d.b) rode a horse on his weekly or fortnightly visits to some of the more distant visits on the east coast, and in 1834 the committee passed a resolution permitting King to build a stable at Te Puna (CMS n.d.b). The later Kerikeri store archives record King's purchases of horse gear. In 1847, he purchased two saddles and one bridle, and another saddle the following year, suggesting that several horses were kept at Te Puna (Kemp, Richard n.d.).

Metal items such as lead and bar iron, supplied in large quantities from the Kerikeri store, indicate that John King may have operated a blacksmithing forge at Te Puna, as may have been the case at each mission station (Middleton 2007d). Iron metal bar as well as lead was recovered from the excavation. In the early 1830s, the Kerikeri mission store was issuing "British and Foreign iron" as well as plate iron to its missionaries (CMS n.d.e).

TOOLS

A number of the metal tools in the assemblage, such as a grubber, a pickaxe, spades, axes, a reaping hook and a scythe, relate to agricultural and building activities. Two axes, each of a different type, were recovered from the line in the excavation where many of the metal artifacts were found (Fig. 4.8; Middleton 2005a,b). Two of these can be compared with others of the same type displayed at the Stone Store, Kerikeri. One of these is of the type Salaman (1975) identifies as a felling axe, with a flared blade and pointed lugs below the eye. It was used with a handle about 3 ft in length, so that it could be held with both hands, and was regarded as "the tree feller's master tool." Another is also a felling axe, of the "improved" or "wedge" type, heavier than the other two. This type of axe has a "plain, stocky wedge-shaped blade weighing from 2 to 7 lb, with somewhat swollen sides and a heavy, flat poll [blunt end]" (Salaman 1975). A third axe is 175-mm long and 70-mm wide, with parallel sides slightly flared toward the blade and no lugs. Its simple shape and construction suggest it may have been locally made from a length of flat iron, manufactured by folding a length of iron around the eye and bending it double to join at the body of the blade.

A metal blade found in the fill of the cellar is similar to those described by Loudon (1871) as either reaping hooks or hedge-bills. Reaping hooks in general, as the name suggests, were used to cut and harvest ripe grain crops, such as wheat. An improvement on the reaping hook for this purpose was the scythe, or as more particularly described by Loudon, the Hainault scythe. An example of such a scythe blade, 540-mm long, was recovered from the bottom of the cellar fill. The blade was attached to a handle some 2–3 ft long, depending on the height of the mower. Loudon describes the scythe being used in tandem with a hook, also attached to a wooden handle.

Other lithic items likely to be associated with mission house domestic activities consist of a flat grindstone and a broken sharpening stone, both of which were recovered from layer one of the eastern area of the excavation, the area where many of the tools and metal items were found.

All these items can be found listed in the goods supplied to the mission families (Table 5.2; Appendix). In the first quarter of 1832 John King received 12 each of axes, hoes, plane irons, and knives as well as one cast steel chisel; in the previous year, he received 11 spades, 15 axes, 15 adzes, and 31 hoes, as well as 48 saw files. Not all of these were intended for King's own use. The accounts King returned to the quarterly committee meetings indicate that stores of tools and other goods were kept at the mission house to be used for trade (Middleton 2007d). In his return to the quarterly meeting for October 1832, he used two hoes along with 20 blankets, 7 iron pots and a quantity of tobacco to pay for "Native food." He lists three hoes, five adzes, and two axes for his own expenditure as well as a similar number of tools for James Shepherd's use, including four spades. In this return, he had a lot of these trade items still on hand: 22 hoes, 6 chisels, 18 plane irons, 11 spades, 21 knives, 14 axes, and 6 adzes (CMS n.d.a); Figure 5.3 ("Tepuna Account of Trade") gives a similar account for goods used in 1836. Store accounts listed in the Appendix also note a number of stones and grinders supplied to missionaries: grind stones, rub stones, and oilstones.

Several other items recovered from the investigation provide information about activities at the mission. A large piece of whalebone, 20-cm long and 70-cm wide, sawn at one end was recovered from the western edge of the excavated area in proximity to a metal artifact tentatively identified as a whaling lance. A second piece of whalebone, worked into a small square tab or preform 5 mm thick, and another piece of bone worked into a shape resembling a small shoe-horn, broken on one edge and burnt, were recovered from the fill near the northern wall of the cellar. These articles suggest the presence of whaling ships in the vicinity, as visitors such as Joseph Orton (below) noted.

A musket ball demonstrates that a musket was present, as does the gunflint (discussed earlier), even though these were once forbidden goods on the missions. Guns may have been a part of the domestic economy at Te Puna, used for killing cattle or perhaps for hunting, as Taylor's account (above) shows. They do not feature in the archival accounts, or does John King mention such goods in his journals or reports. Such items formed part of the "black" economy in the early years of the mission that was beyond the control of the CMS.

HOUSEHOLD AND PERSONAL ITEMS

A number of other miscellaneous items relate to activities in the household, such as a single piece of jewellery (part of a necklace), a candlesnuffer, coins, and clay pipes. Only one of these miscellaneous items, a clay marble, evokes the presence of children. Otherwise, there is no indication of the presence of children, no toys or doll fragments in the entire assemblage. This is remarkable in a household where there were a number of teenaged and younger children growing up. There is also a general absence across all categories of the assemblage of ornaments or frivolous items (Middleton 2005a,b).

Coins

Two coins were found in the cellar fill, both of these bearing the head of George III. One is a penny, dated 1797, while the date and coinage is no longer visible on the second. The 1797 penny is a large, heavy coin with a rough, irregular edge. According to Noel Hume (1969: 156), the 1797 penny was the first English copper penny, known as the "cartwheel" penny, and the first to be struck in the new steam-powered presses. Noel Hume does not explain why this term was used; perhaps it was because the edge is irregular rather than having an even, round surface. Noel Hume (2001: 179) provides some explanation for the size:

> The huge and unwieldy penny and twopenny pieces [were] minted in Birmingham in 1797 in an effort to restore confidence in English copper

currency, which, in the last quarter of the century, was represented by more
underweight forgeries than genuine money from the royal mints. It turned
out that with copper in an era of low market value, the coins had to contain
a great deal of metal to be worth a penny or twopence. Needless to say, this
bureaucratic expedient went with a dull thud into the citizens' pockets and
purses, and was replaced with a more manageable copper currency in 1806.

This also provides a date after which the second coin, probably also a
penny, may have been produced, as it is smaller and lighter. The date
is illegible as the coin has been drilled at the point where the date was
inscribed above the just-visible head of George III. The driller did not
complete the hole, attempted presumably with the intention of wearing
the penny as personal adornment.

Decoration may have been the best use for coins in the pre-1840
Bay of Islands economy, where hard currency was of little value.
Colenso (1888: 43) noted that coins he had with him on landing in
New Zealand in 1834 "remained unused in my desk for many years,"
although American and especially Mexican dollars were in much
demand by some of the storekeepers. Mission staff salaries were presumably not distributed in cash, but in terms of goods and an internal
accounting system. Mission store records note goods "Issued on Private
Account" below settlement issues (CMS n.d.e; Fig. 5.1). By the 1840s,
though John King was purchasing goods from the Kerikeri store, then
privately owned by the Kemp family, with both cash and goods such as
pigs. After 1840, the CMS itself had accounts with the New Zealand
Banking Company at Kororareka (Chap. 3).

Clay Pipes

Clay pipe fragments recovered from the cellar and surrounding
areas produced a minimum number of 64 pipes (Middleton 2005a,b).
None of these were complete, although there were several complete
bowls. Identified makers included McDougall, Davidson, and Balme, all
likely Glasgow manufacturers, as well as one that may be "Williams" of
Kent Street, London, a manufacturer who was operating between the
years 1823 and 1864. Some clay pipes are likely to have been imported
from Sydney. One stem fragment is inscribed with "ELLIOTT" and
"STREET" on the reverse. The likely maker of this pipe was the
Sydney manufacturer Joseph Elliott, who operated between 1831 and
1837 (Gojak and Stuart 1999). Examples of Elliott's pipes excavated in
Parramatta, New South Wales, were engraved with "J. Elliott Maker/
Market St Wharf," but his lettering and style evidently varied consider-
ably. Other examples of this maker's pipes have been found in the Bay of
Islands (Best 2002; Middleton 2005a), as well as in southern-most New

Zealand, on the site of the early sealers' settlement on Codfish Island in Foveaux Strait (Smith and Anderson 2007), and in Tasmanian whaling sites (Lawrence 2006).

Tobacco is included amongst the goods in the store accounts. King was supplied with 40 lbs of this in the first quarter of 1832 (Appendix; Table 5.2) and similar amounts at other times (CMS n.d.e). The CMS accounts also record tobacco imported amongst other goods received from Captain Wright in August 1830 (Appendix), the CMS receiving three kegs (324 lb) of "Negrohead" tobacco for £16-4-0 and three baskets (213 lb) of Brazil tobacco ("Ditto") for £7-19-9. Although there are no pipes listed amongst the goods Wright supplied in this shipment, it is likely they appear amongst others. Examination of the accounts for expenditure from Te Puna King submitted to the CMS committee shows both tobacco and pipes, some of this expended on "Mr. King's exp" and some on purchasing "Native food" (CMS n.d.a). In July 1836, for example (Fig. 5.3), King had 216 pipes "on hand", 72 of these appearing again in the column traded for "Sundries," while he has 46 (lbs) of tobacco "on hand", 8 lbs of this being spent on purchasing "Native food," 10 lbs on "Mr. King's expenditure" and 22 lbs on "Sundries."

Lighting

Fragments of lamp glass were recovered from the cellar and surrounding areas. Lamp oil was supplied regularly to the mission families, listed in the quarterly accounts, as was lamp cotton (Appendix). Captain Wright supplied a variety of different lamps to the mission in August 1830 (Appendix). His list of goods includes two casks containing

A 6 Light Chandelier Complete £5-16
36 Japan Lamps "10 1/2 £1-11-6
12 Do [ditto] for Wall "1/- 12–0

Records do not name the recipient of the chandelier, and it is not recorded in the store accounts. King's returns to the CMS committee in 1832 and 1833 note that he has lamps "on hand" (Table 5.2; CMS n.d.a). He supplied one of these to James Shepherd, but the balance remained. The CMS purchased whale oil directly from whalers that called into the Bay of Islands. An invoice for October 1828 due to Obed Starbuck, no doubt of Nantucket Island whaling fame, details purchases of 252 gallons of sperm oil for £252, and 220 gallons of black (Right whale) oil for £110, half the price of the former. Sperm oil was considered of a high quality, very clean burning, while black oil was considerably inferior. At this quarter's meeting, the committee resolved that oil rations for "Man and Wife" should be three gallons per quarter, increasing to six gallons for "Man and Wife & Nine Children" (CMS n.d.a October 1828).

As von Huegel noted (quoted above) candles were also used for lighting, probably made as part of the regular household activities. Candles were not used in church services, being considered too papist. A candlesnuffer made from a copper alloy was amongst items from the cellar.

CLOTHING, FABRIC, AND TOILETRY: TRANSFORMING THE BODY

Missionary desire to bring about the spiritual and moral transformation of indigenous societies included efforts to remake and clothe the indigenous body, in particular the female body (Commaroff and Commaroff 1992; Johnston 2003; McClintock 1995). As Johnston (2003: 148–149) has pointed out, this incorporated the development of commerce. Clothing was seen as a commodity to be sold or traded; as noted earlier, while initially in New Zealand metal items formed the focus of trade between missionaries and Maori, by the late 1820s blankets had become the desirable trade item, often worn as a garment. Beaudry (2006; http://www.fiskecenter.umb.edu/Magunco%20Hill.htm), commenting on an assemblage of thimbles recovered from the "Praying Indian Town" of Magunco, established by John Eliot in about 1674, notes the symbolic role these small, mass-produced items can play:

> To the colonizer and missionary, thimbles (and, presumably, needles, thread, and textiles – all less likely than thimbles to be found archaeologically) were a prefect medium for conveying a suite of values that linked ideals of femininity and womanhood, cleanliness, and godliness, as well as the production of proper, *modest*, European-style dress.

Beaudry notes that the Magunco thimbles were all child-sized, suggesting that missionaries targeted children, who may have been more receptive than adult women to learning new methods of sewing, along with the values of civilization.

A number of items recovered from the mission house cellar, such as buttons, beads, thimbles, and pins document the presence of women at the mission house, along with activities such as sewing and teaching such skills to Maori women and girls at the schools for women run at each mission station. These are the visible remains of items that endure in an archaeological context, while the associated fabrics and clothing items have decayed. While the women's journals document these activities, John King also noted in 1815 that Hannah King was busy with such tasks (King n.d.c; White n.d.; Williams, Jane n.d.; Williams, Marianne n.d.b; Wilson, Anne C. n.d.). In 1832, writing his first report to the CMS from the Te Puna mission, John King noted that Hannah and their eldest daughter Jane, who was born at Oihi in 1818, continued with this work:

> During the week days school commences at six O'clock in the morning the natives are instructed in reading and writing and in first rules of arithmetic... Mrs King and Jane attends to the Girls in the afternoon on the Sabbaths, and... on week days school and prayers in the evenings. (King n.d.b).

Eliza White gives details of similar organization of the Wesleyan mission families, who she says each had six or so Maori children living with them:

> They do the domestic work in the morning, and in the afternoon go to school, where they are taught to read, write, sum and sew; and they are making considerable progress. Their desire for instruction is great tho none will attend the school who are not fed and clothed. (White n.d.)

Eliza requested her family in England to send

> workbags and thimbles with large needles are the most useful articles ... stout cotton for gowns ... it is exceedingly useful I have made several garments from it. I have now six girls and three boys to look after – their washing, food and clothes...

Other archival sources document the concern for appropriate clothing and appearances and Georgian propriety in an alien world. A single extant letter from Sarah Fairburn (n.d.) to her daughter Elizabeth, then aged 15 and at school at Paihia, from the Puriri mission on the Hauraki Plains in January 1835, informed Elizabeth of the deaths of her grandfather and a young cousin, and noted that "Mrs Wilson and I wished to put you in mourning for your dear grandfather but I am prevented for want of Black to do it with." Sarah did have the material, however, to make Elizabeth a new pair of stays, or corsets, which she sent, hoping they were the right size. It seems likely that Sarah Fairburn's concerns for Elizabeth's proper dress may have been prompted by the advice of the socially rather superior Anne Wilson (Middleton 2007a). Although stays may not have be worn on a daily basis (Ebbett 1977), Marianne Williams (n.d.b) noted the same concerns in her journal of 1844, mentioning that "a woman from Kororareka came to measure me for a pair of stays", and arranging mourning dress for a recently widowed woman.

Jane Williams also documents the amount of time associated with ironing, as does Eliza White. Marianne Williams (n.d.b) had a whole locked room dedicated to this task, but expected her Maori servants to carry out the work. Many of the smaller items in the Te Puna assemblage, as well as some of the heavier, are connected with all these activities.

DRESSING: DOCUMENTARY EVIDENCE

Women's clothing at this time was many-layered (Byrde 1992; Ebbett 1977; Willett and Cunnington 1951). It began with the shift or chemise, a loose garment of about knee length, followed by corset and petticoat (sometimes a number of petticoats), and the gown as the final layer, with additional items possible such as the tippet (a cape covering the shoulders), fichu (a similar item, a triangular piece of fabric covering the shoulders), or an apron for work-wear. A pocket was worn as a separate item, attached around the waist. Knee-length drawers, usually tied at the back and with an open seam from front to back, may have been worn underneath all this, although Willett (1951: 110) states that these were originally an item of male clothing, and were considered "extremely immodest" when first worn by women at the beginning of the nineteenth century.

Ebbett (1977: 11) considers that missionary women in 1814 "wore dresses much more suited to the life ahead of them than their sisters who arrived in 1850" as these were shorter than later fashions, above ground at ankle length. The high-waisted Empire line was then in fashion, with long skirts narrow, rather than later in the century when the narrow waist and crinoline and bustle returned, producing a much fuller look. According to Ebbett (1977: 11), missionary women wore "a minimal amount of underwear," while corsets were "not restricting if worn at all". Willett confirms this, stating that at the beginning of the nineteenth century layers of undergarments may have been reduced. However, several decades later, "tight-lacing became progressively more severe, partly to accentuate the much-admired 'small waist,' and partly as a moral restraint correcting the looser habits of the Regency" (Willett 1951: 130). As noted earlier, "stays" did feature in journals and letters in the 1830s and 1840s, although this may have been a token gesture at formal requirements and not everyday wear. While current fashion may not have been a daily concern, the arrival of Bishop George Selwyn and his wife Sarah in 1842 prompted Marianne Williams to "cut out a brown Holland cloake like Mrs. Selwyn's which had been lent to Mrs. Dudley."

Appropriate headwear signaled the image of the modest, controlled female evangelical body. While suitable outdoors headwear was the bonnet, "metonymic of wider clothing practices, representative of the gender and body politics of Christianity" (Johnston 2003: 149), indoors the cap was a necessity. All the women's journals document a large amount of time spent ironing, sewing, and "stringing" or repairing day caps, an item of headwear tied under the chin with "kissing strings"

(McDowell 1997: 127) that all married women were expected to wear, as well as older "spinsters" (Drummond and Drummond 1967; Ebbett 1977). Jane Williams makes regular references to caps; "Mrs. Stack kindly ironed my caps"; Jane was "busy making up caps and trimming bonnets" (Williams, Jane n.d.); Marianne Williams (n.d.b 20/06/1844) "ironed caps". Eliza White (n.d.) at the Mangungu mission in the Hokianga spent a Saturday evening in August 1833 "mending and stringing my caps for next week," then ironed her husband's shirts. In the earlier years of the mission, Marsden (n.d.a) was ordering large amounts of coarse and fine muslin for caps. These were often embroidered or trimmed with lace and ribbons. Night caps, a less elaborate form of the day cap, were required wearing for bed (Clark 1982; Drummond and Drummond 1967; Ebbett 1977; Willett and Cunnington 1951). A portrait of Hannah King displayed in the Waimate Mission House, reputedly painted posthumously from a photograph, shows her wearing a day cap, while a portrait of Eliza White painted before her marriage shows her bare-headed (Middleton 2005a: Figure 5.52; 2007a: Figs. 9–11). As a married woman, Marianne Williams wears a day cap in her portraits, as does her sister-in-law Jane Williams (see also http://www.matapihi.org.nz). Missionary wives wore these items, while it seems likely that Maori women went bareheaded, unlike missionized women in the Pacific, who had been taught to make themselves straw bonnets (Ellis 1859; Johnston 2003; Edmond 1997). The journals make no reference to Maori women wearing caps, and perusal of historical (later nineteenth century) photographs such as Main (1976) shows Maori women sometimes wearing fashionable hats, but not caps, and mostly bare-headed. Stack (1937) states that Maori women (and men) never wore hats or shoes.

A woman's gown might require six or more yards of fabric, although Ebbett (1977) states up to 20 yards of material could be used; large quantities of fabric may have been required to keep the mission women covered and decent, one of the important preoccupations of the missionaries (White n.d.; Williams, Jane n.d.; Williams, Marianne n.d.b). Jane Williams' (n.d.) journal gives some indication of the use these fabrics were put to, with continual references to cutting out and sewing, all done by hand with a needle and thread. Marianne Williams' (n.d.b) work at the beginning of June, 1844 included cutting out "garments for my infant school", while one of her daughters "undertook to see them made"; ten days later "Catherine and the little natives [were] getting on with their new frocks". A day later Marianne was "cutting out work all day", with her daughter assisting; later again she cut out "checked gingham frocks" which "Takapui and Anato" sewed. Gowns as well as men's clothing were mended, and resewn into new garments. One of Marianne's daughters "finished a very pretty black cloth cap for her boy out of Grandpapa's [Henry Williams] trousers" (Williams, Marianne n.d.b. 4 September 1844). The Williams daughters' own gowns were reworked and mended by "Mrs. Walmsley," one of the European servants, who also sewed day caps for Marianne. These daughters went to "Mrs. Stanley's school," where they were supposed to learn to make garments too; however, their mother "fear[ed] they will never know how to sew" (Williams, Marianne n.d.b 15 July 1844).

Much of the clothing itemized to John King in the store accounts may have been supplied to Maori living at the mission and at the pa, sometimes used as payment for services rendered. For example, Eliza White (n.d. May 1833) gave a red shirt as payment to the man who carried a box of goods that arrived from England for her, from the Bay of Islands to Mangungu. Marianne Williams (n.d.b) collected and counted blankets to use as payment for Maori who worked for her. Certainly by the 1830s Maori often wore European clothing in preference to traditional attire, as von Huegel (n.d.) described Wharepoaka boarding the *Alligator* on its arrival at Rangihoua:

> The chief of Tipuna was amongst them, in European clothing, which he wore like one who knows this style and no other: trousers, socks and shoes were blue, waistcoat and scarf coloured, blue jacket and white hat, very much in fact the dress of the captain of a superior merchant ship; a man of perhaps forty, his hair was trimmed in European style, his face was fully tattooed, and even subsequently I saw no head tattoo better than this which made his face appear black at a short distance and wholly concealed his age.

Waikato was with Wharepoaka, but he had given up European dress, according to von Huegel. The women who visited the ship were dressed only in mats, which required continual adjustment to maintain modesty. In contrast, on Marshall's (1836: 12) visit to Rangihoua Pa with John King, the day after the *Alligator*'s arrival, he noted that most of the women were dressed in English clothing, as was Wharepoaka's wife, "very cleanly and neat in her appearance."

Some of the store records specify that large amounts of fabric were supplied to King for Maori women at the mission (CMS n.d.d), while other accounts only note the yardage without specifying its use. For example, on January 5, 1830, John King received for the "Settlement Girls 11 Girls" 27 1/2 yards of striped cotton and 23 yards of blue linen, as well as "Clothing for Native Girls"; a further 74 yards of blue linen and 60 yards of striped cotton along with over 1 lb of thread as well as tape. Three months later, John King received "for Settlement at Rangihoua" 26 "soldiers' belts" and eight "soldiers' coats", along with 123 yards of "Factory Cloth", the coats and belts no doubt intended for the men of the mission or the pa. However, the missionary himself may have worn a soldier's coat and a scotch cap, items of clothing James Kemp is portrayed wearing as he reads the scriptures to a group of Maori gathered in front of his tent (Fig. 5.4). His Maori audience are dressed in a mixture of European and traditional clothing. The Bay of Islands chiefs Hakiro, Waka Nene, and Rewa wore similar caps, drawn by either James Hutton or William Cotton on their visit in 1844 (Easdale 1991: 17).

Committee minutes record quite strict regulations about mission clothing, which change over time. In 1829, Maori children born in the missions were to receive one [Parramatta] factory cloth garment yearly (CMS n.d.a). Three years later the committee resolved:

> That married women living in the Settlements but not engaged in the domestic affairs of the mission families shall not be allowed any garments except as payments. That the native children – infant schools – one garment each for the next twelve months and that one small garment be provided for each to attend school in. (CMS n.d.a)

Other Europeans provide descriptions of mission clothing. J.W. Stack (1937, 1938; Stack and Stack 1938), son of missionary James Stack senior, was born at the Puriri mission in 1835, and grew up on mission stations on the East Coast of the North Island. According to him, mission Maori were reluctant to wear European clothing, although this was a requirement of mission work:

> The women and girls were supplied with a loose print garment of the ordinary nightgown pattern. But as soon as their work about our house was finished, and they got back to their quarters, they threw aside the foreign garment and put on their favourite waist-mats. (Stack 1937: 80).

In the early mission days, Stack (1937: 80) states that Maori men refused to wear any European garment other than "an ordinary day shirt," while those with tattooed limbs appeared better covered. At the Kohanga mission in the 1850s, boys attending the mission school where Stack taught wore white duck trousers and white smocks in the summer, and white moleskin trousers and blue serge shirts in winter (Stack 1937). After futile washing efforts, Stack himself boiled these in washing soda to remove the grime.

In 1862, on a visit to the Te Papa mission at Tauranga, John Kinder photographed a small group of mission girls in clothing typical of the period (Fig. 5.5).

They are wearing long white dresses of the style described by Stack, standing outside what appears to be a kitchen. A large fireplace can be made out in the building behind them, and a number of cast iron cooking pots, of the kind used over an open fire, are on the ground.

Fig. 5.5 Maori girls, Te Papa Mission, Tauranga, 1862 (Photographer John Kinder, 1819–1903. Auckland Institute and Museum, Auckland, New Zealand. B 8544)

The building in the right foreground appears to be sitting on a stone foundation, above ground level.

Writing to the parent committee in August 1838, the Bay of Islands committee offered an opinion different to that expressed by Stack:

> The Natives living about our families are anxious for European clothing and wear but little else and at their work the Natives generally prefer the Trousers and Shirt as more convenient than their own Clothing but it must be confessed that they never feel themselves so comfortable and respectable as when wrapped up in a Blanket this is applicable to the Christian Natives as well as to those who have no profession of Christianity. (CMS n.d.b)

Several years earlier, Maori of "both sexes, young and old" were employed at the Waimate mission in pulling up and burning fern root before the fields were ploughed. Richard Davis (n.d.) reported that young women formed the largest part of the workforce, "whose object in working is to procure for themselves clothing – in short we now pay but few [hardware] articles for labor of this kind the principal cry of the natives is for books slates and clothing."

Although no clothing or fabric survived in the archaeological context of the cellar, two items of clothing that belonged to the King family are held in the NZHPT collections at Waimate Mission House.

A gown reputedly first worn by Thomas Holloway King, born at Oihi in 1815, on his christening by Samuel Marsden in March of that year is displayed at the Waimate Mission House as well as a shirt belonging to John King, reputedly sewn by Hannah King and worn by him at their wedding in 1812. The gown may have been first worn by Thomas's older brother Philip Hansen King, who was born in NSW in 1813, and by later King children as well as subsequent generations. For example, it features in Ebbet (1977), worn by a King descendant in the 1970s. The hand-sewn shirt is in the traditional "frock" style (discussed later), but is not smocked (Armes 1974; Cave 1965). The body of the shirt is gathered onto the collar, and the sleeves gathered onto the body, with gussets inserted at the side seams and underarm. John King's initials are embroidered near the side opening in a red that has now faded somewhat, and a heart is embroidered in the same thread below the short neck opening. The front opening has small shell buttons, similar to the shell buttons recovered from the mission house investigation. Hannah King was known as an expert needle-woman (Drummond and Drummond 1967; Wordsworth 1981), and may have made the christening gown also, which is embroidered in the traditional Ayrshire style, which was synonymous with christening wear (Bryson 1989; Drummond and Drummond 1967).

In addition to these two items of clothing in the Waimate Mission House, there is a sampler embroidered by Elizabeth Marsden King, the youngest of the children, born in 1837. The smaller thimbles, described earlier, provide clues to the kind of activities expected of girls in nineteenth century households, where needlework was an important accomplishment. Elizabeth completed the sampler in 1853. The Auckland War Memorial Museum collections has two similar items to those described earlier, both donated by the daughter in law of Jane Davis (nee King), Elizabeth Marsden King's eldest sister, in 1923. A sampler, stitched by Jane Holloway King, is exactly the same design as Elizabeth's, although it does not show the date it was stitched. It is likely to have been completed some years earlier than Elizabeth's sampler, as Jane was born in 1818. The other King family item is a shirt, of the same design and with the same red embroidery as John King's wedding shirt. This shirt, reputedly stitched in 1849, is attributed to Elizabeth Marsden King.

Two other artifacts attributed to the King family, displayed at the Waimate Mission House, attest to the meticulous attention women paid to clothing and handwork. A crimping board was used to crimp ruffles on baby clothes and similar small items, while a netting set, a carved ivory or bone cylinder was used to make a lace-like fabric, with twisted, plaited, looped, or knotted threads.

John King's descendant Pam Berry (1981) has described him as of diminutive stature, as the dimensions of his wedding shirt also reveal. Richard Taylor (n.d.) noted in 1839 that John King (aged 52 at the time) was "a white haired old man though not more I should fancy than 55. We slept at his house he reminded me of an English yeoman and his family had much the same appearance." In 1844 the Rev. William Cotton (n.d.) also said that John King, who had "never been outside the heads [the entrance to the Bay of Islands] for this 25 years" had "very silvery hair" and that he still spoke a broad Shire dialect, as did all his family. A year earlier, in 1843, Sarah Selwyn, wife of Bishop George Selwyn, was more specific in her description of John King:

> George went to Te Puna, the station of Mr. King, the oldest member of the Church Mission in the land. He came in more perilous times than these, but he looks as if he had always lived in a retired village in England all his life, his powdered head and spruce appearance might have created wonder and awe in the eye of those who thought of the Maoris as fierce savages only he is just like Scott's description of Owen in Rob Roy. (Quoted in Berry 1981)

THE ARTIFACTS: BUTTONS, BEADS, IRONS, THIMBLES, AND PINS

The documentary evidence (above) has identified the importance of domestic activities such as ironing in the mission stations elsewhere in the Bay of Islands, to maintain suitable standards of dress and appearance. At Te Puna, five domestic irons in a range of sizes, from 115 to 90 mm in length were recovered from the mission house.

Fearn (1990) notes that most British households had a smoothing iron by the end of the eighteenth century. Some models were hollow and filled with charcoal for heating, while the type from Te Puna is solid cast iron, known as the sad or flat iron, "sad" being an obsolete English term meaning solid or heavy. The sad or flat iron was the most popular iron of the nineteenth century, used in pairs, one being in use while the other was heated, usually sitting on a trivet in front of an open fire, or hung from a hook suspended from the fire bars (Sambrook 1983). These should not be confused with the later version of the sad iron with a detachable wooden handle that slotted into the notches on the top of the iron, patented in 1871. Flat irons were manufactured in Britain in the nineteenth century in sizes from 1 to 12 or 14, with no standardization between manufacturers. The smaller sizes, such as the smallest one in the Te Puna assemblage, were used for finer tasks, ironing caps, lace, and similar items. The handles, formed of a more fragile hollow tube of iron, have broken off the Te Puna irons. Irons were in use from the first days of the Oihi mission, a somewhat incongruous activity when the Kings were living in a thatched house "that would keep neither wind nor rain out" (King n.d.d; Chap. 2). However, in January 1815, Samuel Marsden ordered 1 dozen of smoothing irons, along with the same number of coffee mills and pepper mills (Marsden n.d.).

Seven thimbles were recovered from the excavation, six of these from the floor and fill of the cellar and one from layer one of square F21, the western area of the excavation (Fig. 5.6).

The Te Puna thimbles are brass, with the indentations mechanically applied and the rims rolled, manufactured by the deep-drawn

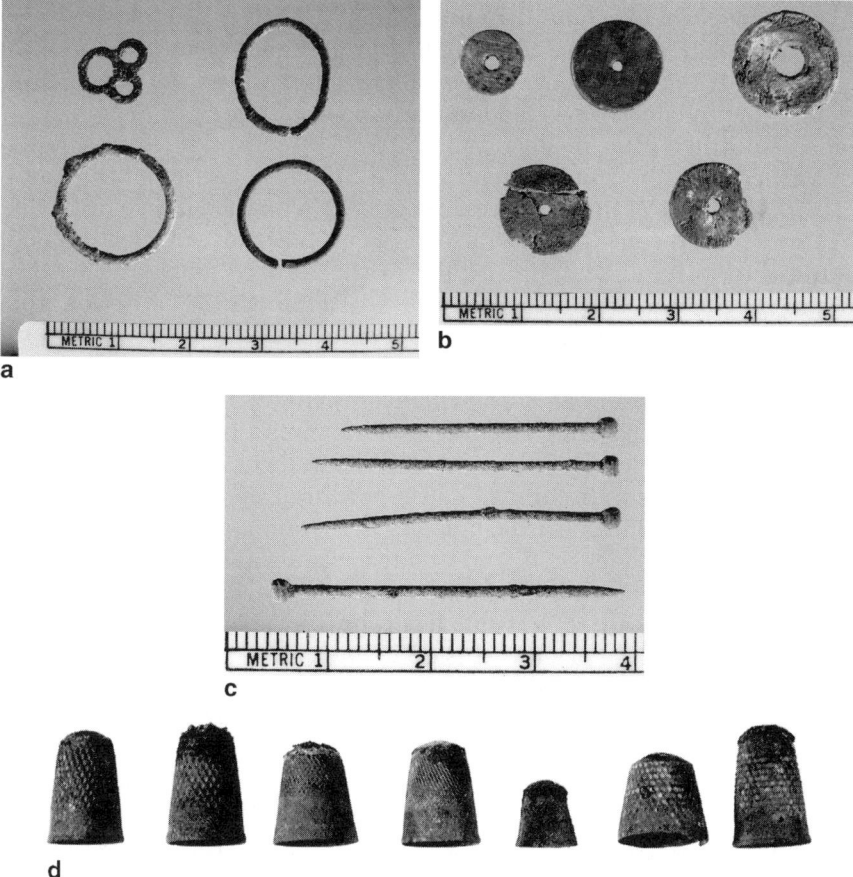

Fig. 5.6 Thimbles, pins, Dorset buttons and rings, and eye from a hook and eye, Te Puna Mission House assemblage

punch and die process (Beaudry 2006; Holmes 1985). The thimbles vary in size, the smallest being 12-mm high and 7-mm wide, the largest, 17-mm wide and 27-mm high. The size of the smallest is comparable with children's thimbles recovered from Spanish colonial sites, where thimbles of approximately 1 cm in height were numerous (Hill 2000). Three other thimbles 16 mm in diameter and 22–26 mm in height appear to be below adult size, while the remaining four are an average size. As with thimbles recovered from the Praying Town of Magunco, Massachusetts, these thimbles could also be interpreted as "gifts with a hidden agenda, as presentation – a gift or offering in fulfilment of a duty or service" (Beaudry 2006: 113), as an encouragement to Maori women and girls to attend school or catechism, to learn the female arts of sewing and needlework, and to wear European clothing, "in the service of the ideology of colonialism and Christianity."

A total of 16 pins were recovered from the cellar floor and beneath the cellar fill (Fig. 5.6). These are thicker and somewhat more substantial than modern pins, the lengths varying from 27 to 37 mm. The heads also differ from modern pins in that they consist of a rounded blob rather than the smaller head with a flat cross-section of the modern pin. This style of head was constructed by a method in use until the early nineteenth century, in which a second piece of wire was turned around the shank of the pin, usually in three turns, anchored with a blow to spread the top of the shank (Noel Hume 1969). The lengths suggest that they are ordinary sewing pins called "short whites" by pin makers (Beaudry 2006: 25).

Buttons are often the only evidence of clothing persisting in the archaeological record after the fabric of garments has decayed. Prior to the appearance of pressed metal buttons and ceramic buttons commonly known as "small chinas," mass-produced by mechanised processes from about 1850 onwards, buttons were handmade from available materials such as bone, shell, and wood (Sprague 2002). Machine made production of buttons manufactured in these materials continued from 1850 also. The majority of buttons from the Te Puna assemblage point to a manufacture date prior to this 1850 date.

A total of 28 buttons was recovered from the cellar and the surrounding area, made from bone, wood, ceramic, shell, and metal (copper alloy).

Three wire rings associated with the manufacture of Dorset disc buttons were also recovered from the cellar floor (Fig. 5.6). These can be matched with five bone discs varying in diameter from 8.5 to 15 mm. These discs, with one central hole, were used in conjunction with metal rings, covered in thread and stitched to form a fabric button. Known as Dorset buttons for the area in Britain where they were made, these had gone out of production by about 1850, when machinery making linen-covered buttons was introduced (Meredith 2000; Peacock 1972). These buttons, covered with silk or linen thread, suggest use on women's garments such as gowns.

Seven of the buttons are shell sew-throughs, six of them four-holed, and a seventh with only three holes, although this example is broken in the center. The shell buttons vary in diameter from 7.35 to 10 mm, and two of them have the "pie crust" (Peacock 1972) decoration of lines radiating from the center. A further seven sew-through buttons are manufactured from bone. One of the smaller examples is three-holed, while the others all have four holes. These small buttons were used on underwear and shirts, while the larger bone buttons are likely to have been used on outer garments (Lindberg 1999; Sprague 2002).

Five of the buttons are metal, two of them four-holed sew-throughs and the other three with a shank. One of the sew-throughs is inscribed "warranted not to cut." All of the metal buttons are of one-piece construction. Two of the buttons are four-holed white ceramic ("small chinas" or "Prosser" buttons), of the kind first manufactured in Britain in the 1840s, but manufactured in France from an earlier date (Peacock 1972; Lindberg 1999; Sprague 2002) also used as shirt or underwear buttons. The only decorative button is a wooden shanked example, 17 mm in diameter.

Buttons similar to those from the Te Puna cellar have been found in many archaeological contexts in both Australia and New Zealand, as well as at the Kerikeri Mission House. In Australia, similar bone and metal buttons are illustrated by Birmingham (1992) from Wybalenna, the Flinders Island settlement established in 1833 and abandoned by 1847, and from the Tasmanian whaling station at Adventure Bay, established in the 1820s (Lawrence 2006). Three-holed bone sew-through buttons from these sites are very similar to one from the Te Puna cellar. Of the Wybalenna buttons, Birmingham (1992: 105) remarks "no other colonial sites so far excavated have so restricted a range and unlike some of the other domestic items it seems to imply a standard range of government institutional cloth and haberdashery issued to the Tasmanians." Although there are more shell and several ceramic buttons from Te Puna, only the broken wooden button could be called decorative, and one is tempted to make a similar judgement about the Te Puna button assemblage and the CMS institution.

Four glass trade beads were recovered from the cellar and eastern area of the excavation, of the kind used to reward children for attendance at school or completion of domestic and handiwork tasks (King n.d.c; Elder 1934). The smallest of these is a tubular drawn bead, of the type Sprague (2000) notes was manufactured by two workmen drawing a tube of hot glass out to a desired length, and later, when sufficiently cool, cutting this to small lengths. The other three beads are round, or spheroid, known as wound beads for the way they were manufactured, a rod of glass being heated over a flame until it was plastic enough to wind around a length of wire, in order to create the central hole for threading. All of these examples are similar to those illustrated by Birmingham (1992), excavated from the Wybalenna site and are of the same kind as beads excavated in North America Indian sites dating to late eighteenth – early nineteenth contexts. Similar beads can also be found on display at the Kerikeri Mission House and Stone Store, recovered from contexts comparable with those from Te Puna. Although glass trade beads such as those from Te Puna seem to be a rare occurrence in the New Zealand archaeological context, Bedford (1994) recovered a large number, a total of 85, from his investigation of the Puriri mission site. Although these were excavated from a later nineteenth century context postdating the mission station, Bedford considered that some of the beads could have originated from the mission.

ARCHIVES: THE STORE ACCOUNTS

Archival sources allow the archaeological assemblages of artifacts associated with sewing, clothing, and fabric to be seen in context. All the missionaries received a constant supply of large quantities of fabric, haberdashery and clothing from the Kerikeri store. In 1820, prior to the establishment of the store, Marsden ordered thimbles, pins and needles, shirt buttons, black and colored, ribbons, 56 yards of linen, 30 yards of check for aprons, dark print, 40 yards of brown twilled stuff, 30 yards of fustian, 10 yards of velveteen, 10 yards of black velvet, 30 yards of calico, 10 yards of muslin, as well as 12 pairs of women's black stockings, six pairs of men's worsted stockings, all "wanted for Mr. King and family" (Marsden n.d.a). Other supplies for the Oihi settlement not intended specifically for the Kings included 1 case of hats for men and boys, 3 dozen of men's black stockings, 2 dozen of women's straw bonnets, 2 dozen of child's straw bonnets, one dozen each men's and women's leather gloves, 6 dozen of woolen nightcaps, 6 dozen of men's woolen stockings, as well as one bale each of blue trousers, duck frocks, and striped cotton shirts and trousers.

In 1831 and 1832, similar goods were still being supplied, although straw bonnets, leather gloves, and woolen nightcaps and stockings seem to have disappeared (see Appendix). Men's clothing appears to have been purchased ready-made, while fabric for sewing women's gowns was supplied from the store and sewn at the missions, as women's gowns were usually sewn by their wearers or custom-made rather than purchased off the rack at this time. Men's clothing consisted of cotton shirts and trousers, red shirts, duck trousers (both common and best), grey trousers, blue trousers, blue jackets, duck frocks, and scotch caps. Duck is a strong untwilled linen or cotton fabric (canvas) used especially for outer clothing, as well as for small sails. "Duck frocks" were a laborer's shirt or smock, a traditional English garment simply constructed from rectangles and squares and gathered (usually smocked) onto the collar or a yoke. These garments were worn both for work and leisure, with those for festive events such as weddings featuring more elaborate embroidery (Cave 1965). The only ready-made women's garments supplied from the store were cotton shifts, a chemise or straight undergarment, often worn beneath a petticoat (Willett and Cunnington 1951). Fabrics purchased included blue linen, striped cotton, twilled factory cloth, "common print," "brown holland," "best chintz and prints," "Bangor fustian," flannel, and calico shirting. "Twilled" cloth is woven so that the fabric has a diagonal line; "untwilled" duck hence has just a plain weave. "Fustian", a thick, twilled linen or cotton, was used to make trousers and jackets for work wear (Maynard 1994; Simpson 1962). Parramatta or factory cloth was woven by convict labor at the Parramatta female factory (Salt 1984). Thread was purchased by the pounds and ounces. Thimbles, needles, and buttons of different types ("metal" and "shirt"), as well as tape were all supplied for sewing, although pins do not appear on the lists for 1831 and 1832. Household linen may have been hand-stitched from "cotton sheeting" and "Russian towelling". Rugs and blankets, popular trade items, were supplied regularly to King and other mission families (Table 5.2; Appendix).

Both "English" and "colonial" shoes were supplied from the store, "colonial" implying that they were made in NSW. In October 4, 1831, John King received "on private Acct. 6 pair Boys Shoes viz. 2 largest size 2 No.11 2 No. 13 6 Pieces Tapes 4 pair men's shoes" (CMS n.d.d). Although King was initially employed by the CMS as a shoemaker he no longer continued this activity after 1822, precipitating a strongly worded complaint from Marsden (Chap. 2).

King's returns to the quarterly committee meetings indicate that quantities of fabric and clothing as well as blankets supplied from the Kerikeri store were kept at the Te Puna mission as trade goods. In his return for October 1833 (Table 5.2), King has "on hand" ten blankets, Parramatta cloth ("P Cloth"), shirts, trousers, jackets and caps (presumably men's "Scotch" caps) as well as hardware and similar items. Six blankets and a quantity of Parramatta cloth, as well as other goods were used to purchase pigs. One blanket and one iron pot were used to "Redeem a slave," no doubt the young woman John Wilson wrote about in some detail (Chap. 3). Three years later, King's return for July 1836 (Fig. 5.3) lists fewer fabric and clothing items, although blankets and trousers remain and "drawers", another ready-made item for women, seem to have appeared.

TOILETRIES

McClintock's (1995: 209) *Imperial Leather* uses soap and its advertising as a trope for the processes of imperialism within the African continent during the Victorian fetishism of the later nineteenth century. Elements of her argument resonate with the earlier concern of the CMS with cleanliness and the dispensation of soap. McClintock (1995: 209) argues, "The cult of domesticity became indispensable to the consolidation of British national identity, and at the center of the domestic cult stood the simple bar of soap." Soap was an "exemplary mediating form" of the cult of domesticity, a single household commodity embodying the "imperial civilizing mission ('washing and clothing the savage')," amongst other middle class values (McClintock 1995: 208). Soap became associated with cleansing the great unwashed and imbued with racial overtones, "magically embodying the spiritual ingredient of the imperial mission itself" (McClintock 1995: 211), while overtly, cleanliness was next to godliness.

Sarah Selwyn's description (earlier) of John King's "powdered head and spruce appearance" confirms the maintenance of Georgian (and subsequently Victorian) standards of propriety and appearance amongst the CMS brethren, both men and women. Journals, especially those written by women, document the concern with personal cleanliness and instilling these values in their charges at the mission schools, although bathrooms were unlikely to have been found within any of the mission houses at this time, and bathing itself was a "cursory activity at best" at the beginning of the nineteenth century (McClintock 1995: 207).

Soap was amongst the basic goods issued to the missions every 3 months. John King received a total of 75 lbs of this for the last quarter of 1831, and the same amount in the following quarter, January to March 1832 (Table 5.2; CMS n.d.e; Appendix). But the CMS apparently gave up encouraging young boys in this respect, the committee resolving in 1832 (CMS n.d.a) "That the ration of soap hitherto allowed to the Native boys be dispensed with." Other goods in the accounts relate to toiletries and personal items. William Yate's (n.d.) 1832 crockery order for the CMS included one crate containing 30 white wash hand basins and ewers and another crate containing five dozen of white chamber pots, essential items for bedrooms in the days before household plumbing. However Eliza White (n.d.) went to greater lengths in the Hokianga, and noted on Monday Jan 30, 1832, "Mrs Hobbs [her close friend and neighbor] and I went in a shower bath," an apparently unusual event. In 1836, builder Benjamin Nesbitt also built a "shower bath" at Kerikeri (James Kemp journal in Pickmere 1994: 29). In the Williams (Williams, Marianne n.d.b) household, occasional mention is made of "tubs", such as "the foot tub" and a tub of warm water for bathing in.

John King certainly makes no mention of such personal events, and the archaeological investigation revealed only one item of this nature, fragments of a chamber pot (Fig. 5.7), which, when refitted, revealed a blue-and-white transfer print identified rather ironically as "Village Church" (Coysh 1974: 101).

Fig. 5.7 (**a**) Village Church pattern chamber pot, Te Puna Mission House assemblage; (**b**) Hannah King's toilet box, NZHPT collections, Kerikeri Mission House; (**c, d**) Village Church pattern toilet box, NZHPT collections, Waimate Mission House, attributed to King family donation

This has a blue and white floral border around the rim and part of a landscape scene on the body. The large area of transfer print on the main part of the body of the chamber pot has been misprinted, with half of the house, complete on the other side of the body, replaced by mismatched tree/landscape, suggesting that this was a seconds quality item.

Examination of the NZHPT ceramic displays at the Kerikeri and Waimate Mission Houses revealed two further items of the same pattern (Fig. 5.7). Figure 5.7b, a toilet dish identified as Hannah King's, displayed in the Kerikeri Mission House, shows the entire version of this pattern, complete with church and tower, as does a similar square box with its lid missing, from the Waimate Mission House (Fig. 5.7c, d). These items formed part of a toilet set, usually consisting of chamber pot, toilet dish (used to contain toothbrush and related items), washbowl and ewer (Coysh and Henrywood 1982: 365). Although the chamber pot does not have any maker's mark, the toilet box at Waimate Mission House has an "Iron of Mars" mark on the reverse. Kowalsky and Kowalsky (1999: 328) note that this mark is the continuation of John and George Rogers, c.1815–1841. That the chamber pot was possibly of "seconds" quality reinforces again the austerity of the mission economy.

METAL FRAGMENTS: LAUNDRY AND OTHER HOUSEHOLD ACTIVITIES

In a world where metal and plastic containers did not exist, iron hoop-bound wooden tubs and similar vessels were used for a number of functions, including, as mentioned above, for personal washing. Missionary William Bambridge kept a record of his family life in New Zealand, drawing family members and interiors of houses they lived in. While he did not live at Te Puna, Bambridge's sketches provide another glimpse into mission households of the time, contextualizing the interior of the Te Puna house. William Bambridge's wife Sophia is shown using two of these handled containers, presumably for washing clothes (Fig. 5.8).

The wooden vessels are constructed in a manner similar to barrels and bound with hoop iron. It is interesting to note that Sophia is wearing a cap as she does this housework. Her gown is low-waisted, rather than of the earlier Regency high-waisted style, and it does not have the exaggerated full skirt created by wearing a crinoline or bustle beneath it in the fashion of the day. The line at the side of the skirt suggests she may be wearing a long apron (also known as a petticoat at this time) for working in over the gown, and she has a fichu, a square of fabric, worn across her shoulders.

Fig. 5.8 Sophia Bambridge washing laundry (Artist William Bambridge, 1844 [?]. Alexander Turnbull Library. MS-0131-106)

As Bambridge's caption points out, the washing is not being done in a space dedicated to this activity, but in his office. Such containers, being portable, may have allowed different activities in a number of spaces and rooms may not have had a fixed function in the way they do now. For example, Marianne Williams (n.d.b) noted "Catherine took the foot tub to Mr. Cotton's room (the little old study)."

A total of 22.275 kg hoop iron was recovered from the investigation, demonstrating the presence of these kinds of containers in the mission house, as well as barrels and crates. The largest proportion of this, 17.197 kg, came from the cellar, suggesting that it may have contained a large number of barrels before the house was abandoned. Barrels were ubiquitous containers of many different materials, also used to hold salted pork and beef. Orders from the Kerikeri mission store were provided to mission families in these containers, for example flour, supplied by the cask (CMS n.d.f). Another form of container for a variety of goods was the crate, a wooden box with metal strapping, as Yate (n.d.; see ceramics section below) noted in his crockery order, which may account for some of the other metal fragments.

KITCHEN AND COOKING

Journals and letters, principally written by missionary wives, provide information about daily life, the preparation of food, and some of the social rituals concerned with its consumption. In a letter to her parents in England, written in September 1833, Eliza White detailed her domestic life at the Mangungu Wesleyan mission. Two of the live-in Maori girls did

> all the washing, and nearly all the Ironing and Cleaning, I have two who do most of the plate washing, and the rest fetch firewood, and fern to put at the doors to wipe feet on – which saves matting and keeps the floor clean. Their kitchen is a large place with a fire place and large iron pot fixt in one side which serves for a copper – any saucepans, firewood, pails and such utensils are kept there, but I do as little cooking there as I can help, as it is too full of Natives and too many of their appendages about it. I have a good fireplace in my sitting room, and we have a good oven in Mrs. White-ly's kitchen, where I do most of my Casking [preserving in small wooden casks] – we bake and boil almost everything. I have been at it nearly all the morning today, preparing food for Mr. W to take out with him next week. (White n.d.)

While Eliza and William White were living on the west coast, about two days walk from the Bay of Islands, and Hannah King's domestic life at Te Puna was likely to consist of a similar routine, with Maori women living as part of the household. Eliza White evidently had a separate building as a kitchen at Mangungu, not the case at Te Puna where the kitchen was most likely to have been situated in the west lean-to of the house, where drawings place the house's single chimney. Cooking is likely to have been done over an open fire in the kitchen, as White describes above, with firedogs and hooks for cast iron pots and pans. It is possible Hannah King may have had a brick oven of the kind William Hall had described building at Oihi some years earlier, or all the cooking, including bread baking may have been done over an open fire. A brick oven was heated by lighting a fire inside it, and the embers raked out before the food was put in it (Macgregor 1975).

The kitchen sketched by William Bambridge of his family quarters (Fig. 5.9) provides an image of a similar structure to the Te Puna mission house kitchen lean-to.

This drawing shows a lean-to with a sloping ceiling, the room lined with wooden boards, as mentioned by Thomas Surfleet Kendall (Chap. 4). Bambridge's wife Sophia sits beside the grated fireplace, where the cooking would have been done, although the view of this is truncated. A lit candle is placed next to her, and in the middle of the table a quill for writing rests in an inkwell or similar object. An open book rests on

Fig. 5.9 Sophia Bambridge in the family kitchen (Artist William Bambridge, 1844 [?].
Alexander Turnbull Library, Wellington, New Zealand, MS-0130-280)

the table. An array of everyday objects is stored around the walls, on
shelves, and on the mantelpiece above the fireplace.

The Investigation: Kitchen and Cooking Vessels

Cast iron cooking vessels recovered during the investigation of
the mission house confirm Eliza White's "baking and boiling everything" style of cooking, as does the soup style of dinner plate recovered,
more useful for stewed and liquid food rather than a flat dinner plate
(Middleton 2005a,b).

While the cast iron vessel fragments from the Te Puna mission
house are very rusted, rim dimensions and other details suggest a minimum number of three vessels, two with the small "ear"-shaped handle
of the three-legged goashore cauldron, and a third with a long handle
suspended across the vessel. Included in the fragments were three legs
of two different sizes, puzzling artifacts when looked at in isolation.

Goashores, round-bellied and round-bottomed, were so named because they could be taken from ships to cook on shore, standing over a fire. This type of pot could also be suspended above a fire from a metal handle attached to the two "ear" handles. Similar vessels from the Stone Store at Kerikeri display one of the weaknesses of pots of this type – the tendency to lose or break a leg, leaving a hole in the base of the pot. This may explain their use as broken fragments for packing in postholes.

Cooking vessels of these styles can be compared with those illustrated in Fearn (1990: 6), where the goashores of the type from Te Puna are identified as "bake pan". The third pot is of an oblong shape and flat base with a handle for suspending the pot from a hook over a fire. Eveleigh (1997) notes that by 1844 the three-legged cauldron had disappeared from use in Britain, replaced by the flat-bottomed type, which could be stood flat on the newly developed kitchen ranges and hobs. It is unlikely that a cast-iron range was used in the Te Puna kitchen. No pieces of cast iron from a range were recovered, although missionary households may have had such things, as Marianne Williams mentions "boiling on the oven" in her 1844 journal (Williams, Marianne n.d.b).

Iron pots were also a trade item. King had eleven of these "on hand" in July 1836 and used one on his own account (Fig. 5.3). At other times he used them to purchase "Native food" and pigs, for sundry items and to pay sawyers, as well as to redeem a slave (CMS n.d.a).

DINING AND DRINKING

Food: Documentary evidence

The Kings kept poultry and turkeys from the first days of the mission at Oihi, with John King occasionally complaining in his reports to the CMS that some of these had been stolen by people from the pa (King n.d.a, n.d.b).

Although it is possible pigs were raised at Te Puna, these were a food item consistently purchased from Maori, as journals and accounts note (White n.d., Williams, Marianne n.d.b; Table 5.2). King's (CMS n.d.a) accounts submitted to the quarterly committee meetings regularly note the trade expended in buying pigs. For example in July 1832, he traded hoes, blankets, iron pots, and rugs in return for pigs, but he does not give the quantity he received. He exchanged the same sort of items the following year, with books also now included in the trade goods. In July 1833, he makes a passing reference: "I have bought food for the Settlement, killed the pigs etc," the only reference that appears in his reports and journals to slaughtering animals, something that was likely to have been a regular event.

Rabbits were also kept at Oihi, as Thomas Surfleet Kendall (n.d.) noted above that he had made a rabbit coop, and domestic rabbits kept for food may have been the source of faunal remains at the Te Puna house. Visitors to Te Puna, such as von Huegel (above), noted that cows were kept there, and CMS journals report the difficulties that missionaries experienced retrieving wild cattle until fencing and improved farming methods solved this problem (Kemp, James n.d.). Bambridge (n.d.) notes that the wildest of the oxen were caught at Waimate with a lasso. William Marshall (1836) took onions, pumpkins, and cabbages back to the *Alligator* from the mission garden as well as potatoes purchased from the pa. Marshall also enjoyed eating kumara at the Wilsons' dinner table, although he does not mention whether it was grown at the mission or the pa.

In the 1820s and 1830s, flour, tea, sugar, soap, salt, and lamp oil were supplied from the Kerikeri mission store every three months, "fine" flour being supplied to Europeans and "second" quality flour being supplied to the pa (Appendix; CMS n.d.e). Rice was also a staple in the missionary diet, with Marsden commenting in 1819 that this was the cheapest food to supply (Elder 1932: 231). Wheat (inventoried separately as wheat, following flour) continued to be supplied from the CMS store, imported from NSW, after earlier attempts to grow this at Oihi proved difficult, and Marsden's initial plans for the Oihi settlement to be self-supporting had to be modified. Even the planned CMS farm at the Waimate mission was eventually considered a failure, following futile attempts to plough land prolific in fern root (*Pteridium esculentum*), a staple of the Maori diet (Standish 1962; Leach 1984; Davis n.d.). In 1840, Henry Williams (in Standish 1962: 26) conceded that Waimate "was nothing short of a Sinking Fund … Flour can be bought in New Zealand much cheaper than it can be grown". Colenso (1888: 29) pointed out that due to the cost of carting flour from Waimate "across a rough country with no roads" to Kerikeri and from there to other stations by boat, the price of Waimate flour was nearly double the price of flour imported from Sydney.

Goods supplied to King for the first quarter of 1832 (Appendix; CMS n.d.e) are representative of rations for this period. For 14 Europeans (seven children and seven adults), and 31 Maori King received nearly 20 lbs of tea, 176 lbs of sugar, 75 lbs of soap, 1,014 lbs of "fine," and 705 lbs "seconds" flour. No rice, arrowroot, salt or saltpetre was supplied this quarter, but on other occasions quantities of these were supplied, with large amounts of salt and saltpetre used in preserving meat, and 312 lb of "biscuit", possibly ship's biscuit, supplied to King in the second quarter of 1831. Accounts note that goods such as flour were supplied in casks; this may account for some of the metal, in particular hoop iron, recovered from the cellar floor. Rations supplied for numbers of "Natives" could not be expected to feed the whole pa, but related to those associated with the mission. The number of 14 Europeans includes both the King and Shepherd families, with an annotation to the accounts for July to September 1831 noting that King's account included 6 months supplies for Mr. Shepherd. The King family numbered nine at this time, and the Shepherd family five. Although the total number of children and adults at Rangihoua (or Te Puna) remains the same, the ratio of adults to children increases over the years as the children grew older, being accounted for as adults from the age of 15 (CMS n.d.a). In 1842, the committee changed this, supplying adult rations to children over the age of ten (CMS n.d.b). There was little variation in CMS food items inventoried, the "biscuit" being the only example of this.

The surviving parts of Marianne Williams' (n.d.b) journal for 1844 provide more information about everyday food, as well as variations that may not have appeared in the missionary diet a decade earlier, such as dates. Amongst her domestic tasks in July 1844, she made pork pies, bought a small pig "which Honi killed," supervised bread and soup making, and "saw the pig cut up and more sausage meat [made]." Her daughter Sarah cooked a goose. A quarter of beef was salted and pickled in casks, as pork was. Meat preserved in this way could last for up to 2 years (Brewis 1982). Mutton also formed part of the diet. Biscuits were baked (in an oven). Kumara was made into puddings in this household, but Williams gives no more details about these. At one point, Marianne Williams (July 26) notes that "Joe brot. me beef and shin and head etc.," indicating that the cuts of butchery waste may have been used regularly. Jelly was made from the hooves, boiled in water with sugar, and egg whites added (Brewis 1982). Honey had recently made its appearance at the mission for the first time, brought in by the CMS visitor Rev. William Cotton, and beehives were a focus of some attention in the Williams' garden. The garden contained asparagus beds, along with more mundane items such as potatoes, and apple and pear trees. Captain Clendon purchased goods for the Williams in Sydney. Kororareka featured once as a shopping destination. On Tuesday October 29th, Marianne went there with Henry to purchase goods "before some of the shops had cleared off in the 'panic'," the "panic" likely to be that provoked by Hone Heke's assault on the flag pole in the town, which developed in the ensuing months into the "War in the North" (Belich 1986; Buick 1926).

Marianne Williams (n.d.b) appears very partial to tea-drinking; she and Henry "staid for one cup of tea" with Mrs. Busby, (wife of

James, British Resident at Waitangi from 1834 to 1840), and they "had a second tea" on returning home; two days later (20th July) she "drank tea in the front room" with Mr. and Mrs. Clendon. She regularly notes going to tea with Mrs. Busby or Mrs. Stanley. Other favorite visitors included Mrs. Martin, wife of Judge Martin, and Sarah Selwyn, wife of Bishop George Selwyn. In the case of Marianne Williams, this was part of a busy social round of which the Williams household formed the centre. This was not so at Te Puna, by the 1840s a more isolated outpost of the CMS where there may have been few visitors. However, as the ceramic assemblage indicates, tea drinking was likely to have been a daily ritual there, too.

Eliza White also recorded food eaten in their Wesleyan household at Hokianga, and provided a recipe for sourdough yeast, used regularly to make bread. At the right season, corn, peaches, and apples were plentiful. In May 1832, she purchased potatoes, kumara, corn, pigeons, pork, and fish from Maori in trading canoes. "We are now living on the Fat of the Land," she commented, noting that these provisions should be stored away for winter and scarcity. Two days later, more canoes came to trade. Eliza purchased:

> a pig for a small blanket
> 8 baskets (1 bushel) of corn for a spade
> the same number of baskets for a Hoe
> 1 basket for a negrohead of Tobacco
> 2 for a comb
> 2 for a bottle of oil

At other times of the year pork was the cheapest, most available food:

> I have eaten rather too freely of meat lately, owing to the high price of flour. Have made very few puddings, and been careful to use little bread. Pork is so cheap that it is a constant article of diet at every meal except tea; but it does not suit me more than once a day. (White n.d. Wednesday Feb. 10 1836)

Eliza was at Paihia for the marriage of William Puckey and Matilda Davis, held at the household of Henry Williams. Food for this festive event included "fine white bread – cake and strawberries – in the center was a large seed cake, which showed the occasion for which we were met" (White n.d.).

The existing garden at Te Puna also provides some evidence of fruit grown here, although some of this planting may relate to the later nineteenth century occupation. Several large fig trees are still standing (Middleton 2005a: Fig. 5.29). In 2001, two pear trees identified as dating from the mission settlement (Ross n.d.; S. Mountain pers. commun.), located about 100 m from the mission house on the slope below P05/915 were still producing fruit, although this was quite inedible and woody, as Ruth Ross (n.d.) had remarked about the same trees on a visit to Te Puna in February 1965. A later visit in 2002 showed the trees broken by recent strong winds (Middleton 2005a: Fig. 5.30).

The Investigation: Faunal and Midden Remains

Faunal remains from the cellar indicate that pig, sheep, beef, and poultry, as well as some duck and turkey, formed a regular part of the King family's diet, along with fish, particularly snapper, and a small amount of eel remains (Stuart Hawkins pers. commun. 20/22/2003; Middleton 2005a,b).

Total counts of mammal remains for the cellar floor, fill, other features and topsoil indicate that pig and sheep were the most frequently consumed species, with cattle following, although cattle would have returned a greater weight per NISP (number of identified specimens, i.e., the number of complete and fragmentary items identified to a category within an archaeological assemblage). Consideration of the mammal remains by layer indicates change over time in species consumed. The larger number of sheep and cattle recovered from the topsoil layer is likely to be the result of recent farming activities rather than any result of food consumption during the mission house occupation, and can be effectively disregarded in this context. However, the remains recovered from the sealed deposit of the cellar floor demonstrate that pig was the dominant species consumed, as does the cellar fill, with a lesser amount of goat or sheep (as it is difficult to distinguish between species from bones), and a small amount of cattle. The proportion of goat or sheep and cattle consumed appears to have increased over time, with pig still predominating. This is congruent with Watson's (2000) findings that pig was the most commonly consumed animal in New Zealand historic sites. Watson (2000: 145) suggests that pigs were an important food source because they grew rapidly to maturity and then bred prolifically, sows producing two litters a year. They also required little care and attention, and ate anything.

Stuart Hawkins (pers. commun. November 2003) suggests that sheep and pigs were slaughtered and consumed on the site, with a broader range of body parts present than cattle. Cattle are represented by "what appears to be butchery waste (crania, mandibles, metacarpals/ metatarsals, phalanges, carpals, tarsals etc) with only a few vertebra, ribs and long bones. Most of these have been consumed and/or deposited elsewhere" (Hawkins pers. commun. 20/11/2003). Fishes are predominantly represented by snapper (*Chrysophyrs auratus*) and terakihi (*Nemadactylus macropterus*), with a single example of a sting ray (*Elasmobranchii*) recovered from the topsoil. Once again, examination of the cellar floor deposit and fill demonstrates that snapper was the most commonly consumed fish at the mission house, with single examples of long fin eel (*Anguilla dieffenbachia*), kahawai (*Arripis trutta*), and Labridae (banded wrasse, *Notolabrus fucicola*), and one MNI (minimum number of items; the smallest number of complete items needed to account for fragments/specimens recovered) of the short fin eel (*Anguilla australis*), although these may be under represented in the faunal remains as the bones are poorly preserved. Poultry also formed an important food source, with 50 chickens represented, as well as two ducks and two turkeys. From the cellar floor and fill, an MNI of four rabbits were also identified, two of these bones with cut marks pointing to the use of these animals for food. Rats appear to have infested the cellar, with 15 MNI identified from the floor and fill, although this may have occurred after abandonment and demolition. Cat remains also found are more likely to be associated with the occupation of the mission house. Eel is quite likely to have come from the stream and swamp nearby.

Shellfish from the nearby shoreline were also exploited, with nerita (*Nerita atramentosa*) the most-commonly eaten species. Other shellfish used for food included cockle (*Austrovenus stutchburyi*), cats eye (*Turbo smaragdus*), rock oyster (*Crassostrea glomerata*), spotted top shell, blue mussel (*Mytilus edulis*) and pipi (*Paphies australis*). The habitat of the majority of these species is the rocky shoreline, while several live in sand and mudflats (Crowe 1999), all of which may have come from the nearby beach and rocky coast at Rangihoua Bay. Spines of kina (*Evechinus chloroticus*) were also present in the cellar fill and other features. Nearly all of the above species were staple or favorite foods of the Maori (Crowe 1999), and a small number of Maori were living at the mission on a daily basis, as King's reports regularly record, so the shellfish remains may represent the results of their food collecting.

It appears from the species represented here that those at the mission house ate well, from a broad range of local resources that they exploited to the full. Hawkins, who has also carried out analysis of faunal material from the Kerikeri Mission House (Best 2003a), suggests that those at the Te Puna mission fared better than occupants of the Kerikeri house (S. Hawkins pers. commun. November 2003).

Ceramics

The ceramic material constituted one of the smaller portions of the total artifact assemblage. Analysis of the pieces excavated provides some insight into the economy of both the King family at Te Puna and the CMS mission generally in the Bay. Likely dates of particular patterns provide confirmation of the age of the site, and are useful to assess which pieces may have arrived at Oihi, prior to the establishment of Te Puna, a site that predates most other European sites investigated in New Zealand (an exception to this is Smith and Gillies' (1997, 1998) work in Dusky Sound, in the far south of the country).

Although the artifact assemblage demonstrates that the family had a supply of china, the more durable pewter plates are the only form of dinnerware recorded in the CMS store accounts in 1831 and 1832, and in the 1820s. Pewter plates from the King family are in the NZHPT collections at Waimate Mission House, as well as a pewter christening mug that belonged to Elizabeth Marsden King. This suggests that the household economy was poor, with no luxury goods such as decorative and nonutilitarian items present. No complete ceramic vessels were discarded at the Te Puna mission house. Refitted items point to these being broken prior to deposition. While the items were all functional and utilitarian, tea ware predominated, including single fragments of at least ten London-style cups of unidentified patterns. This suggests that at Te Puna, as well as at the more sociable mission stations such as Paihia, the English tea drinking custom was practiced, and matching sets of tea wares were used. However, such goods were not supplied by the CMS, as they were not included in the Kerikeri store's accounts and Yate's (n.d.; see later) order of 1832 notes that these ceramics were to be supplied on the mission families' private accounts.

As in local historic sites (for example, Plowman 2000), as well as in other British colonies such as Cape Town in South Africa (Klose and Malan 2003), the ubiquitous Willow pattern predominates in the Te Puna ceramic assemblage. This assemblage demonstrates Te Puna's connections, through its material culture, with the wider trade networks of the British Empire.

Some archaeological sherds were matched to a small number of other complete vessels of the same patterns (such as Willow, Rhine, and Wild Rose) and potentially of the same sets displayed in the Kerikeri Mission House and the Waimate Mission House, donated by the daughters of John and Hannah King in the late nineteenth century. This suggests that china may have been a valuable resource for the King family, difficult or expensive to obtain and replace in this remote part of the world, and that complete items were cared for and passed on within the women of the family (Berry 1981), and eventually to the NZHPT collections. The ceramics assemblage can also be compared with archaeological collections recovered from the Kerikeri Mission House and Stone Store (Best 1995, 1997, 2003a; McLean 1994). These pieces may have come from the same CMS sources as the Te Puna ceramics. Imperfections in the glazes and patterns of some vessels point to purchases of seconds quality china. Once again, this points to the utilitarian economy of the CMS itself, with its members being provided with only basic requirements.

Visitors who were invited to take tea in the mission house parlor would have done so from elegant cups and saucers. The small assemblage of china fragments recovered from the Te Puna cellar evokes English table manners and tea-drinking habits, while some of the patterns depict far-distant idyllic English pastoral landscapes. Brooks (1999) explains the symbolic role of such imagery in conveying messages of a "calm and prosperous rural Britain," ironically reminiscent of a distant home. Such imagery on blue and white tea wares evokes the social rituals associated with the cult of domesticity and the genteel aspects of the middle class family. This is also shown in the matching of fragments from the archaeological context with complete vessels from the NZHPT collections in the Kerikeri and Waimate mission houses, pointing to the use of matching sets of tablewares, one of the markers of domestic gentility (Fitts 1999). While the Kings at Te Puna may not have met all the requirements of decorum in the closed New Zealand missionary circle, the family home and mission station contained the trappings of such respectability in its tableware and other items of material culture.

In October 1815, John King noted in a report to the CMS: "We have received one crate of earthenware. The other is at Port Jackson." (King n.d.c). He did not apparently note the arrival of the second crate of earthenware, and there is little other archival record of ceramics arriving at Oihi or Te Puna, apart from one bulk order for china requested from the CMS by William Yate (n.d.) in 1832. Yate's order requested, on the mission families' "private accounts"

1 Crate containing meat-pudding and cheese plates, ea, 30 doz
1   „   meat pie and vegetable dishes, ea, 10 sets
1   „   blue and white basins in sizes 30 doz
1   „   white wash hand basins and ewers, ea,
1   „   White Chambers 5 doz
1   „   blue and white breakfast cups and saucers 30 doz
1   „   Jugs in sizes 30 doz
1 Cask containing plain pint decanters one doz and plain strong tumblers & wine glasses, ea 30 doz.

While some patterns can be compared with those recovered from urban archaeological sites in Auckland (for example, Plowman 2000), these urban sites post date the 1840 annexation of New Zealand by Britain, but CMS material is generally from a pre-1840 context. Ceramics destined for the CMS in New Zealand were purchased privately by the CMS in Britain and shipped to New Zealand, as Yate's order demonstrates. Supplies may also have been sourced from NSW merchants. Other goods, such as clay pipes produced in Sydney by merchant Joseph Elliott were recovered at Te Puna and Kororareka. This process differs from later urban colonial markets, such as Auckland, where ceramics were imported in bulk from Britain and sold by merchants (Plowman 2000).

Table 5.3 lists all the ceramics recovered from the mission house investigation and Table 5.4 lists vessel color (Middleton 2005a,b). All the dinner plates were of the "soup" style. Blue and white transfer-printed vessels dominated the assemblage, with a total MNI of 63 of these vessels represented (61%). Some items are described below. The chamber pot is discussed in the section on toiletries (above).

A number of London-style teaware items have been partially refitted (Fig. 5.10). This pattern features an inside border of flowers and

Table 5.3 Ceramic vessels by ware, Te Puna Mission House assemblage

| Vessel | Refined earthenwares | | | Porce-lain | Stone-ware | Total |
	White-ware	Blue bodied	Red bodied			
Dinner plate	19					19
Side plate	13					13
Bowl (tea)	28					28
Bowl (kitchen)	1					1
Cup	15	1	–	–		16
Coffee can	1	–	–	–	–	1
Saucers	5	1	–	–		6
Ashet	2	–	–	–	–	2
Jug	2	–	–	–	–	2
Teapot	1					1
Tableware nk	–	–	1	1	–	2
Chamber pot	1	–	–	–	–	1
Tile	1	–	–	–	–	1
Candlestick	–	–	–	1	–	1
Bottle/jar	–	–	–	–	3	3
Total	89	2	1	2	3	97

Table 5.4 Ceramic vessel color, Te Puna Mission House assemblage

Color	Number of fragments
Blue	539
White	156
Nil (salt glazed)	59
Brown	25
Green	15
Mocha	9
Nk (burnt)	5
Black	3
Yellow	2
Grey	1

leaves between a narrow outline of bells at the rim of the vessel, and a lower outline of a narrow irregular zigzag, similar to the "Rose Border Series" (Coysh and Henrywood 1982). The outside decoration consists of a landscape scene, while the fragment of the largest bowl shows a woman standing behind a cow, repeated on one of the flatware fragments, suggesting Coysh and Henrywood's (1989: 137) "Milkmaid" pattern. A match for this pattern can be found in Williams and Weber (1986: 447), where it is only identified as an "unascribed genre pattern". The "London-style" tea wares also included elegant teapots and sugar boxes, with lids and handles, both vessels of an oblong shape (Miller 1983: 225). At the Waimate Mission House other items of the same pattern, and arguably of the same tea service, are displayed, provenanced to the King family. A sugar box of the type described displays the complete pattern of which the items from the Te Puna cellar show only fragments (Fig. 5.10). Here, the entire "milkmaid" can be seen along with her cows. A complete plate of the same pattern is also pictured.

The predominance of the London-style teawares confirms ceramic dates in the first half of the nineteenth century. Spode first introduced this shape around 1813, and while it became popular by about 1820, Miller (1983: 225) notes that by about 1827, when Minton began to manufacture teawares in this style, calling it "cottage," "the round plan was again fashionable for the major pieces of a tea service. Thus, the London shape was relegated from the fashionable drawing-room to the humble cottage." Both Whiter (1970) and Miller (1983: 225) note that there are minor variations of the London-style cup, attributable to many different manufacturers including Minton, Ridgeway and

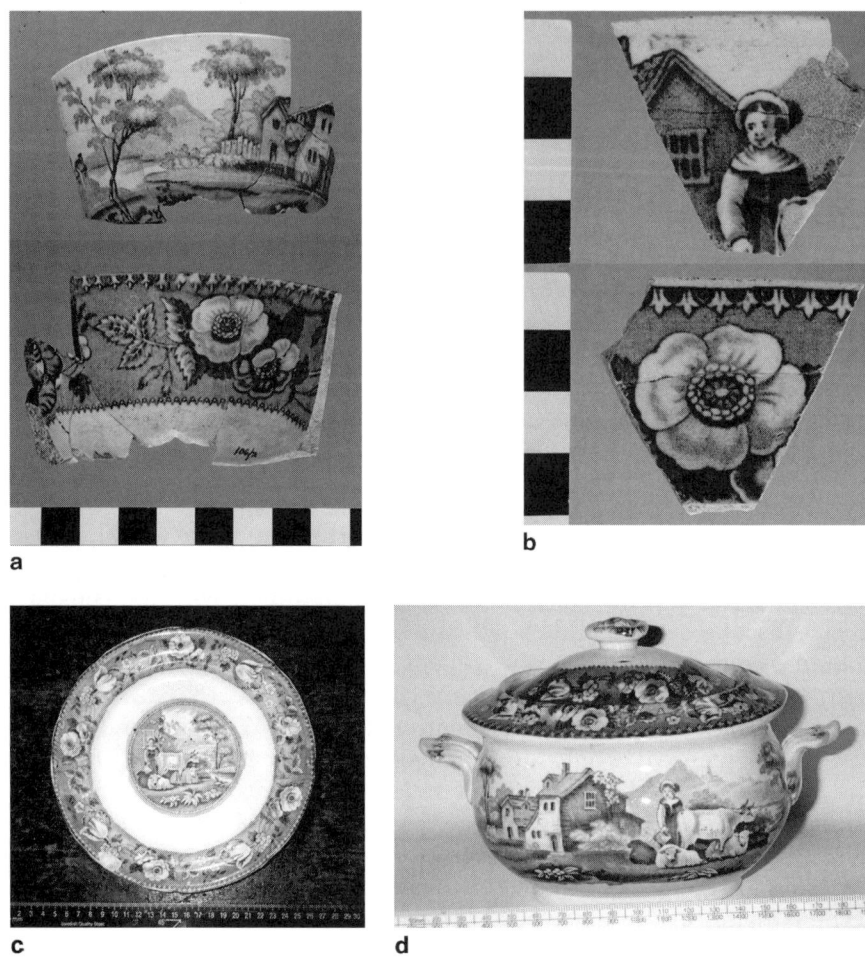

Fig. 5.10 (**a, b**) London-style teaware fragments (Te Puna Mission House assemblage), (**c**) table plate, and (**d**) sugar box, NZHPT collections, Waimate Mission House, attributed to King family donation (pattern unidentified)

Bourne, often "bearing cheap cottagey patterns," which could well describe that on the tea ware discussed above.

Other fragments are representative of patterns popular in the early to mid nineteenth century, in particular Willow. Of the total of 539 blue and white transfer-printed fragments, 246 of these, or just under half, were of Willow design, producing a MNI of 17 plates (12 dinner plates, all of the "soup" style and 5 side plates) and 2 hollow ware vessels

(18.5% of the total assemblage). All the Willow pattern vessels are of the standard Willow design in common use, but there are variations in print, ware colour and surface quality such as stippling. The standard Willow pattern was first produced at the end of the eighteenth century and "by 1814, Willow had been set aside as the cheapest available transfer printed pattern in the potters' price fixing lists" (Miller 1991: 8). This may account for the large proportions of this pattern found in New Zealand historic assemblages (Best 2002; Plowman 2000). Complete Willow pattern dinner plates (soup style) belonging to the King family can also be found amongst the Waimate Mission House material, with the same scalloped rims as those from the Te Puna Mission house cellar.

Several rim fragments from a straight-sided vessel (or coffee can) of the Wild Rose pattern (Coysh and Henrywood 1982: 401; Noel Hume 2001) and a single fragment from a table plate rim of the same pattern can be matched with a mug (or coffee can) displayed at the Waimate Mission House as King family memorabilia. This pattern was manufactured by a number of different potteries, and its popularity was well established by the 1830s. Noel Hume (2001) provides evidence of it first being used sometime between 1809 and 1823, while Coysh (1974: 48) gives a slightly later date, c. 1834–1844, pointing out that "This pattern, named after its border, came second only to the standard willow pattern in popularity between about 1830 and 1855."

Fragments of Broseley pattern hollow ware were also identified. Broseley presents a mirror image of the standard Willow pattern, with only two figures on the bridge instead of three, and was used more commonly on porcelain than on earthenware according to Coysh and Henrywood (1982: 62). Whiter (1970) states that Broseley was amongst Spode's early patterns, with other variations of it, including "Pale Broseley" introduced in 1817 and 1818, a date that varies little from Willow itself. At the Kerikeri Mission House, Broseley fragments were excavated from an early context dating between c. 1820–1832 (Best 2003a; Clunie pers. commun. 2002).

Other patterns identified include Muleteer, manufactured by Davenport, c. 1815–1830 (Coysh 1974: 32), Fiber, Cable, Rhine, mocha, edge-banded and shell-edged ware, while an Asiatic Pheasant patterned serving dish or ashet was recovered from above the cellar fill, post dating the occupation of the house itself. All these patterns are commonly recovered from New Zealand historic archaeological sites (Best 2002; Plowman 2000). While Coysh (1974) names Wild Rose as second in popularity to Willow pattern up to about 1855, he states elsewhere (Coysh and Henrywood 1982: 29) that in the second half of the nineteenth century and later, Asiatic Pheasant held this place in popularity. Coysh and Henrywood also list a large number of makers of this pattern as it was widely copied and produced prior to 1880.

The shell edged blue ware is also likely to date to the earlier decades of the nineteenth century. The same pattern has also been found in excavations at the Kerikeri Mission House (Best 1995, 1997, 2003a). Noel Hume (2000: 228) states that shell-edged plates were first produced in the late eighteenth century, and continued into the middle of the nineteenth century. Other examples of shell edged ware have been recovered from early (predating 1840) New Zealand contexts, from both the northern and southern extremes of the country (Fraser 2004; Harris 2005; Smith and Anderson 2007). The same pattern was also recovered from the Mission Houses Museum, Honolulu, illustrated (but not identified) in an archaeological report (Puette and Dye 2003: 13), and in whaling sites in Tasmania (Lawrence 2006).

Patterns such as Wild Rose and Muleteer have production dates of c. 1830s, a date that is concurrent with the move to the Te Puna mission house by the King family. However, some account needs to be taken of the time lag for the arrival of such wares in New Zealand from the country of manufacture, at a time when it could take 2 years for missionaries in the Bay to receive responses to their letters to the CMS in Britain.

While Brooks (1999, 2003) has examined the patterns of nineteenth century Staffordshire potteries in terms of their meaning and symbolism in relation to British identity, Klose and Malan (2000: 58, 2003) have looked at the same wares, recovered from nineteenth century Cape Town archaeological sites, as a "mirror of social class, values and trade networks, that may be compared with contemporary sites elsewhere." From the 1790s to the early 1900s, South Africa was a British colony. Even though the British population was in the minority for much of this time, by the middle of the century Cape Town was identifiably British and it "became the rage to copy everything English" (Klose and Malan 2000: 50). Ceramics excavated from Tennant St in urban Cape Town display similar patterns to those from Te Puna such as mocha, edge-banded wares, shell-edged and Willow, as well as other decorative techniques identified in New Zealand urban sites such as sponged and hand-painted white ware (Plowman 2000). In Cape Town, Willow pattern tableware predominates, as at Te Puna, in other nineteenth century New Zealand sites, and in households at Dolly's Creek, a gold mining township in Victoria, Australia, as well as whaling sites in Tasmania (Lawrence 2000, 2006). Klose and Malan's examination of mass-production and consumption in one corner of the globe during the nineteenth century raises useful questions about trade networks and nineteenth century globalization. As they note,

Studying the material culture of nineteenth-century colonies is related to a question of scale, ranging from the global dimension to richly textured local manifestations. An archaeology of the modern world must address the fact that objects, images and people circulated across oceans and through continents (Hall 2000). (Malan and Klose 2003: 191)

Nineteenth century ceramics, produced in Staffordshire potteries in Britain, provide an ideal marker of the extension of empire throughout the globe, from Hawaii to South Africa, to Australia and New Zealand.

Bottle Glass

The bottle glass, weighing a total of 106 kg, formed the largest component of the total artefact assemblage from the mission house, with a minimum number of 266 bottles recovered and a total of 26 of these complete (Table 5.5). Bottle glass fragments and complete bottles were classified by type according to glass color, base diameter and features and other bottle morphology according to the methods outlined in Smith (n.d.). Type 1 bottles (Table 5.5; Fig. 5.11) are of a dark olive glass, square bodied, with the pig-snout finish typical of the case gin

Table 5.5 Glass vessel types by identifying portions

Color	Type	Complete	MNI
Dark olive	1	7	28
	2	5	34
	3	5	68
	4	–	9
	5	5	9
	6	–	4
	7	–	4
	2–7?	–	65
Light olive	8–17	3	16
Green	18–20	1	4
Aqua	21–26	–	6
Clear	27–35	–	9
Opalescent	36–39	–	4
Blue	40–41	–	2
Blue (light)	42	–	1
White	43	–	1
Pink	44	–	1
Brown	45	–	1
Total		*26*	*266*

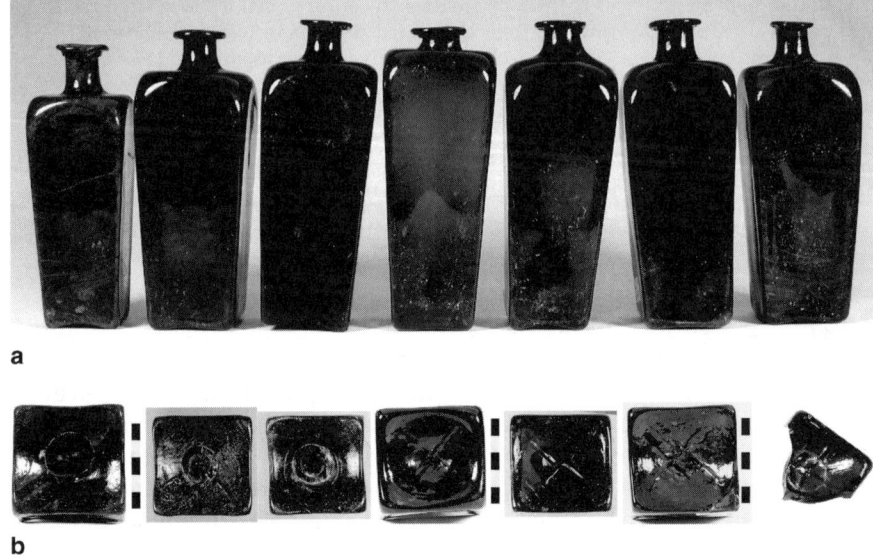

Fig. 5.11 Type 1 complete bottles and bases, Te Puna Mission House assemblage

Fig. 5.12 Type 2 and type 18 complete bottles, Te Puna Mission House assemblage

bottle. Bases (Fig. 5.11b) show glass pontil marks as well as mould marks, one of the same type as illustrated in Jones (2000; Fig. 14). Other dark olive bottles with a round cross-section, defined as types 2–7 according to a variety of sizes and base features, were the kind of bottle often described as "black beers" (Fig. 5.12; Middleton 2005a,b).

Morphology demonstrates that bottles in the Te Puna assemblage were manufactured by two main techniques, the cup or dip mould, developed in the late eighteenth century and used into the early nineteenth century, and the hinged three-piece mold, used from about 1821 until the mid to late nineteenth century (Jones 1986). It is also possible that some of the examples in this assemblage were free-blown, rather than blown into a mould. In these cases, there is no evidence of seams anywhere on the bottle, and the glass has a smooth, regular surface. The shape of the bottle may also be asymmetrical. The bottle shown in Fig. 5.13 is likely to have been made by this method. The uniformity of techniques used in manufacture of the bottles demonstrates that the Te Puna glass assemblage is consistently early, dating to the first half of the nineteenth century, with none of the glass showing features resulting from mechanized manufacture developed later in the nineteenth century. The majority of bottle bases were hand-tooled, many of these with a variety of different pontil marks. Few were molded or embossed. Many of the finishes were also simply constructed, with a string rim or similar lip. A seal embossed "Vieux Cognac" pointed to its origin on a French cognac bottle, and three other seals, one on a complete bottle, were embossed "Dumon F es F. Duran Vivez", suggesting a Portuguese or Spanish origin.

As there was no firmly established glass production industry in Australia until approximately 1872 (Morgan 1990: 10) and in New Zealand until the early twentieth century (Tasker 1989), all bottles used here up until this time came from Europe or North America, a valuable commodity. Jones (1986) states that empty bottles were shipped out of Britain throughout the nineteenth century, stowed loose on board ships, the cost of exporting them barely covered.

All the complete bottles were recovered from the cellar, and nearly all of these from the floor, suggesting that many of the bottles were stored in the cellar and discarded there after the house was abandoned. Other bottle fragments were found throughout the fill layers and in the eastern area of the excavation. The case gin bottles, found in situ on the cellar floor lying end-on-end in proximity with metal staples, were likely to have been stacked in wooden boxes. This suggests that they were stored in the cellar as a resource, but finally no longer needed.

There is a certain austerity and consistency about this assemblage. Only one of the vessels was likely to be a pickle or oil jar, only one fragment was possibly tableware (a tumbler), and only two bottle types are likely to be from perfume or similar style bottles, amongst an artifact assemblage where the presence of women is identified by thimbles, pins, beads, buttons, and cooking items. The glass assemblage suggests almost no decorative or ornamental items. This points to an

a   b

Fig. 5.13 Type 8 bottle, refitted from two fragments, showing a double string rim finish and glass pontil mark on the base, Te Puna Mission House assemblage

economy at Te Puna where resources were scarce and basic domestic items not readily discarded, as the historic record also testifies. It indicates an austerity and lack of the frivolous within the missionary world, or at least at the Te Puna mission. The consistently early nature of the assemblage demonstrates that most of the bottles were likely to have been acquired during the first decade or so of the Te Puna settlement, or acquired earlier and brought there from the Oihi mission, rather than accumulating from use or consumption during the approximately 40 years of habitation in the mission house.

Alcohol Bottles: Consumption or Conservation?

Despite remonstrances about alcohol, it was acceptable for missionary consumption, in addition to being considered medicinal. In 1816, John King complained to his CMS mentor Daniel Wilson that he and Hannah had "Not a drop of wine or spirits to help either of us out of our sickness" (King n.d.c), and in 1834 Anne Wilson (n.d.), writing from Puriri to her husband John, noted that "There was no brandy in the *Karire* [missionary boat] for anyone. Perhaps you had best get some." Alcohol was also considered appropriate for daily use. Easdale (1991: 52) notes that hospitality received by Marianne Williams at Kerikeri in 1823 included "English bottled porter." Alcohol was purchased in bulk by the CMS and divided amongst its members. In 1827, the CMS (n.d.a) wrote to Marsden

> The mission Families wish to purchase on private account to be divided and charged to their respective accounts in New Zealand
> 1/2 pipe Best port Wine, and if 1/2 pipe cannot be procured a Whole Pipe may be sent
> 1/4 Cask of Best Madeira

A "pipe" in this context was a tube of wood used as a container for liquids (Oxford English Dictionary). Alcohol bought in this way may have been decanted into bottles in the process of being divided amongst the mission families. As seen above (ceramics section), William Yate's 1832 order for crockery included one dozen "plain pint decanters" and 30 dozen each "plain strong tumblers and wine glasses," also items purchased on the missionaries' private accounts. Other references to purchases of alcohol do not appear regularly in the CMS archives, and it is not an item listed in the store accounts supplied to the mission families.

In 1819, Marsden (Elder 1932: 180, 231) extolled the virtues of New Zealand's suitability for growing the grapevine, and planted "about a hundred grape vines of different kinds" near the Kerikeri settlement on this visit, along with fruit trees. The vines were in leaf before he left about 2 months later. Wine was also required for communion. The Waimate Mission House has in its collections a small wooden barrel and funnel noted as the vessel used by John King to carry wine for communion to villages lying beyond Rangihoua and Te Puna.

The cellar of a mission house filled with the remains of over two hundred bottles of styles commonly known as 'case gins' and 'black beers', as well as cognac and champagne bottles raises questions about consumption, use and the domestic economy of missionary life.

As in the case of the ceramics, the archaeology again demonstrates aspects of the material culture and economy of the mission household rarely revealed in other sources. In this case, the presence of so many bottles in the cellar is a surprising aspect of the archaeological assemblage, and presents the possibility of the consumption of a large, or regular, amount of alcohol by members of the King family, away from the eyes of other members of the Church Missionary Society. This may explain, or may have contributed to, the apparent social ostracism of Hannah King by the likes of Marianne Williams (Middleton 2007a). However, in an environment where domestic resources were scarce, and items like ceramics appear to have been precious, bottles may also have been containers valued for use in a variety of domestic tasks. Bottles of late eighteenth/early nineteenth century manufacture may have arrived at Oihi with John and Hannah King and other missionaries in 1814, and subsequently been moved to Te Puna with the family. While the only liquid included in the store accounts is oil, that is whale oil, used for lighting, other household liquids would have included water, milk, vinegar, wine (for communion as well as household consumption), medicines, and cleaners such as lye.

Jones (1986) has also noted that large quantities of old bottles survive in private cellars in England and points out that vessels commonly known as wine or beer bottles may have contained a number of different liquids apart from alcohol, including vinegar, mineral waters and oil, and may have had a number of different uses as containers, in a number of different contexts. Reuse of bottles was commonplace throughout the nineteenth and up to the middle of the twentieth centuries (Busch 1987). Analysis or interpretation of glass assemblages on the basis of "original contents" is limited, in terms of both vessel form and typology, as well as the ongoing use such vessels may have had in historical contexts, in a household economy where a number of liquids were used and few containers were available.

No similar bottle glass assemblage has been recovered from any of the other mission sites discussed here, such as Waimate or Kerikeri, and examination of the New Zealand archaeological literature reveals that there are few other bottle glass assemblages of a comparative date, that is, from contexts predating 1840 (Best 2002; Bedford 1986, 1994; Brassey 1989; Brassey and Macready 1994; Felgate 1998; Prickett 1981, 1994; Robinson 1995). The unique nature of the Te Puna bottle glass assemblage, with its consistently early nineteenth century bottle glass features and lack of the whole range of domestic bottle types that constitute later nineteenth century assemblages, suggests that although they may have arrived complete with alcohol contents that was consumed, the bottles recovered from the Te Puna cellar were used as containers for a range of household liquids, and may have been the only type of container available to the house's residents. The low number of stoneware vessels recovered (an MNI of only three) also suggests this, stoneware bottles being the other common liquid container of the nineteenth century.

Although glass bottles may have been a resource during the years when the mission house was inhabited by the King family, by the later decades of the nineteenth century, when the house was abandoned and demolished, these may no longer have been considered of use. The Bay of Islands economy had changed over the course of the nineteenth century. By the 1870s, the likely date of the abandonment and demolition of the mission house, the Bay of Islands had a thriving European population, with sources of European goods at a number of different locations. Old bottles may no longer have had a domestic use and the cellar may have been considered a dump for such unwanted items after the house was abandoned.

CMS missionaries regarded the presence of the shipping in the Bay of Islands as anathema, usually avoiding both crew and captains as an evil influence amongst their flocks. However, the large quantity of bottles in the cellar does point to a trading relationship with ships coming into the Bay of Islands, the most likely source of such bottles being ships trading full bottles or off-loading empty bottles. Te Puna played an important role in the early years of the nineteenth century as an anchorage for ships (Lee 1915; Middleton 2003; Savage 1973 (1807)), but even in 1833 the Rev. Joseph Orton (n.d.) when visiting the Bay of Islands, complained that the Te Puna mission "was by no means a promising station; its immediate connection with a roadstead for Shipping has proved very detrimental to the successful operations of the missionaries." Von Huegel and Marshall's mention of Maori women in relation to the *Alligator* when they visited the following year, 1834, reinforces Orton's point. Consumption or purchase of alcohol may have been another factor in this disapproval.

TE PUNA: ABANDONMENT AND DEMOLITION

Recovery of artifacts from the Te Puna mission house site, and in particular its cellar, has revealed the detritus of everyday life there, beginning in 1832 when the King and Shepherd families moved to the houses they had spent several years building on the shore of Rangihoua Bay. The same artifacts, examined alongside documentary sources, facilitate the recreation of daily life at the mission station. Although the archival records provide the evidence for the move from Oihi to Te Puna, nothing is written about the demise of the mission station over the years following John King's death in 1854, when his children remained living there (Chap. 4). During these years, John Wheeler King and his unmarried sisters Hannah and Mary were the likely inhabitants of the mission house, with the addition of their brother William Spence King and his family between the years 1867 and 1871 (Berry 1981; *Weekly News* 1896). Samuel Leigh King, who also like his brother John and his two sisters, never married, was also living at Te Puna where he died in 1871 at the age of 49, the cause noted as "debility". He was buried in the family plot at Oihi (Berry 1981). By 1874, the year John Tollis Hansen purchased the King family land and the 16 acres of CMS land, including the mission house (LINZ n.d.), the King family had evidently all moved on. Anything of value, including family china and furniture once used at Oihi and Te Puna, stayed in the ownership of the youngest daughter, Elizabeth Marsden King, who bequeathed many of these to the Waimate mission house (Berry 1981).

The nature of the artifact assemblage demonstrates its early nineteenth century origins, consistent with abandonment of the mission house by this date. This has been shown to be particularly so in the case of the nail assemblage (Middleton 2005c). This suggests that by about 1874, or some time soon after, the remains of the mission house were demolished. The house may have been in a poor state by this time; even in June 1850 John King had complained to the committee of the "bad repair" of the house (Chap. 3). Chimney bricks, weatherboard timbers, and roof shingles were pushed into the cellar cavity on top of the household goods such as bottles and barrels that had accumulated and been abandoned there. The large round tree trunks, used as posts to support the main structure of the house, were pulled out of the postholes around the perimeter of the cellar; as they were removed, some of the old bottles stored there collapsed into the postholes. Other goods had also been left behind or lost; books perhaps, although nothing remained of them some 130 years later; clothing and shoes apparently rotted, leaving only the visible markers of buttons and buckles; coins, never of much use in the mission days of the Bay, anyway, were abandoned with other useless mementoes and forgotten items – a few old pins, thimbles once used by children to stitch clothing and samplers, discarded clay pipes; glass trade beads, once stored on a shelf, stayed tucked into the clay recess of its support. After much of the upper structure was thrust into the cellar, a fire burned in one corner, reducing some of the timbers and other remains to ashes; a few sherds of broken china showed the fire's effects, but still cross matched with undamaged sherds from beyond the cellar to reconstruct a cup, a plate, a bowl, a chamber pot. The fire died out before it got to the square glass bottles stacked end-on-end in wooden crates on the cellar floor, although other bottles smashed when the timbers and bricks collapsed. Some of these items, useful for a variety of household purposes, were moved from Oihi to Te Puna in the early days, along with all the other household goods, either in a small boat sailing or rowed the short distance across the bay, or perhaps carried over the pathway that runs above the cliff, between the two mission sites. Outside the cellar, a lean to and outbuilding stood to the east; a fence may once have run between these. The fence and outbuilding remained standing after the demolition of the house itself. Tools were left leaning against it, or against the wall; a pickaxe, a bolt, a long hinge off a door. When the wall collapsed, they fell onto the ground surface, covered in time by topsoil and grass, as was the cobbled surface alongside. In the postholes supporting the outbuilding and lean-to, the smaller timbers rotted away, while the fragments of broken goashore cooking pot, brought to Oihi in the first days of the mission, were used to shore up the supports after it was no longer of use in the kitchen. An old iron was put to the same use – in the days before the mixing of cement, these discarded, heavy cast iron things were useful for other purposes, such as building foundations, too. With the leveling of the structure into the cellar and eventual demise of the outbuilding, the site of the mission house was incorporated into the surrounding pasture, nothing marking the surface to indicate what had once stood there, apart from the remnants of the garden alongside.

The mission past of Te Puna was subsumed into the renowned history of the Oihi mission, identified and memorialized by the Marsden Cross, erected in 1914 to commemorate the centenary of Samuel Marsden's first church service and the reserve status of the mission land. While Oihi became something of a pilgrimage destination for following generations, the significant "mythic" history of Te Puna was forgotten, the site of the mission erased from the landscape.

CONCLUSION (SECTION 2)

The archaeology of the mission house reveals long discarded every-day objects that evoke daily activities. The household, once considered an unproblematic realm controlled by the male head of the household where women carried out chores of little consequence, such as food preparation (Allison 1999; Hendon 1996; Spencer-Wood 1999, 2004) is revealed as a domain of the wider society, where the values of nine-teenth century mission life were maintained, revealed in items of mate-rial culture and the documentary record. Both men and women carried out "culturally recognised tasks" in culturally constructed gender roles (Hendon 1996: 46). While the analysis of gender is not a central focus here, the historically specific (Lawrence 1999) roles of men and women in the domestic realm are significant. The archaeology of the mission household demonstrates the presence of women, a voice that is missing in the official documentary record of the CMS. Within the wider CMS society, women were subordinated, but played a vitally important role in constructing and maintaining home life, in the "cult of true woman-hood" and the cult of domesticity that was central to nineteenth century Christian ideology and the imperial mission (Davidoff and Hall1991; Fitts 2001; Grimshaw 1989a,b; McClintock 1995; Spencer-Wood 1999). At the same time, Hannah King was further subordinated within the class structure of the CMS in the Bay of Islands (Middleton 2007a). The material culture of the archaeological assemblage as well as items displayed at the Kerikeri and Waimate mission houses brings the pres-ence of Hannah King and her daughters to life, while John King's story is more readily accessible through his journals and letters.

Food preparation is often defined as an essential function of the household, or even "its primary reason for existing" (Hendon 1996: 50), and forms a fundamental part of the economy of any social system. CMS records along with faunal remains and kitchen artifacts facilitate the reconstruction of the mission house economy and the wider CMS econ-omy in the Bay of Islands. Accounts from the CMS store and returns to the committee meetings supply a detailed record of most goods that were used in the mission stations. Goods were supplied to the missions from the Kerikeri store. Returns to the committee detailed how these goods had been disposed of and what remained "on hand", the mission in effect functioning as a trading post. The accounts and returns are used to expand on artifacts recovered from the archaeological record to produce a more detailed reconstruction of everyday life at the Te Puna mission, along with objects held in the collections of the NZHPT at the Kerikeri and Waimate Mission Houses. All the goods supplied from the store were sourced from Britain or Port Jackson, as were the ceramics and bottles, which do not appear on the regular accounts or returns.

The large number of bottles recovered from the cellar suggests that the consumption of alcohol may have been a regular event at the mission. An alternative or concurrent explanation may be that these were used as containers of household liquids, stored for use and reuse, one of the few types of container available at the time. The manufacture evidence dates the majority of the bottle types to the first half of the nineteenth century, and the lack of other household glass such as sauce and pickle bottles differentiates this assemblage from other later nineteenth century glass assemblages. The lack of decorative and nonfunctional glass items points to the austerity of the assemblage and to the austerity of the economy.

The small number of ceramics recovered from the mission house site, and the table wares in the collections of the NZHPT at the Kerikeri and Waimate Mission Houses provenanced to the King family suggest that household china was valued and cared for in the household, perhaps difficult to replace if broken, or an expensive item to be charged to John King's "personal account." This is confirmed by the fact that no complete ceramic items were recovered from the archaeological context, although items were refitted from fragments evidently broken prior to deposition. These same matching wares point to one of the markers of gentility, that is, complete sets of china tableware, as well as the matching toilet set, provenanced to Hannah King. Ceramic assemblages have been examined elsewhere (Klose and Malan 2000; Malan and Klose 2003) as markers in the process of globalisation that occurred with the expansion of the British Empire into the New World. The Te Puna ceramic assemblage has similarities to assemblages excavated from nineteenth century contexts in urban Cape Town, providing evidence connecting this remote mission station with other parts of the British colonial world.

It is interesting to note that there is very little evidence of artifacts relating to children in the archaeological assemblage, in a household where there were a number of children in the King family as well as children from the *pa*. This is similar to Lawrence's (2000: 135) findings at Dolly's Creek, where "no archaeological evidence of children" was found, although the site related to families. At Te Puna, only two of the items recovered from the investigation can be associated with children, the very small thimble and the clay marble. The thimble is not an item associated with children's play, but rather with diligence in sewing clothing or perhaps a sampler of the sort done by Elizabeth King. It is clear that a family unit lived at Te Puna for a long time, with a number of children from the *pa* continuously present. The lack of this kind of material in the Te Puna assemblage has several possible explanations: that the mission economy did not lend itself to the purchase of toys that would persist in the archaeological record, such as teacups and dolls with porcelain limbs; that the children at the mission may have had wooden or fabric toys which were no longer evident in the archaeological record; or that toys were not present at all in the Te Puna household. This adds to the austere and stringent economy of the household suggested by the whole assemblage. The presence of the marble suggests that toys may have been present, but no evidence of them remains in the archaeological context. Children's toys do not appear in the store accounts, but are the kind of item the Williams children may have received in boxes sent by relatives in England, mentioned by Marianne Williams from time to time.

The lack of artifacts relating to children, along with the austerity of the glass and the ceramic assemblages and the signs that some of these wares were of seconds quality, provides evidence of a frugal, subsistence household without access to luxury goods. The Te Puna economy was a poor one, and the Kings stood on the lower rungs of the missionary social scale. Basic rations such as flour, sugar, and tea, which Colenso (1888; Chap. 2) stated were barely adequate, provided from the mission store, were supplemented with foods locally available. Seafood and fish was collected from the nearby shoreline. Pigs were purchased from Maori and slaughtered at the mission along with other meat like beef. Rabbit may have been consumed, as it was earlier at Oihi, and vegetables and fruit were grown in the garden. Although the assemblage demonstrates frugality, it also points to domestic work associated with the effort involved in maintaining appropriate standards of appearance, even in a remote household where visitors were few. This was an essential aspect of the culture of the CMS, and an essential role for missionary women. Artifacts associated with women's work like ironing point to the other parts in this process, that is, washing, and starching clothes and linen. Buttons, pins, and the netting set displayed at Waimate Mission House are the surviving archaeological evidence of hand-sewn clothing and finely detailed needlework.

Where is the evidence of the mission station in the archaeological assemblage? The assemblage does not in itself provide any particular confirmation of mission activities. While the small number of Maori artifacts has been interpreted as the presence of Maori in the household, these could equally have been interpreted as curio collecting. The slate pencils and fragments do not in themselves provide proof of mission school activities. It is only through the combined archival and archaeological evidence that a full interpretation of the household activities can be achieved.

Discussion and Conclusion | 6

The archeology and history of the Te Puna mission clearly demonstrates the nature of the early CMS missions in New Zealand. Te Puna was typical of mission stations in the Bay of Islands in the first half of the nineteenth century: a simple house lived in by the missionary, his wife, and their family, along with a small number of children from the nearby pa. In this way the missionary and his wife presented the model of the ideal monogamous Christian family, the foundation of civilization, to the "heathen," essential to the converting, civilizing, and eventually, colonizing processes. The "rituals of domesticity" (McClintock 1995: 35) of the mission station are shown in both the archeological assemblage and the archival material. The journals and reports that John King sent back to the CMS in London detail his battles against the "Prince of Darkness," who appeared in the various cultural practices and beliefs of Maori. Success was demonstrated when these practices changed and died out, alongside conversions to Christianity. The archeological assemblage demonstrates these rituals through artifacts associated with the daily practice of the cult of domesticity - the matching sets of ceramic tablewares and teawares, the irons used to produce smooth fabrics, thimbles and pins used to make lace trimmed caps and bonnets, worn to show the modesty of the married woman. At the same time it also shows the marginalization of the Kings within the wider framework of missionary society, which attempted to replicate the class structure of its home society. However, this attempt at replication occurred in a new situation that gave the likes of John and Hannah King the opportunity for choice and agency. It allowed them to purchase land and establish a greater degree of economic independence than they would have had in Britain. The presence of the mission also provided Maori with new opportunities that they pursued to their own advantages.

Te Puna demonstrates the "household" type of mission station, also found in the CMS and other evangelical missions throughout the Pacific and in parts of Protestant North America. This mission was a

A. Middleton, *Te Puna: A New Zealand Mission Station*,
DOI:10.1007/978-0-387-77622-4, © Springer Science+Business Media, LLC 2008

humble, austere affair, as contrasted with the "institutional" mission found in Spanish North America and Australia, often associated (in North America) with monumental architecture, highly institutionalized organization, and the incarceration of inmates.

As McClintock (1995) has noted, domestic rituals, encapsulating the cult of domesticity and practiced across the globe, brought women and indigenous people into a colonized state. Households are mirrors of the ways people saw their worlds, representing their values and culture (Deetz 1982), one of the most basic places for sharing and acquiring (or learning) culture. The Te Puna mission household was the place where CMS culture and values were replicated within the King family and passed on to other household members, such as the children of the pa who lived there. While the role of wives such as Hannah King was to maintain material standards of propriety within the private realm of the home, missionary wives also carried out public roles in the missionary world, teaching school and visiting villages, as John King's journals and the eulogy to his wife demonstrated.

The archeological assemblage represents a diverse range of activities, and the artifacts do not demonstrate that this was a specialist mission site. Primarily it represents a household economy in an isolated rural location, with tools associated with farming and pastoralism. While artifacts associated with the work of the mission - slate pencils and boards and glass trade beads - were also found, they do not present evidence of the mission on their own account. This is provided in association with the documentary material. The material culture has demonstrated the presence of women and men within the household; however, Maori and children remain barely visible. The Oihi mission and its later continuation at Te Puna were both established because of the proximity of the Maori population at the pa, but the artifact assemblage from Te Puna reveals little direct evidence of Maori themselves. Obsidian and other flaked tools in the assemblage suggest the presence of Maori at the mission house. However, Maori were living there within a European context; the lack of Maori artifacts speaks loudly about this changing cultural context into which they were incorporated. The Maori presence is also demonstrated through indirect evidence such as food remains like pig bones and shellfish, trade items in the daily accounts and the purchase of labor, as well as schooling. King's reports consistently record the numbers of Maori residents at the mission, with names also noted from time to time. John King's details of his regular visits to villages along the coastline are also a reminder of the presence of Maori in the wider landscape.

The documentary material also indicates that the mission functioned as a trading post, with quantities of goods stored to be used to pay for food and labor from Maori, as well as extraordinary events such as the purchase of a slave. This was a frontier household, with an economy based on goods and exchange, largely controlled by the CMS, with goods supplied from Britain and Port Jackson, bringing New Zealand into the sphere of a global material culture and economy. At the same time, in the early years of the mission there was a "black" economy that functioned outside the CMS to some extent. This was originally demonstrated in the trade in muskets that the missionaries participated in, and possibly continued in the "alcohol" bottles in the Te Puna assemblage.

The artifacts in the Te Puna assemblage have a demonstrably British provenance, as the documentary evidence confirms, with Staffordshire ceramics displaying the patterns of idyllic pastoral scenes and a bottle assemblage manufactured in English glass factories. This is symbolized by the heavy, cumbersome George III penny, recovered from the Te Puna cellar, on the other side of the world from its British origins. This British provenance is also tempered with bottles of a European origin, as shown by the embossed seals, and one clay pipe stem with a Sydney maker.

While the mission house was built from local timber, with bricks and hearthstones possibly from Port Jackson, little of the assemblage reveals adaptation to the New Zealand environment. This is to be expected at a time well before any local manufacturing of goods. Faunal remains also suggest a dependence on traditional English meat sources, such as pork, beef, sheep, and rabbit. At the same time small amounts of locally sourced food such as fish, shellfish, and eel appear. These amounts are much smaller than one could expect to find from an equivalent Maori context of the same time period.

Missions throughout the new world have been held responsible for the beginnings of colonization and cultural change, as was the case in New Zealand. At Te Puna, the simple assemblage of the mission represents New Zealand's grand historical themes of colonization and the extraordinary times of first contact between Maori and Pakeha. The examination of the material culture and economy of the Te Puna mission household has revealed the actual processes of colonization in daily life and everyday events, reflected in items of material culture such as spades and other tools, ceramic tea wares, cast iron cooking pots and irons, buttons, thimbles, and pins, as well as in the processes of the mission - the schooling, church services, purchase of food and domestic labor, the purchase of land, building of houses, and the teaching of needlework. While history has glorified (and critiqued) the signing of the Treaty of Waitangi in the Bay of Islands in February 1840 as the definitive moment of colonization and the seminal event of the Maori and Pakeha relationship, historical archeology reveals the beginnings of these processes at least two decades earlier, in the household and daily life of the mission, established within the patronage of Rangihoua pa. These "grand narratives" took place in an austere, material manner, within the mission household and the broader landscape of the subsistence farm.

Dietler (1998) provides insight into the processes of colonization, the predicted and unpredicted outcomes of cultural contact. A focus on consumption in the initial phases of cross-cultural encounters leads to the "entanglement of indigenous and colonial societies" from which the conditions for other unanticipated kinds of colonial relationships develop (Dietler 1998: 298). Colonization was not a systematic, planned activity but a "congeries of activities and a conjunction of outcomes that, though related and at times coordinated, were usually diffuse, disorganized, and even contradictory," through which structures of colonial dependency and domination were gradually created (Dirks in Dietler 1998: 298). Dietler (1998: 299) describes colonization as

> an active process of creative transformation and manipulation played out by individuals and social groups with a variety of competing interests and strategies of action embedded in local political relations, cultural perceptions, and cosmologies. People use alien contacts for their own political agendas and they give new meanings to borrowed cultural elements according to their own cosmologies.

Te Pahi, Ruatara, Hongi Hika, and their like were agents in the Maori world. Their forays into the European arena were undertaken as leaders, in order to explore the benefits of new technologies and goods available. On the other side, Governor King, Samuel Marsden, and John King also acted as individuals, driven to their interaction with Maori by different social and political forces. Governor King was ordered to bring New Zealanders to Norfolk Island to teach flax weaving. Tuki and Huru, and later Te Pahi impressed him. His parting gifts to Tuki and Huru of potatoes and pigs, and subsequent gifts to Te Pahi of the same kind of goods, contributed to the growing Maori trade in provisioning ships, and the ascendancy of the place of Te Puna and Te Pahi as principal chief in the Bay of Islands.

Maori agency continued as Marsden and the first missionaries came to Rangihoua at the invitation of Ruatara, who planned to export wheat to Port Jackson and to build a European-style town on the slopes of Te Puna, under his own jurisdiction as chief. These ambitions were cut short by his death, from an illness likely to have been of western causes, an event Salmond (1997: 508) describes as a "cosmological collision," where ideas of Christianity and *tapu* competed in the ether. At the same time, a more earthed debate was also taking place. Missionaries were desirable to Maori of Rangihoua not for the catechisms, prayers, and Bibles they brought with them, but for the metal axes and other tools their blacksmith forged at Oihi. As Marsden had realized, the ideas of Christianity would be unacceptable unless dressed in more attractive attire, that of material goods and the "spirit of trade" or commerce that accompanied "civilization." While Owens (1968: 37) considered that literacy was the Trojan Horse that carried the "otherwise unacceptable ideas" of Christianity into the Maori camp, Binney (1969: 152) retorted a year later that this Trojan Horse was trade. Binney (1969: 152) considered that "missionaries succeeded in making themselves indispensable to the Maoris through trade," skills and techniques which appeared to be ideologically neutral. Examination of missionary journals and accounts of the CMS store and the returns made to the committee meetings demonstrates that this was the case. Children were rewarded for attendance at school and church services with fishhooks and glass beads. Adults traded potatoes and pigs for iron tools, and Maori labor was also exchanged for these goods. However, the idea that this Trojan horse fooled or tricked Maori needs to be qualified. Marsden's idea that the mission might be able to control Maori through material goods was often ironically transposed. As this study has demonstrated, in the early days of the mission, missionaries were often at the mercy of their Maori patrons. Maori retained and still today do retain agency and control, taking advantage of economic opportunities. Maori trade grew under the influence of Hongi Hika, as did the ascendancy of the greater Ngapuhi *iwi* with Hongi as nominal leader (Hohepa 1999; Cloher 2003). Hongi's quest for *mana* and *utu* took him to Britain seeking muskets, and drew the missionary Kendall into his sphere. The Ngapuhi control of food supplies, such as pork and potatoes, and their quest for muskets, usually traded from visiting ships, led to missionaries at Oihi and Kerikeri being drawn into this exchange, and was a further cause of conflict among the mission brethren.

Mission literature identifies Henry Williams as a strong leader of the CMS, responsible for the ultimate success of the missions, and his arrival in the Bay of Islands with his wife Marianne in 1823 was one of the turning points in CMS policy. Henry Williams did away with Marsden's strategy of commerce before conversion to Christianity. He was clear that "Christianization" should take priority above commerce. This was all very well for Williams, but had he arrived in 1814 his terms may have proved quite unacceptable to Maori. Certain factors stood in Williams' favor. From about 1823, the trade in muskets in the Bay of Islands declined, possibly because warriors were all equipped with a gun by then (Binney 1969). As the committee minutes note, blankets were a more desirable trade item in the late 1820s than hardware or metal goods. This was better basis for mission trade, and contributed to the economic independence of the missions, a crucial factor in their success or failure. Williams built a ship in order for the missions to obtain food supplies directly from Port Jackson as well as other parts of the country, contributing to mission economic independence. The *Herald* was launched in 1827, followed by two others, the *Karere* and *Columbine*, after the Herald's demise on the Hokianga bar. The death of Hongi in 1828, five years after Williams' arrival, also brought about a new dynamic. During Hongi's lifetime, missionaries were suffered only on Maori terms; Hongi considered that Christianity was irrelevant to a nation of warriors (Binney 1969; Hohepa 1999; Cloher 2003). After his death, the balance of power began to change as the number of conversions to Christianity grew, and missions could obtain food independently from Maori.

John King, a rather humble man from a small rural village in Britain, was driven to join the CMS by the social forces he was subject to, those of evangelical revivalism at the turn of the eighteenth century, as were many others of the time. Samuel Marsden was a more important link in the chain of revivalists. His networks encompassed NSW, Britain, the Pacific, and New Zealand as well as several missionary societies, the CMS, LMS, and WMS. Through the dynamics of his friendships with Te Pahi and Ruatara, through, in terms of Maori cosmology, the intermingling of the *hau*, Marsden was compelled to find the resources to establish an evangelical mission to New Zealand, under the patronage of Ruatara and subsequently Hongi Hika. Due to these "cultural entanglements" (Dietler 1998: 298) and first exchanges, the transformations and events that led to colonization were set in motion.

For missionaries trade was the means to gain access to the prime target of conversion of Maori to Christianity and to wage a war on Maori social customs. Practices such as *hahunga, hakari*, and *tangi* came under attack and by the mid 1830s appeared to be less commonly practiced, or perhaps had gone to ground. However, a decade later John King was complaining about the revival of "old customs," and as Oppenheim (1973) has demonstrated, traditional customs persist into the present in altered forms. As elsewhere in the newly Christian world, as had taken place in Hawaii and Tahiti, syncretic forms of Christianity appeared in the Bay of Islands, incorporating aspects of the new religion along with traditional Maori customs.

The Te Puna assemblage represents the arrival of the "global spirit of commerce," the arrival of the first days of the global "consumer society" (Comaroff and Comaroff 1991). As the Comaroffs (1991: 9) explain:

> The impact of Protestant evangelists as harbingers of industrial capitalism lay in the fact that their civilizing mission was simultaneously symbolic and practical, theological and temporal. ...[These goods and techniques] were vehicles of a moral economy that celebrated the global spirit of commerce, the commodity, and the imperial marketplace. Indeed it is in the signifying role of evangelical practice - often very mundane, material practice - that we begin to find an answer to the most basic, most puzzling question about the historical agency of Christian missionaries: how is it that they, like other colonial functionaries, wrought such far-reaching political, social, and economic transformations in the absence of concrete resources of much consequence?

Settler society in New Zealand provides an example of a historicized study of a local context in the manner that Beaudry (2003: 294) has called for, leading to a more "nuanced understanding of the plurality of colonizing endeavors and their continuing effects" (Thomas in Beaudry 2003: 294). As Gibbons (2002: 7) points out,

> The New Zealand past since Europeans first appeared over the horizon is not *sui generis*, but a component of a much wider process, the expansion of European power into the global arena from the fifteenth century onwards.

The CMS settlers predated the post-1840 settler society Gibbons discusses, but anticipated and embodied significant aspects of it. John King's journals and reports clearly articulate his attachment to place, his connection to Te Puna, partly because of the family burials at Oihi but also for other more subtle reasons; his relationship to the people of Rangihoua Pa, his relationship with the place. King also expresses the same kind of connections for his children (although they have left no record of this themselves), through their association with the land and its people, as Richard Davis also did. Gibbons (2002: 8) considers that later generations born into or brought up within the settler society differ from the first generation of migrants, "very unsettled people" who have left behind much of what is meaningful and familiar in their lives, that is "kin, community, and accustomed landscape." While migrants make efforts to transform their surroundings into something similar to their homelands, the later generations have

> no direct experience of the old world, or very little, as an internalized, remembered frame of reference, so they cannot be shocked by the contrast between old and new to the extent the migrants once were. Nor, as a consequence, do they feel so obsessively impelled to transform the 'wilderness'. (Gibbons 2002: 8)

In this sense, King's children can be seen to "become 'native,' to belong to this place"; as John King claimed in 1842 (Chap. 3), the "Natives have always considered them as virtually belonging to the Tribe they were born among." They and later generations became Pakeha, the light-skinned people Maori first acknowledged arriving on the shores in the late eighteenth and nineteenth centuries (Hall n.d.), and later as non-Maori partners in the Treaty of Waitangi (King 2003). This hybridization of the migrant from settler to Pakeha is created through the relationship with Maori and with place.

John and Hannah King and their family anticipated the later settler society in other ways, through their farming and subsistence practices, and the transformation of the Te Puna landscape that predicted the later land transformation on a nation-wide scale through fern and bush clearance in order to establish pastoral farming and the rural economy that the country came to depend upon. CMS missionaries, despite their claim of holding Maori land in trust for its original owners, also began the process of alienating Maori from their land (Walker 1990). Maori and settlers had incompatible ways of using the land, and competed for its possession (Sinclair 1969). Maori cultivated small areas, and relied on the interwoven network of rights to much larger areas for resources that the forest and coast offered, while settlers burnt the forest and fern land to plant grass seed. "To the settlers, land was money; but to the Maoris it was life itself and more" (Sinclair 1969: 113). The typical nineteenth century settler farm holding has echoes of the King family farm:

> The small farm of a few acres, worked by the owner, or lessee, and his family, became the characteristic unit of European agriculture, market gardening and dairying. Sometimes the family would live off their land; more often, perhaps, the men would supplement their income by casual labouring, and by other means, such as buying a team of bullocks and contracting to plough for neighbouring farmers. According to Sir George Grey the majority of the population consisted of these small landed proprietors. (Sinclair 1969: 95)

These settlers startled members of the English upper classes by their republican attitudes and their "delight in a forced equality" (Sinclair 1969: 96), anathema to the original intentions of the New Zealand Company. While there were rich and poor among the settlers, there was little that resembled the English class system. The reality of owning one's own piece of land was a strong incentive for migration and settlement for Britain's urban poor, and came to represent the ability to climb into the middle class of this new "classless" society. To the nineteenth century settler New Zealand represented the "ideal society," a country of Arcadian natural abundance where working class, laboring people could be independent and the middle class free from anxiety and the fear of economic failure (Alley and Hall 1941; Arnold 1981, 1994; Fairburn 1989; King 2003). The myth of this Arcadian society (Fairburn 1989) drove a quest for freehold ownership of land, an aspiration of many English tenant farmers, and the espousal of the yeoman world and countryside (Arnold 1994).

Arnold (1994: 281) considers "the emerging triumph of the yeoman ideal" the most significant trend of the late nineteenth century settlers' world, where bush frontiers were being cleared for new domains and the "enterprising landless laborer" could work his way to owning a substantial mixed farm, focused on a practical family life and community conviviality. John King, born in the eighteenth century, a humble man from a small English village who reminded Richard Taylor (n.d.) of "an English yeoman" on his first visit to Te Puna in 1839, represents this later nineteenth century settler ideal.

This examination of New Zealand mission archeology provides a detailed description of the material culture and economy of a New Zealand settler household over the period from 1832 to about 1874. This time span frames the transition that took place from early European settlement to formal colonization, providing perhaps the first detailed example of the process of "becoming Pakeha" for the members of one missionary family.

However, the archival record of the detailed CMS store accounts provides an excellent source to expand and contextualize not only the material culture and trading economy of the Te Puna mission, but also of the wider CMS in the first decades of the mission. This is a rich source that has not yet been exploited to its full archeological potential.

The initial contact between Maori and European in the Bay of Islands and the role that the CMS mission played in the processes of colonization have also been examined. In this respect, the CMS mission in New Zealand embodied many of the contradictions that missions in other parts of the New World have demonstrated. Within the mission itself, the class distinctions of the home society were reproduced. The mission played an important role in bringing innovative skills to Maori society, such as literacy, along with new items of material culture. As part of this process, missionaries participated in the commodification of Maori land and watched the burgeoning settler population, leading to the eventual ceding of sovereignty by Maori. While missionaries had seen themselves as protectors of Maori, guarding them from the effects of colonization, they found themselves part of this process. Some of these contradictions are mirrored in the moves of the mission from Oihi to Te Puna, and Te Puna's transition from Maori land to mission station and then to pastoral landscape.

The study of Te Puna initially placed the mission within a Maori physical and cosmological landscape. Over time, this landscape changed to become a mission station and subsistence farm within a surrounding Maori landscape, until by the beginning of the twentieth century this was a European pastoral landscape with relict features of Maori occupation. The history of occupation and change is registered in the archeological landscape as much as in the documents and archeological materials recovered. The site of the mission station and its environs was well preserved archeologically, as the pastoral farming activities that took place there up until the end of the twentieth century left subsurface remains intact. The landscape study contributes important insights. It has demonstrated the implicit contradictions the mission first faced at Oihi, with the injunction from Marsden and the CMS to become self-sufficient through agriculture in a location where it was nearly impossible to carry this out. For Maori, access to good horticultural land was facilitated by mobility, with access to a range of resources in different places, while the mission was restricted to Oihi only. Te Puna, with somewhat better agricultural land, offered the possibility of the self-sufficiency that Marsden and the CMS had earlier demanded, where the King family were able to develop a subsistence economy on their land. The landscape study also demonstrates the waxing and waning of the importance of place as larger political and social events are played out over time. At the beginning of the nineteenth century, Te Puna and Rangihoua were the pre-eminent locations in the Bay of Islands, the home of paramount chiefs such as Te Pahi and Ruatara and the focus of European visitors such as Savage. This provided the rationale for the location of the mission at Oihi in 1814. By the mid 1820s, this focus had shifted. The importance of Rangihoua and Oihi waned as Hongi Hika came to prominence, with his central village at Kerikeri (Binney 2007). By 1830, this focus moved again to Kororareka, the preferred port of call for ships. With the arrival of Governor Hobson in 1840, the seat of government was established in the Bay of Islands at Okiato, but by February 1841 Hobson had moved his government to Auckland, the Bay of Islands itself losing its formerly prominent position in this shift. Hone Heke's response to British annexation and the resulting war in the north in 1845-1846 temporarily raised the centrality of the Bay again, but ultimately this waned in favor of the growing importance of Auckland and other later urban centers.

By 1850, Te Puna and Oihi had become a largely nostalgic landscape as the CMS went on to expand in other locations, eventually developing into the New Zealand Anglican church. Even in 1844 William Cotton (n.d.) considered Te Puna "quite mythic ground," the place where John and Hannah King "held on steadily...during all the turbulent times." Oihi remains a sacred place in New Zealand's past because of its religious connections, as the site of New Zealand's first mission station, the site of first European settlement, the place where Samuel Marsden preached the first sermon on New Zealand soil, and the site of the burials of those associated with the mission, in particular members of the King family. It is also sacred for its proximity to Rangihoua pa, where the first close connections between Maori and European were forged. Te Puna, the place where the relationship with the people of Rangihoua was continued, shares this quality of "sacred site." This important aspect of the Te Puna mission was lost during the many decades that it was farmed. The site of the house was obliterated and its history gradually forgotten. However, the archeological investigation of this site has returned it to its place of significance in New Zealand's history, for its demonstration of a particular kind of mission station, operated by the humble missionary and his family living under sometimes difficult, straightened circumstances, and for the role that it played in the emergence of a new kind of society in New Zealand during the nineteenth century.

Appendix

Complete list of all items in CMS store, April 1831– March 1832

	Items listed in store inventory	Received at store from Capt Wright Aug 1830	Supplied to John King April 1831–March 1832				Represented in Excavation
			Apr–May	July–Sept	Oct–Dec	Jan–March 1832	
Food	Tea		1 lb	24 lb 9 oz	19 lb 10 oz	19 lb 10 oz	
	Sugar		16 lb	219 lb 12 oz	176 lb 8 oz	176 lb 8 oz	
	Fine flour	12,475 lb		1,166 lb	1,014 lb	1,014 lb	
	Seconds flour	12,407 lb	405 lb	728 lb	796 lb	705 lb	
	Arrowroot	1 cask 750 lb		11 lb	17 lb		
	Salt lbs		240 lb	60 lb	416 lb		
	Saltpetre				5 lb		
	Biscuit		312 lb				
	Rice			160 lb			
	Wheat						
Sundries	Tobacco	3 Kegs & 3 Baskets	4 lb	51 lb		40 lb	
	Pipes						X
	Fishhooks			200	200		X
Household	*Kitchen / dining*						
	Pewter plates						
	Iron spoons						X

Item						
Tin pots						
Tin pans						
Knives	17		3		12	X
Kettle pans	300 × 3 sizes					
Iron pots	80				4	X
Tin cans						
Lighting						
Lamp oil		13 gal 2 qt		10 gal 2 qt	9 gal 2 qt	
Lamps						X
Lamp cotton						
Cleaning						
Broom heads						
Ground brushes						
Scrubbing brushes						
Water						
Pump boxes	5					
Iron pump	1					
Wooden pump	1					
Bedding						

(continued)

| | Items listed in store inventory | Received at store from Capt Wright Aug 1830 | Supplied to John King April 1831–March 1832 | | | | Represented in Excavation |
			Apr–May	July–Sept	Oct–Dec	Jan–March	
	Blankets	1,002	24	18	30	30	
	Toiletries						
	Razors						
	Soap			61 lb 8 oz	85 lb 1 oz	75 lb 14 oz	
	Horn and bone combs			12		12	
	Ivory combs	12 dozen					
	Miscellaneous						
	Case of medicines	1					
	Scissors						
	Glue						
Reading and Writing	Pens and quills				25		X
	Ink powder						
	Blotting paper						
	Brown paper						
	Foolscap						
	Letter paper						

	Item							
	Slates							X
	Slate pencils							X
	Black lead pencils	6 dozen						X
	Native books	530 Books of native language	12					
	Books	6 blank minute						
	Scriptures							
	Catechism							
	L Books							
	P Books							
	Sealing Wax	6 lb				0.5 lb		
Clothing	*Men's wear*							
	Belts	397 Soldiers						X?
	Red shirts	150 Men 50 boys	6		6			
	Cotton shirts	150 Men 50 boys	6	8				
	Duck frocks							
	Duck trousers							
	Cotton trousers							
	Gray trousers		7					
	Best duck Trousers	144 pr						

(continued)

	Items listed in store inventory	Received at store from Capt Wright Aug 1830	Supplied to John King April 1831–March 1832				Represented in Excavation
			Apr–May	July–Sept	Oct–Dec	Jan–March	
	Blue jackets	150 Men 50 boys		20			
	Scotch caps	300 Men					
	Women's wear						
	Cotton shifts	36 Stripe		9			
	Shoes						X
	Children's shoes	240 pr					
	English shoes						
	Colonial shoes						
Fabric	Canvas						
	British duck				50 yard		
	Std cotton						
	Stripe cotton		3 yard	24 yard		42 yard	
	Cotton shirting						
	Print						
	Common print			50 yard			
	Best prints Chintz						
	Shirting calico						

Std linen					
Blue linen		18 yard		42 yard	
Factory cloth	10 Bundles		53 yard		
Parramatta cloth					
Flannel					
Sheeting					
Cotton sheeting					
Russian toweling					
Worsted		7 yard			
Fustian	53 yard Fine				
Brown Holland					
Bunting					
Haberdashery — Shirt buttons					X
Metal buttons					X
Brace buttons					
Thread	60 lb	8 oz	12 oz	1 lb	
Needles					
Thimbles					X
Braces					
Handkerchiefs				5	
Tapes pieces		1.5	3 Pieces	4	

(continued)

| Building | Items listed in store inventory | Received at store from Capt Wright Aug 1830 | Supplied to John King April 1831–March 1832 | | | | Represented in Excavation |
			Apr–May	July–Sept	Oct–Dec	Jan–March	
	Materials						
	Bricks	6,000					X
	Hearthstones	4					X
	Brick moulds					24	X
	Window glass panes					55 lb	X
	Copper sheet						
	Fasteners						
	Screws	2 gross			4 gross	1 gross	X
	Spike nails						X
	Nails sizes			142 lb	105 lb	296 lb	X
	Iron boat nails						X?
	Copper boat nails	14 lb				2 lb	X
	Flat clout nails						X
	Brads					9 lb	X
	Tin tacks						X
	Rivets						
	Hardware						
	T Hinges pr				6		X
	Box hinges pr						

	Item	Qty	A	?
	Butt hinges pair			?
	Door locks		4	10
	Chest locks			10
	Door bolts			
	Norfolk latches			
	Drawer locks			
	Joinery			
	Sash			
	Sash lines	31		
	Sash pulleys	8 dozen		
	Sash weights	8 dozen		
	Paint and Plaster			
	Plasterers hair	6 Bags		
	Plasterers brushes		2	
	Paint lb		56	56
	Paint Oil gal		6	6
	Whitening lb		12	
	Turpentine			1 gal 2 qt
	Building			
	Plane irons			12
Tools	Bench plane			

(continued)

Items listed in store inventory	Received at store from Capt Wright Aug 1830	Supplied to John King April 1831–March 1832				Represented in Excavation
		Apr–May	July–Sept	Oct–Dec	Jan–March	
Chisels				12		
Saw files	36			48		
Plasterers trowel						
Augers						
Lime sieves						
Hand saws						
Tennon saws				2		
Pit saws						
Picks						X
Squares						
Hammers				2		
Trowels						X
Gimblets				36	22	
Cast steel chisels					1	
Pincers						
Drawing Knives						
Gouges						
Coopering						

Coopers adzes				
Drawing knives				
Spoke shaves				
Hooks and bands				
Coopers tools				
Coopers rivets				
Smithing				
Blacksmith files				
Plate iron				X
Iron	480 lb			X
British and foreign iron		224 lb		X?
Stones & grinders				X
Grind stones				
Rub stones				
Oil stones				
Stone chisels				
Agriculture Hay forks	24			
Reap hooks	24			X
Garden rakes	24			
Hatchets		3		X

(*continued*)

Items listed in store inventory	Received at store from Capt Wright Aug 1830	Supplied to John King April 1831–March 1832				Represented in Excavation
		Apr–May	July–Sept	Oct–Dec	Jan–March 1832	
Dung and potato forks	24					
Hay and dung forks						
Axes		11	4	12		X
Adzes		15				
Hoes	400	13	18	12		X
Spades	100	11				X
Scythes						X
Turnip and garden hoes						?
Barrow wheels						
Grass seeds	2 Casks					
Powder						
Horse gear — Saddles						
Bridles	1					X?
Harness cases						
Dray						
Miscellaneous — Anticorrosive powder						

Tin funnels	4					
Shaving boxes				6		
Tents						
Rope coils	3					
Blocks						
Planks set						

Glossary

Hahunga	Disinterment of bones of the dead for removal to a final resting place
Hakari	Feast
Hangi	Earth oven for cooking
Hapu	Subtribe
Iwi	Tribe, people
Kaheru	Spade, digging stick
Kainga	Village
Kawanatanga	Government
Kumara	Sweet potato
Makutu	To bewitch; spell, incantation
Mana	Authority, control, influence, prestige
Mana whenua	Power associated with the possession of land
Moko	Tattoo
Noa	Free from tapu
Pakeha	Non-Maori, European
Rangatiratanga	Sovereignty
Taiaha	Carved wooden spear
Take	Issue, cause
Tangi	Funeral; to cry or lament
Tapu	Sacred, forbidden; under religious restriction
Taua muru	Plundering party, war party
Tohunga	Priest, expert
Tuku whenua	Use of land by another party that does not extinguish the owner's rights
Utu	Return for anything, satisfaction, reward, reply
Wahi tapu	Sacred place

Whangai	To adopt or foster a child
Whanau	Family
Whata	Storage platform
Whenua	Land

References

Adams, Peter, 1977. *Fatal Necessity: British Intervention in New Zealand 1830–1847.* Auckland University Press, Auckland, New Zealand.

Adams, W., 2002. Machine Cut Nails and Wire Nails: American Production and Use for Dating 19th-Century and Early-20th-Century Sites. *Historical Archaeology*, 36(4):66–88.

Allen, Harry, 1996. Horde and Hapu: The Reification of Kinship and Residence in Prehistoric Aboriginal and Maori Settlement Organisation. In *Oceanic Culture History: Essays in Honour of Roger Green*, edited by J.M. Davidson, G. Irwin, B.F. Leach, A. Pawley, and D. Brown, pp. 657–674. New Zealand Journal of Archaeology Special Publication, Auckland, New Zealand.

Alley, Geoffrey, and David Hall, 1941. *The Farmer in New Zealand*. Department of Internal Affairs, Wellington, New Zealand.

Allison, Penelope (Ed.), 1999a. *The Archaeology of Household Activities*. Routledge, London, New York.

Allison, Penelope, 1999b. Introduction. In *The Archaeology of Household Activities*, edited by Penelope Allison, pp. 1–18. Routledge, London, New York.

Anderson, Atholl, 1991. *Race Against Time*. Hocken Library, University of Otago, Dunedin, New Zealand.

Anderson, Grahame, 2001. *The Merchant of the Zeehaen*. Te Papa Press, Wellington, New Zealand.

Armes, A., 1974. *English Smocks*. Dryad Press, Leicester, UK.

Arnold, Rollo, 1981. *The Farthest Promised Land*. Victoria University Press, Wellington, New Zealand.

Arnold, Rollo, 1994. *New Zealand's Burning*. Victoria University Press, Wellington, New Zealand.

Axtell, James, 1982. Some Thoughts on the Ethnohistory of Missions. *Ethnohistory*, 29:35–41.

Bagnall, Austin, and George Petersen, 1948. *William Colenso*. A.H. & A.W. Reed, Wellington, New Zealand.

Ballara, Angela, 1973. Warfare and Government in Ngapuhi Tribal Society Institutions of Authority and the Function of Warfare in the Period of Early Settlement 1814–1833, in the Bay of Islands and Related Territories. MA thesis, University of Auckland, Auckland, New Zealand.

Ballara, Angela, 1998. *Iwi: The Dynamics of Maori Social Organisation from c. 1769 to c. 1945*. Victoria University Press, Wellington, New Zealand.

Ballara, Angela, 2003. *Taua: 'musket wars', 'land wars' or tikanga?: Warfare in Maori Society in the Early Nineteenth Century*. Penguin Books, Auckland, New Zealand.

Bambridge, William, n.d. *Diaries*. MS-copy-micro-0501, Alexander Turnbull Library, Wellington, New Zealand.

Barber, Ian, 1989. A Classification System for Traditional Maori Horticultural Ditches. *New Zealand Journal of Archaeology*, 11:23–50.

Barile, K., and J. Brandon (Eds.), 2004. *Household Chores and Household Choices*. University of Alabama Press, Tuscaloosa.

Barker, J., 2005. Where the Missionary Frontier Ran Ahead of Empire. In *Missions and Empire*, edited by Norman Etherington, pp. 86–106. Oxford University Press, Oxford, UK.

Barnes, n.d. Statements from Two of the Seamen Involved in the Reprisal Raid on Te Pahi Island in 1810, to the Thames Water Police. Public Records Office London, UK.

Barton, J.R., 1927. *Earliest New Zealand*. Palamontain & Petherick, Masterton, New Zealand.

Bawden, Patricia, 1976. *Christian Beginnings in New Zealand. The Historical Significance of the Oihi, Rangihoua, Te Puna Area*. Scholar in Theology Diploma, St. John's Theological College, Auckland, New Zealand.

Beaglehole, John C. (Ed.), 1955. *The Journals of Captain James Cook on His Voyages of Discovery*. The Hakluyt Society, London, UK.

Beaudry, Mary, 1999. House and Household: The Archaeology of Domestic Life in Early America. In *Old and New Worlds*, edited by G. Egan, and R. Michael, pp. 117–126. Oxbow Books, Oxford, UK.

Beaudry, Mary, 2003. Concluding comments: Disruptive narratives? Multidimensional perspectives on Britishness. In *Archaeologies of the British*, edited by Susan Lawrence, pp. 290–295. Routledge, London, UK.

Beaudry, Mary, 2006. *Findings: The Material Culture of Needlework and Sewing*. Yale University Press, New Haven and London.

Bedford, Stuart, 1986. *The History and Archaeology of the Halfway House Hotel Cromwell Gorge*. Unpublished report to N.Z. Historic Places Trust, Cromwell, New Zealand.

Bedford, Stuart, 1994. Tenacity of the Traditional: A History and Archaeology of Early European Maori Contact, Puriri, Hauraki Plains. MA thesis, University of Auckland, Auckland, New Zealand.

Bedford, Stuart, 1996. Post-Contact Maori – The Ignored Component in New Zealand Archaeology. *Journal of the Polynesian Society*, 4:411–439.

Bedford, Stuart, 2004. Tenacity of the Traditional: the First Hundred Years of Maori-European Settler Contact on the Hauraki Plains, Aotearoa/New Zealand. In *The Archaeology of Contact in Settler Societies*, edited by Tim Murray, pp. 144–154. Cambridge University Press, Cambridge, UK.

Belich, James, 1986. *The New Zealand Wars*. Penguin, Auckland, New Zealand.

Bell, Leonard, 1980. *The Maori in European Art*. Reed, Wellington, New Zealand.

Bell, Leonard, 1992. *Colonial Constructs: European Images of Maori 1840–1914*. Auckland University Press, Auckland, New Zealand.

Bender, D., 1967. A Refinement of the Concept of Household: Families, Co-residence and Domestic Functions. *American Anthropologist* 69:493–505.

Berry, Pam, 1981. *The Kings of Te Puna*. P. Berry, Whangarei, New Zealand.

Best, Simon, 1995. *The Stone Store Drains*. Unpublished report to NZHPT, Auckland, New Zealand.

Best, Simon, 1997. *More Stone Store Drains and Things; Archaeological Restoration of the CMS Ground Surface Stone Store Kerikeri Site P05/617*. Unpublished report to NZHPT, Auckland, New Zealand.

Best, Simon, 2000. *Purakau Catholic Mission Site Hokianga*. Unpublished report to NZHPT, Auckland, New Zealand.

Best, Simon, 2001. *Drainage and Cable Laying Excavations at Pompallier and Clendon House Russell: Archaeological Testing and Monitoring.* Unpublished report to NZHPT, Auckland, New Zealand.

Best, Simon, 2002. *Guns and Gods the History and Archaeology of Rewa's 'Pa' Kororareka.* Unpublished report for Department of Conservation, Northland Conservancy, New Zealand.

Best, Simon, 2003a. *The Kerikeri Mission House Archaeology in Shell Paths and Flower Beds Church Missionary Society to Historic Places Trust.* Unpublished report to NZHPT, Auckland, New Zealand.

Best, Simon, 2003b. *Archaeology at Wairoa Bay Purerua Peninsula Bay of Islands.* Unpublished report to NZHPT, Auckland, New Zealand.

Binney, Judith, 1966. Papahurihia: Some Thoughts on Interpretation. *Journal of the Polynesian Society,* 321–330.

Binney, Judith, 1969. Christianity and the Maoris to 1840: a comment. *New Zealand Journal of History,* 3(2):143–165.

Binney, Judith, 1970. Introduction. In W. Yate, *An Account of New Zealand,* edited by Judith Binney, pp. v–xxi. Irish University Press, Shannon, Ireland.

Binney, Judith, 1997. Ancestral Voices: Maori Prophet Leaders. In *The Oxford Illustrated History of New Zealand,* edited by Keith Sinclair, pp. 153–185. Oxford University Press, Auckland, New Zealand.

Binney, Judith, 2005. *The Legacy of Guilt.* Bridget Williams Books, Wellington, New Zealand.

Binney, Judith (Ed.), 2007. *Te Kerikeri 1770–1850: The Meeting Pool.* Bridget Williams Books, Wellington, New Zealand.

Binney, Judith, Judith Bassett, and Erik Olssen, 1990. *The People and the Land an Illustrated History of New Zealand.* Allen & Unwin, Wellington, New Zealand.

Birmingham, Judith, 1992. *Wybalenna: The Archaeology of Cultural Accommodation in Nineteenth Century Tasmania.* Australian Society for Historical Archaeology, Sydney, Australia.

Birmingham, Judith, 2000. Resistance, creolization or optimal foraging at Killalpaninna Mission, South Australia. In *The Archaeology of Difference,* edited by R. Torrence, and A. Clarke, pp. 360–405. Routledge, London, UK.

Bozic-Vrbancic, Senka, 2006. *Celebrating Forgetting: The formation of identities and memories by Maori and Croats in New Zealand.* University of Otago Press, Dunedin, New Zealand.

Bragdon, Kathleen, 1988. The Material Culture of the Christian Indians of New England, 1650–1775. In *Documentary Archaeology in the New World,* edited by Mary Beaudry, pp. 126–131. Cambridge University Press, Cambridge and New York.

Bragdon, Kathleen, 1996a. *The Native People of Southern New England, 1500–1650.* University of Oklahoma Press, Norman.

Bragdon, Kathleen, 1996b. Gender as a Social Category in Native Southern New England. *Ethnohistory,* 43(4):573–592.

Brandon, K., and K. Barile, 2004. Introduction. In *Household Chores and Household Choices,* edited by K. Barile, and J. Brandon, pp. 1–12. University of Alabama Press, Tuscaloosa.

Brassey, Robert, 1989. *Rediscovering Fort Ligar: Archaeology at R11/656, Auckland. Rep. Science and Research Internal Report No. 41,* Department of Conservation, Wellington, New Zealand.

Brassey, Robert, and S. Macready, 1994. *The History and Archaeology of the Victoria Hotel, Fort St, Auckland (Site R11/1530).* Unpublished report, Department of Conservation, Auckland, New Zealand.

Brewis, Jill, 1982. *Colonial Fare*. Methuen, Auckland, New Zealand.

Brink, Yvonne, 2004. The Cape during the rule of the Dutch east India Company. In *The Archaeology of Contact in Settler Societies*, edited by Tim Murray, pp. 91–108. Cambridge University Press, Cambridge, UK.

Brock, Peggy, 1988. The Missionary Factor in Adnyamathanha History. In *Aboriginal Australians and Christian Missions*, edited by T. Swain, and D. Rose, pp. 277–291. Australian Association for the Study of Religions, Bedford Park, Australia.

Brock, Peggy, 1993. *Outback Ghettos*. Cambridge: Cambridge University Press, UK.

Brock, Peggy, and D. Kartinyeri, 1989. *Poonindie, the Rise and Destruction of an Aboriginal Community*. South Australia Government Printer, Netley, South Australia.

Brook, J., and J. Kohen, 1991. *The Parramatta Native Institution and the Black Town*. New South Wales University Press, Kensington, NSW, Australia.

Brooks, Alasdair, 1999. Building Jerusalem: Transfer-Printed Finewares and the Creation of British Identity. In *The Familiar Past?* Edited by Sarah Tarlow, and Susie West, pp. 51–65. Routledge, London, UK.

Brooks, Alasdair, 2003. Crossing Offa's Dyke: British Ideologies and Late Eighteenth- and Nineteenth-Century Ceramics in Wales. In *Archaeologies of the British*, edited by Susan Lawrence, pp. 119–137. Routledge, London.

Bruce, George, n.d. (1817). *The Life of a Greenwich Pensioner*. MS-0337. Alexander Turnbull Library, Wellington, New Zealand.

Bryson, A., 1989. *Ayrshire Needlework*. Batsford, London, UK.

Buick, Thomas L., 1926. *New Zealand's First War, or the Rebellion of Hone Heke*. Government Printer, Wellington, New Zealand.

Busch, J., 1987. Second Time Around. *Historical Archaeology*, 21(1):67–80.

Butler, John, n.d. John Butler to Samuel Marsden. *Transcripts of Selected Items from the Four Volumes of Samuel Marsden*, MS-0057a Hocken Library, Dunedin, New Zealand.

Byrde, P., 1992. *Nineteenth Century Fashion*. Batsford, London, UK.

Carleton, Hugh, 1948. *Life of Henry Williams*. Reed Books, Wellington, New Zealand.

Carson, V., 1992. Submitting to Great Inconveniences. In *Mission and Moko*, edited by R. Glen, pp. 56–72. Latimer Foundation, Christchurch, New Zealand.

Casella, Eleanor, 2001a. Every Procurable Object: A Functional Analysis of the Ross Female Factory Archaeological Collection. *Australasian Society for Historical Archaeology*, 19:25–38.

Casella, Eleanor, 2001b. To Watch or Restrain: Female Convict Prisons in 19th-Century Tasmania. *International Journal for Historical Archaeology*, 5(1):45–72.

Cave, O. 1965. *English Folk Embroidery*. Mills & Boon, London.

Challis, Aidan, 1993. Bedggood Buildings, Te Waimate, Bay of Islands: Excavations on the Site of the Blacksmith's Shop, 1986. *New Zealand Journal of Archaeology*, 15:17–37.

Challis, Aidan, 1994. *Edmonds Ruins, Kerikeri Inlet, Bay of Islands: The Stone Structures and the Artefact Assemblage*. Department of Conservation Science and Research Series No.68, Wellington, New Zealand.

Clark, Fiona, 1982. *Hats*. Batsford, London, UK.

Clarke, George, n.d.a. *G. Clarke to the Secretaries*. MS-0498 (Folder 12), Hocken Library, Dunedin, New Zealand.

Clarke, George, n.d.b. *Letters and Journals*. MS-vol. 60/PC-054, Hocken Library, Dunedin, New Zealand.

Cloher, Dorothy, 2003. *Hongi Hika Warrior Chief*. Viking, Auckland, New Zealand.

Clunie, Fergus, 1998. *Historic Bay of Islands a Driving Tour*. Reed Books, Auckland, New Zealand.

Clunie, Fergus, 2002 March and September. Personal communication.

CMS, 1830. *Missionary Register*. L & G Seeley, London, UK.

CMS, n.d.a. *Minutes of Missionaries' Meetings*. CMS archives microfilm 79–326 (CN/04). University of Auckland Library, Auckland, New Zealand.

CMS, n.d.b. *Minutes of Missionaries' Meetings*. CMS Archives microfilm 79–327 (CN/04). University of Auckland Library, Auckland, New Zealand.

CMS, n.d.c. *Sydney Correspondence*. CMS archives microfilm 79–328 (CN/05) University of Auckland Library, Auckland, New Zealand.

CMS, n.d.d. *Daybook Journal Te Kiddee Kiddee Store*. CMS MS1122(6) XKH902. Kerikeri Mission House and Stone Store, Kerikeri, New Zealand.

CMS, n.d.e. *General Account of Stores Issued Te Kiddee Kiddee Store*. CMS MS1122(7) XKH905. Kerikeri Mission House and Stone Store, Kerikeri, New Zealand.

CMS, n.d.f. *Journal Te Kiddee Kiddee Store*. CMS MS1122(7) XKH904. Kerikeri Mission House and Stone Store, Kerikeri, New Zealand.

Cole, Keith, 1971. *History of the Church Missionary Society of Australia*. Church Missionary Historical Publications Trust, Melbourne, Australia.

Cole, Keith, 1988. Anglican Missions to Aborigines. In *Aboriginal Australians and Christian Missions*, edited by T. Swain, and D. Rose, pp. 174–184. Australian Association for the Study of Religions, Bedford Park, Australia.

Coleman, H., 1865. *A Memoir of the Reverend Richard Davis*. James Nisbet, London, UK.

Colenso, William, 1880. On the Vegetable Food of the Ancient New Zealanders before Cook's Visit. *Transactions of the New Zealand Institute*.

Colenso, William, 1888. Fifty Years Ago in New Zealand. *New Zealand Philosophical Institute*.

Comaroff, John L., and Jean Comaroff, 1986. Christianity and Colonialism in South Africa. *American Ethnologist*, 13:1–22.

Comaroff, John L., and Jean Comaroff, 1991. *Of Revelation and Revolution*. University of Chicago Press, Chicago and London.

Comaroff, John L., and Jean Comaroff, 1992. *Ethnography and the Historical Imagination*. Westview Press, Boulder.

Comaroff, John L., and Jean Comaroff, 2000a. *Civil Society and the Political Imagination in Africa*. University of Chicago Press, Chicago.

Comaroff, John L., and Jean Comaroff, 2000b. Cultivation, Christianity and Colonialsim: Towards a New African Genesis. In *The London Missionary Society in Southern Africa, 1799–1999*, edited by John De Gruchy, pp. 55–81. Ohio University Press, Athens, Ohio.

Connah, Graham, 1993. *The Archaeology of Australia's History*. Cambridge University Press, Cambridge, UK.

Cotton, W.C., n.d. *Journal*. DLMS 40–42 Mitchell Library, Sydney, Australia.

Coysh, A.W., 1974. *Blue and White Transfer Ware 1780–1840*. David and Charles, London, UK.

Coysh, A.W., 1989. *Dictionary of Blue and White Printed Pottery 1780–1880*. vol. 2. Antique Collectors Club, Woodbridge.

Coysh, A.W., and R.K. Henrywood, 1982. *Dictionary of Blue and White Printed Pottery 1780–1880*. vol. 1. Antique Collectors' Club, Woodbridge.

Crowe, Andrew, 1999. *Which Seashell?* Penguin, Auckland, New Zealand.

Cruise, R.A., 1974. *Journal of a Ten Month's Residence in New Zealand*. Capper Press, Christchurch, New Zealand.

Cunningham, A. n.d. *Papers 1819–1828* (N.Z. Journal September to November 1826). Acc 141–702–703 [59,60], Alexander Turnbull Library, Wellington, New Zealand.

Cusick, James, 1998a. Historiography of Acculturation: An Evaluation of Concepts and Their Application in Archaeology. In *Studies in Culture Contact*, edited by James

Cusick, pp. 126–145. Center for Archaeological Investigations, Southern Illinois University Occasional Paper No. 25, Carbondale, Illinois.

Cusick, James (Ed.), 1998b. *Studies in Culture Contact: Interaction, Culture Change, and Archaeology*. Center for Archaeological Investigations, Southern Illinois University Occasional Paper No. 25, Carbondale, Illinois.

Cusick, James, 2000. Creolization and the Borderlands. *Historical Archaeology*, 34:46–55.

Davidoff, Leonore, and Catherine Hall, 1991. *Family Fortunes: Men and Women of the English Middle Cass, 1780–1850*. Chicago University Press, Chicago.

Davidson, Janet, 1984. *The Prehistory of New Zealand*. Longman, Auckland, New Zealand.

Davies, John, 1961. *The History of the Tahitian Mission 1799–1830*, edited by C. W. Newbury. Cambridge University Press, Cambridge, UK.

Davis, Richard, n.d. *Letters and Journals 1824–1863*. MS-vol. 66, Hocken Library, Dunedin, New Zealand.

Davison, P., 1985. *The Manga-Manda Settlement, Phillip Creek*. James Cook University of North Queensland, Townsville, Queensland.

De Cunzo, Lu Ann, 1995. Reform, Respite, Ritual: An Archaeology of Institutions; The Magdalen Society of Philadelphia 1800–1850. *Historical Archaeology*, 29(3):iii-168.

De Cunzo, Lu Ann, 2001. On Reforming the "Fallen" and Beyond: Transforming Continuity at the Magdalen Society of Philadelphia, 1845–1916. *Historical Archaeology*, 5(1):19–43.

De Cunzo, Lu Ann, 2006. Exploring the Institution: Reform, Confinement, Social Change. In *Historical Archaeology*, edited by Martin Hall, and Stephen W. Silliman, pp. 167–189. Blackwell Publishing, Malden.

De Gruchy, John (Ed.), 2000. *The London Missionary Society in Southern Africa, 1799–1999*. Ohio University Press, Athens, Ohio.

Deagan, Kathleen, 1983. *Spanish St. Augustine: The Archaeology of a Colonial Creole Community*. Academic Press, New York.

Deagan, Kathleen, 1993. St. Augustine and the Mission Frontier. In *The Spanish Missions of La Florida*, edited by Bonnie McEwan, pp. 87–110. University Press of Florida, Gainsville.

Deagan, Kathleen, 1996. Colonial Transformation: Euro-American Cultural Genesis in the Early Spanish-American Colonies. *Journal of Anthropological Reseach*, 52:135–160.

Deetz, James, 1977. *In Small Things Forgotten*. Anchor Press, Garden City, New York.

Deetz, James, 1978. Archaeolgical Investigations at La Purisima Mission. In *Historical Archaeology: A Guide to Substantive and Theoretical Contributions*, edited by Robert Schuyler, pp. 160–190. Baywood Publishing Company, Farmingdale.

Deetz, James, 1982. Households: A Structural Key to Archaeological Explanation. *American Behavioral Scientist*, 25:717–724.

Deetz, James, 1988. American Historical Archaeology: Methods and Results. *Science*, 239:326–367.

Deetz, James, 1993. *Flowerdew Hundred. The Archaeology of a Virginia Plantation*. University Press of Virginia, Charlottesville and London.

Dening, G. (Ed.), 1974. *The Marquesan Journal of Edward Robarts*. Australian National University Press, Canberra.

Dietler, M., 1998. A Mediterranean Colonial Encounter. In *Studies in Culture Contact*, edited by James Cusick, pp. 288–315. Center for Archaeological Investigations, Southern Illinois University, Occasional Paper No. 25, Carbondale, Illinois.

DNZB, 1998. *Dictionary of New Zealand Biography*. vol. I. Auckland University Press, Auckland, New Zealand.

Drummond, Alison, and L. Drummond, 1967. *At Home in New Zealand*. Blackwood and Janet Paul, Auckland, New Zealand.

Duff, Roger, 1956. *The Moa Hunter Period of Maori Culture*. Government Printer, Wellington, New Zealand.

Dunmore, John, 2006. 'Surville, Jean François Marie de 1717–1770'. Dictionary of New Zealand Biography. URL: http://www.dnzb.govt.nz/

Earle, Augustus, 1909. *A Narrative of a Nine Months' Residence in New Zealand in 1827*. Whitcombe & Tombs, Dunedin, New Zealand.

Easdale, Nola, 1991. *Missionary and Maori Kerikeri 1819–1860*. Te Waihora Press Lincoln, New Zealand.

Ebbett, Eve, 1977. *In True Colonial Fashion*. A.H. & A.W. Reed, Wellington, New Zealand.

Edmond, Rod, 1997. *Representing the South Pacific*. Cambridge University Press, Cambridge, UK.

Edwards, P. (Ed.), 1999. *The Journals of Captain Cook*. Penguin, London, UK.

Elder, John R., 1932. *The Letters and Journals of Samuel Marsden 1765–1838*. Coulls Somerville Wilkie Ltd. and A.H. Reed, Dunedin, New Zealand.

Elder, John R., 1934. *Marsden's Lieutenants*. Coulls Somerville Wilkie and A.H. Reed, Dunedin, New Zealand.

Ellis, William, 1859. *Polynesian Researches*. vol. III. Henry G. Bohn, London, UK.

Etherington, Norman, 2005. *Missions and Empire*. Oxford University Press, Oxford, UK.

Evans, Rex, 1989. *The Descendants of Captain Thomas Hansen and His Wife, Hannah Coats, through Hannah Hansen*. Evagean Publishing, Auckland, New Zealand.

Eveleigh, D., 1997. *Old Cooking Utensils*. Shire Publications, Buckinghamshire, UK.

Fairburn, Miles, 1989. *The Ideal Society and Its Enemies*. Auckland University Press, Auckland, New Zealand.

Fairburn, Sarah, n.d. *Sarah Fairburn Letter to Elizabeth Fairburn*. MS-papers-3234. Alexander Turnbull Library, Wellington, New Zealand.

Farnsworth, P., 1989. Native American Acculturations in the Spanish Colonial Empire: The Franciscan Missions of Alta California. In *Centre and Periphery: Comparative Studies in Archaeology*, edited by T. Champion, pp. 186–206. Unwin Hyman, London, UK.

Farnsworth, P., 1992. Missions, Indians and Cultural Continuity. *Historical Archaeology*, 26:22–36.

Fearn, J., 1990. *Cast Iron*. Shire Album, Buckinghamshire, UK.

Felgate, Matthew, 1998. *His Majesty's Theatre Site Excavations (Site R11/1624) Final Archaeological Report*. The Pacific Dynasty Group, Auckland, New Zealand.

Fitts, Robert K., 1999. The Archaeology of Middle-Class Domesticity and Gentility in Victorian Brooklyn. *Historical Archaeology*, 33(1):39–62.

Fitts, Robert K., 2001. The Rhetoric of Reform: The Five Points Missions and the Cult of Domesticity. *Historical Archaeology*, 35(3):115–132.

Fitzgerald, Catharine (Ed.), 2004. *Letters from the Bay of Islands: The Story of Marianne Williams*. Penguin, Auckland, New Zealand.

Fitzgerald, Tanya, 1995. In a Different Voice. A Case Study of Marianne and Jane Williams, Missionary Educators in Northern New Zealand 1823–1835. PhD thesis, University of Auckland, Auckland, New Zealand.

Fraser, Janice, 2004. Browne's Spar Station Ceramic Analysis, Report prepared for Auckland Regional Council.

Funari, P.A., M. Hall, and S. Jones (Eds.), 1999. *Historical Archaeology Back from the Edge*. Routledge, London and New York.

Garrett, John, 1982. *To Live among the Stars: Christian Origins in Oceania*. World Council of Churches and University of the South Pacific, Geneva, Switzerland, and Suva, Fiji.

Gibbons, Peter, 2002. Cultural Colonization and National Identity. *New Zealand Journal of History*, 36(1)"5–17.

Gillespie, Pamela, 1996. Gifted Words the Life and Writing of Marianne Coldham Williams. MA thesis, University of Auckland, Auckland, New Zealand.

Glen, Robert (Ed.), 1992. *Mission and Moko: The Church Missionary Society in New Zealand 1814–1882*. Latimer Fellowship, Christchurch, New Zealand.

Goffman, E., 1962. *Asylums*. Aldine Publishing, Chicago.

Gojak, Dennis, and Iain Stuart, 1999. The Potential for Archaeological Studies of Clay Tobacco Pipes from Australian Sites. *Australasian Society for Historical Archaeology*, 17:38–49.

Goldsbury, S., 1986. Behind the Picket Fence: The Lives of Missionary Wives in Pre-Colonial New Zealand. MA thesis, University of Auckland, Auckland, New Zealand.

Golson, Jack, 1959. Culture Change in Prehistoric New Zealand. In *Anthropology in the South Seas*, edited by J.D. Freeman, and W.R. Geddes, pp. 29–74. Thomas Avery & Sons, New Plymouth, New Zealand.

Gould, E., 2005. Prelude: The Christianizing of British America. In *Missions and Empire*, edited by Norman Etherington, pp. 19–39. Oxford University Press, Oxford, UK.

Graham, Elizabeth, 1998. Mission Archaeology. *Annual Review of Anthropology*, 27:25–62.

Griffin, Darren, 2000. A Christian Village of South Australian Natives: A Critical Analysis of the Use of Space at Poonindie Mission, South Australia. BA (hons) thesis, Flinders University, South Ausralia.

Grimshaw, Patricia, 1983. Christian Woman, Pious Wife, Faithful Mother, Devoted Missionary: Conflicts in Roles of American Missionary Women in Nineteenth Century Hawaii. *Feminist Studies*, 9(3):489–521.

Grimshaw, Patricia, 1989a. New England Missionary Wives, Hawaiian Women and "The Cult of True Womanhood". In *Family and Gender in the Pacific*, edited by Margaret Jolly, and Martha Macintyre, pp. 19–44. Cambridge University Press, New York and Cambridge, UK.

Grimshaw, Patricia, 1989b. *Paths of Duty: American Missionary Wives in Nineteenth-Century Hawaii*. University of Hawaii Press, Honolulu, Hawaii.

Grimshaw, Patricia, and E. Nelson, 2001. Empire, 'the Civilising Mission' and Indigenous Christian Women in Colonial Victoria. *Australian Feminist Studies*, 16(36):295–309.

Groube, Les, 1965. Excavations on Paeroa Village, Bay of Islands. *Historic Places Trust Newsletter*, 9, Wellington, New Zealand.

Groube, Les, 1966. Rescue Excavations in the Bay of Islands. *New Zealand Archaeological Association Newsletter*, 9:108–114.

Gunson, Neil, 1978. *Messengers of Grace*. Oxford University Press, Melbourne, Australia.

Hall, Martin, 1993. The Archaeology of Colonial Settlement in Southern Africa. *Annual Review of Anthropology*, 22:177–200.

Hall, Martin, 1994. The Secret Lives of Houses: Women and Gables in the Eighteenth-Century Cape. *Social Dynamics*, 20:1–48.

Hall, Martin, 2000. *Archaeology and the Modern World: Colonial Transcripts in South Africa and the Chesapeake*. Routledge, London, UK.

Hall, William, n.d. *Diary 1816–1838*. MLMS1597, Mitchell Library, Sydney.

Hansen, Kath, 1994. *In the Wake of the Active*. Kathleen Ann Hansen, Auckland, New Zealand.

Hargreaves, R.P., 1962. Waimate – Pioneer New Zealand Farm. *Agricultural History*, 36(1):38–45.

Hargreaves, R.P., 1963. Changing Maori Agriculture in Pre-Waitangi New Zealand. *Journal of the Polynesian Society*, 72:101–117.

Harris, J., 1984. *The Waimate Mission Station*. New Zealand Historic Places Trust, Wellington, New Zealand.

Harris, J., 1990. *One Blood 200 Years of Aboriginal Encounter with Christianity*. Albatross Books, Sutherland, Australia.

Harris, Jayden, 2005. *The Material Culture of the Oashore Whalers*. MA thesis, Department of Anthropology, University of Otago, Dunedin, New Zealand.

Havard-Williams, P. (Ed.), 1961. *Marsden and the New Zealand Mission*. University of Otago Press, Dunedin, New Zealand.

Hawkins, Stuart, n.d. 2003, November. Personal communication.

Heap, W., 1964. The First Christmas. *Northland*, October 28:7–14.

Hendon, J., 1996. Archaeological Approaches to the Organization of Domestic Labor: Household Practice and Domestic Relations. *Annual Review of Anthropology*, 25:45–61.

Higgins, T., 2001. *Soles and Soles*. Tony Higgins, Swerford, UK.

Higham, Tom, and Martin Jones, 2005. Chronology and Settlement. In *Change through Time*, edited by Louise Furey, and Simon Holdaway, pp. 215–234. New Zealand Archaeological Association Monograph, Auckland, New Zealand.

Hill, E., 2000. Thimbles and Thimble-Rings from the Circum-Carribean Region, 1500–1800. In *Approaches to Material Culture Research for Historical Archaeologists*, edited by David Brauner, pp. 309–317. The Society for Historical Archaeology, Pennsylvania.

Hill, Jonathan D., 1998. Violent Encounters: Ethnogenesis and Ethnocide in Long-Term Contact Situations. In *Studies in Culture Contact: Interaction, Culture Change, and Archaeology*, edited by James Cusick, pp. 146–171. Center for Archaeological Investigations, Occasional Paper No. 25, Southern Illinois University, Carbondale, Illinois.

Hohepa, Pat, 1999. My Musket, My Missionary, My Mana. In *Voyages and Beaches: Pacific Encounters 1769–1840*, edited by A. Calder, J. Lamb, and B. Orr, pp. 180–201. University of Hawaii Press, Honolulu, Hawaii.

Holmes, E., 1985. *A History of Thimbles*. Cornwell Books, London, UK.

Horrocks, Mark, S. Nichol, D. D'Costa, P. Shane, P. Augustinus, T. Jacobi, and A. Middleton, 2007. A Late Quaternary Environmental Record of Natural Change and Human Impact from Rangihoua Bay, Bay of Islands, Northern New Zealand. *Journal of Coastal Research*, 23(3):592–604.

Hughes, Robert, 1987. *The Fatal Shore*. Pan Books, London, UK.

Humphreys, A., 1989. The Archaeological Setting of Genadendal, the First Mission Station in South Africa. *The Digging Stick*, 6:2–4.

Jenkins, Kuini, 1991. Te Ihi, te Mana, te Wehi o te Ao Tuhi. Maori Print Literacy from 1814–1855. Literacy, Power and Colonisation. MA thesis, University of Auckland, Auckland, New Zealand.

Jeppson, Patrice, 2005. Material and Mythical Perspectives on Ethnicity: An Historical Archaeology Study of Cultural Identity, National Historiography, and the Eastern Cape Frontier of South Africa, 1820–1860. PhD thesis, University of Pennsylvania, Pennsylvania.

Johnston, Anna, 2003. *Missionary Writing and Empire*. Cambridge University Press, Cambridge, UK.

Jolly, Margaret, 1991. 'To Save the Girls for Brighter and Better Lives': Presbyterian Missions and Women in the South of Vanuatu: 1848–1870. *Journal of Pacific History*, 26:27–48.

Jolly, Margaret, 1993. Colonizing Women: The Maternal Body and Empire. In *Feminism and the Politics of Difference*, edited by S. Gunew, and A. Yeatman, pp. 103–128. Allen and Unwin, Sydney, Australia.

Jolly, Margaret, and Martha Macintyre (Eds.), 1989. *Family and Gender in the Pacific*. Cambridge University Press, Cambridge, UK.

Jones, Olive, 1986. *Cylindrical English Wine and Beer Bottles 1735–1850*. Environment Canada, Ottawa, Canada.

Jones, Olive, 2000. Glass Bottle Push-Ups and Pontil Marks. In *Approaches to Material Culture Research for Historical Archaeologists* (2nd ed.), edited by David Brauner, pp. 149–160. Society for Historical Archaeology, Pennsylvania.

Kelly, Lesley, 1951. *Marion Dufresne at the Bay of Islands.* A.H.& A.W. Reed, Wellington, New Zealand.

Kemp, James, n.d. *Journal.* NZ MSS 60. Auckland Public Library, Auckland, New Zealand.

Kemp, Richard, n.d. *Kerikeri Store Account Book 1843–1850.* ANG 63/2/4. St. John's Theological College, Auckland, New Zealand.

Kendall, Thomas, n.d.a. *Journal of a Journey from Port Jackson to New Zealand.* MS-0154, Hocken Library, Dunedin, New Zealand.

Kendall, Thomas, n.d.b. *Letters.* CY 1564, Mitchell Library, Sydney, Australia.

Kendall, Thomas Surfleet, n.d. *Diary.* Ms 0071, Hocken Library, Dunedin, New Zealand.

Kennedy, Jean, 1969. *Settlement in the South East Bay of Islands, 1772.* Department of Anthropology, University of Otago, Dunedin, New Zealand.

King, John, n.d.a. *Letters and Journals 1819–1853.* MS-0073 (PC152), Hocken Library, Dunedin, New Zealand.

King, John, n.d.b. *Letters and Reports 1820–1850.* CMS archives C.N./0 54 microfilm 79–338, University of Auckland Library, Auckland, New Zealand.

King, John, n.d.c. *Transcripts of Selected Items from the Four Volumes of Marsden Correspondence.* MS-0057a, Hocken Library, Dunedin, New Zealand.

King, John, n.d.d. Letter to Daniel Wilson. *Samuel Marsden Correspondence 1814–1815.* PC-119, Hocken Library, Dunedin, New Zealand.

King, John, n.d.e. *Old Land Claim Records.* AREPRO 4711/202, National Archives, Auckland, New Zealand.

King, Michael, 1997. *God's Farthest Outpost: A History of Catholics in New Zealand.* Viking, Auckland, New Zealand.

King, Michael, 2003. *The Penguin History of New Zealand.* Penguin Books, Auckland, New Zealand.

King, Phillip Hansen, n.d. *CMS London Additional Papers Relating to the N.Z. Missions.* MS-0498 Hocken Library, Dunedin, New Zealand.

Kirch, Patrick, and Marshall Sahlins, 1992. *Anahulu: The Anthropology of History in the Kingdom of Hawaii,* vol. 2. University of Chicago Press, Chicago.

Klose, Jane, and Antonia Malan, 2000. The Ceramic Signature of the Cape in the Nineteenth Century, with Particular Reference to the Tennant Street Site, Cape Town. *South African Archaeological Bulletin,* 55:49–59.

Kowalsky, A., and D. Kowalsky, 1999. *Encyclopedia of Marks on American, English, and European Earthenware, Ironstone and Stoneware 1780–1980.* Schiffer, Atglen, Pennsylvania.

Langmore, Diane, 1989a. *Missionary Lives Papua 1874–1914.* Centre for Pacific Islands Studies, University of Hawaii Press, Honolulu, Hawaii.

Langmore, Diane, 1989b. The Object Lesson of a Civilised, Christian Home. In *Family and Gender in the Pacific,* edited by Margaret Jolly, and Martha Macintyre, pp. 84–94. Cambridge University Press, Cambridge, UK.

Larsen, C., 1993. On the Frontier of Contact: Mission Bioarchaeology. In *The Spanish Missions of La Florida,* edited by Bonnie McEwan, pp. 322–356. University Press of Florida, Gainsville.

Larson, D., J. Johnson, and J. Michaelsen, 1994. Missionization among the Coastal Chumash of Central California: A Study of Risk Minimization Strategies. *American Anthropologist,* 96:263–299.

Law, R.G., 1968. Maori Soils in the Lower Waikato. *N.Z.A.A. Newsletter,* 11(2):67–75.

Lawrence, Susan, 1999. Towards a Feminist Archaeology of Households: Gender and Household Structure on the Australian Goldfields. In *The Archaeology of Household Activities*, edited by Penelope Allison, pp. 121–141. Routledge, London.

Lawrence, Susan, 2000. *Dolly's Creek: An Archaeology of a Victorian Goldfields Community*. Melbourne University Press, Melbourne, Australia.

Lawrence, Susan (Ed.), 2003. *Archaeologies of the British: Explorations of Identity in Great Britain and its Colonies 1600–1945*. Routledge, London, UK.

Lawrence, Susan, 2006. *Whalers and Free Men: Life on Tasmania's Colonial Whaling Stations*. Australian Scholarly Publishing, Melbourne, Australia.

Leach, Helen, 1984. *1,000 Years of Gardening in New Zealand*. Reed Books, Wellington, New Zealand.

Leach, Helen, 2001. European Perceptions of the Roles of Bracken Rhizhomes (Pteridium esculentum) (Forst. F. Cockayne) in the Traditional Maori Diet. *New Zealand Journal of Archaeology*, 22(2000):31–43.

Leach, Helen, 2003. Fern Consumption in Aotearoa and its Oceanic Precedents. *Journal of the Polynesian Society*, 112(2):141–156.

Lee, I., 1915. *The Logbooks of the Lady Nelson*. Grafton & Co, London, UK.

Lee, Jack, 1983. *The Bay of Islands*. Reed Books, Auckland, New Zealand.

Lee, Jack, 1993. *The Old Land Claims in New Zealand*. Northland Historical Publications Society, Kerikeri, New Zealand.

Lemert, C., and A. Branaman (Eds.), 1997. *The Goffman Reader*. Blackwell Publishers, Malden, Massachusetts.

Lightfoot, Kent, 1995. Culture Contact Studies: Redefining the Relationship between Prehistoric and Historical Archaeology. *American Antiquity*, 60:199–217.

Lightfoot, Kent, 2005. *Indians, Missionaries, and Merchants*. University of California Press, Berkley, California.

Lightfoot, Kent, 2006. Missions, Furs, Gold, and Manifest Destiny: Rethinking an Archaeology of Colonialism for Western North America. In *Historical Archaeology*, edited by Martin Hall and Stephen Silliman, pp. 272–292. Blackwell Publishing, Malden, Massachusetts.

Lightfoot, Kent, A. Schiff, and T. Wake, 1997. *The Alaskan Neighborhood a Multiethnic Community at Fort Ross*. Archaeological Research Facility Berkeley, California.

Lindbergh, Jenny, 1999. Buttoning Down Archaeology. *Australasian Society for Historical Archaeology*, 17:50–57.

Lineham, Peter, 1992a. This is My Weapon: Maori Response to the Maori Bible. In *Mission and Moko*, edited by Robert Glen, pp. 170–178. Latimer Fellowship, Christchurch, New Zealand.

Lineham, Peter, 1992b. To Make a People of the Book. In *Mission and Moko*, edited by Robert Glen, pp. 152–169. Latimer Fellowship, Christchurch, New Zealand.

LINZ, n.d. *R427–567*. Land Information New Zealand, Auckland Office, New Zealand.

Little, Barbara, 1994. People with History: An Update on Historical Archaeology in the United States. *Journal of Archaeological Method and Theory*, 1(1):5–40.

Lorrain, D., 1968. An Archaeologist's Guide to Nineteenth Century American Glass. *Historical Archaeology*, 5(12):35–44.

Loudon, J.C., 1871. *An Encyclopaedia of Agriculture* (7th ed.). Longmans, Green, and Co., London, UK.

Lundsgaarde, H.P. (Ed.), 1974. *Land Tenure in Oceania*. University of Hawaii Press, Honolulu, Hawaii.

Lydon, Jane, 2000. Regarding Coranderrk: Photography at Coranderrk Aboriginal Station, Victoria. PhD thesis, Australian National University, Canberra, Australia.

Lydon, Jane, 2002. This Civilising Experiment: Photography at Coranderrk Aboriginal Station during the 1860s. In *After Captain Cook: The Archaeology of the Recent Indigenous Past in Australia*, edited by R. Harrison, and C. Williamson, pp. 60–74. Sydney University Archaeological Method Series. Sydney, Australia.

Lydon, Jane, 2005a 'Men in Black': The Blacktown Native Institution and the Origins of the 'Stolen Generations'. In *Object Lessons: Archaeology and Heritage in Australia*, edited by Jane Lydon, and Tracy Ireland, pp. 201–224. Australian Scholarly Publishing, Melbourne, Australia.

Lydon, Jane, 2005b. 'Watched over by the indefatigable Moravian missionaries': Colonialism and Photography at Ebenezer and Ramahyuck. *The La Trobe Journal*, 76:27–48.

Lydon, Jane, 2005c. 'Our Sense of Beauty': Visuality, Space and Gender on Victoria's Aboriginal Reserves, South-Eastern Australia. *History and Anthropology*, 16(2):211–233.

Lydon, Jane, Alasdair Brooks, and Zvonika Stanin, 2004. *Archaeological Investigation of the Mission-House Ebenezer Mission, Victoria*. Centre for Australian Indigenous Studies, Monash University, Melbourne, Australia.

Macgregor, Miriam, 1975. *Petticoat Pioneers: North Island Women of the Colonial Era*. A.H. and A.W. Reed, Wellington, New Zealand.

Main, William, 1976. *Maori in Focus*. Millwood Press, Wellington, New Zealand.

Maingay, Joan, 1993. *James Callaghan's Tannery: A Nineteenth Century Industry in the Bay of Islands*, Department of Conservation, Northland Conservancy, New Zealand.

Malan, Antonia, and Jane Klose, 2003. Nineteenth-Century Ceramics in Cape Town, South Africa. In *Archaeologies of the British*, edited by Susan Lawrence, pp. 191–210. Routledge, London, UK.

Mandell, Daniel, R., 1996. *Behind the Frontier: Indians in Eighteenth-Century Eastern Massachusetts*. University of Nebraska Press, Lincoln.

Maning, F.E., 1973 (1887). *Old New Zealand*. Golden Press, Auckland, New Zealand.

Markham, Edward, 1963. *New Zealand or Recollections of It*. Government Printer, Wellington, New Zealand.

Marsden, J.B. (Ed.), 1857. *Memoirs of the Life and Labours of the Rev. Samuel Marsden of Parramatta and of His Early Connection with the Missions to New Zealand and Tahiti*. Religious Tract Society, London, UK.

Marsden, George, M., 2003. *Jonathan Edwards A Life*. Yale University Press, New Haven.

Marsden, Samuel, n.d.a. Transcripts of Selected Items from the Four Volumes of Marsden Correspondence. MS-0057a, Hocken Library, Dunedin, New Zealand.

Marsden, Samuel, n.d.b. *Samuel Marsden, Cartwright and Youl to Josiah Pratt*. PC-131 March 27 1817. Hocken Library, Dunedin, New Zealand.

Marsden, Samuel, 1831. Rangihoua. *Missionary Register*, pp. 116. L&G Seeley, London.

Marshall, W.B., 1836. *A Personal Narrative of Two Visits to New Zealand, in His Majesty's Ship Alligator, A.D. 1834*. James Nisbet and Co., London.

Martin, Ron, 1990. *The First Family: Captain Thomas and Hannah Hansen and Their Children*. Hansen Celebration Committee, Auckland, New Zealand.

Matunga, H., 1994. Waahi Tapu: Maori Sacred Sites. In *Sacred Sites, Sacred Places*, edited by D. Carmichael, J. Hubert, B. Reeves, and A. Schanche, pp. 217–226. Routledge, London, UK and New York.

May, Helen, 2003. *School Beginnings: Missionary Infant Schools for Maori 1830s-1840s*. Institute for Early Childhood Studies, Victoria University of Wellington, Wellington, New Zealand.

Maynard, Margaret, 1994. *Fashioned from Penury*. Cambridge University Press, Cambridge, UK.

McClendon, Thomas, 2004. The Man Who Would Be Inkosi: Civilising Missions in Shepstone's Early Career. *Journal of Southern Africa Studies*, 30(20):339–358.

McClintock, Anne, 1995. *Imperial Leather*. Routledge, New York and London, UK.

McCormick, E.H., 1966. *Narrative of a Residence in New Zealand - Journal of a Residance in Tristan da Cuhna, by Augustus Earle*. Clarendon Press, Oxford, UK.

McDowell, C., 1997. *Hats Status Style and Glamour*. Thames and Hudson, London.

McEwan, Bonnie (Ed.), 1993. *The Spanish Missions of La Florida*. University of Florida Press, Gainesville.

McKenzie, D.F., 1985. *Oral Culture, Literacy and Print in Early New Zealand*. Victoria University Press, Wellington, New Zealand.

McLean, Gavin, 1994. *No Continuing City*. NZHPT, Wellington, New Zealand.

McNab, Robert, 1908. *The Historical Records of New Zealand*. vol. I. Government Printer, Wellington, New Zealand.

McNab, Robert, 1914. *From Tasman to Marsden. A History of Northern New Zealand from 1642 to 1818*. J. Wilkie and Co., Dunedin, New Zealand.

McNair, W., and H. Rumley, 1981. *Pioneer Aboriginal Mission; The Work of Wesleyan Missionary John Smithies in the Swan River Colony 1840–1855*. University of Western Australia Press, Nedlands, Western Australia.

Meredith, A.G., 2000. *Buttons*. Shire Album, Buckinghamshire, UK.

Middleton, Angela, n.d. *Otuihu: An Outline from 1814 to 1845*. Unpublished research paper, University of Auckland, Auckland, New Zealand.

Middleton, Angela, 2003. Maori and European Landscapes at Te Puna, Bay of Islands, New Zealand. *Archaeology in Oceania*, 38(2003):110–124.

Middleton Angela, 2005a. *Te Puna: The Archaeology and History of a New Zealand Mission Station 1832–1874*. PhD thesis, University of Auckland, Auckland, New Zealand.

Middleton, Angela, 2005b. *The Archaeology of the Te Puna Mission House, Bay of Islands*. Unpublished report to NZHPT, Auckland, New Zealand.

Middleton, Angela, 2005c. Nail Chronology: The Case of Te Puna Mission Station. *Australasian Society for Historical Archaeology*, 23:55–62.

Middleton, Angela, 2007a. Silent Voices, Hidden Lives: Archaeology, Class and Gender in the CMS Missions, Bay of Islands, New Zealand, 1814–1845. *International Journal of Historical Archaeology*, 11(1):1–31.

Middleton Angela, 2007b. Potatoes and Muskets: Maori Gardening at Kerikeri. In *Te Kerikeri 1770–1850: The Meeting Pool*, edited by Judith Binney, pp. 33–39. Bridget Williams Books, Wellington, New Zealand.

Middleton, Angela, 2007c. The Kerikeri Kainga - Kirikokai? In *Te Kerikeri 1770–1850: The Meeting Pool*, edited by Judith Binney, pp. 72–80. Bridget Williams Books, Wellington, New Zealand.

Middleton, Angela, 2007d. Mission Station as Trading Post: The Economy of the Church Missionary Society in the Bay of Islands, New Zealand, 1814–1845. *New Zealand Journal of Archaeology*, 28(2006):51–81.

Miller, C., 1985. Domesticity Abroad: Work and Family in the Sandwich Island Mission, 1820–1840. In *Missions and Missionaries in the Pacific*, edited by C. Miller, pp. 65–90. Edwin Mellen Press, New York.

Miller, G., 1991. A Revised Set of CC Index Values for Classification and Economic Scaling of English Ceramics from 1787 to 1880. *Historical Archaeology*, 25(1):1–25.

Miller, Philip, 1983. The 'London-Shape Teawares. In *Staffordshire Porcelain*, edited by G. Godden, pp. 219–235. Granada, London, UK.

Mitchell, Peter, 2002a. The Archaeology of Colonialism. In *The Archaeology of Southern Africa*, edited by P. Mitchell, pp. 380–412. Cambridge University Press, Cambridge, UK.

Mitchell, Peter, 2002b. *The Archaeology of Southern Africa*. Cambridge University Press, Cambridge, UK.

Moon, Paul, 2002. *Te Ara Ki Te Titiri*. David Ling, Auckland, New Zealand.

Moon, Paul, and S. Fenton, 2002. Bound into a Fateful Union: Henry Williams' Translation of the Treaty of Waitangi into Maori February 1840. *Journal of the Polynesian Society*, 111(1):51–63.

Moorhead, Alan, 1966. *The Fatal Impact: An Account of the Invasion of the South Pacific 1767–1840*. Hamish Hamilton, London, UK.

Morgan, P., 1990. Glass Bottles from the William Salthouse: A Material Culture Analysis. BA hons dissertation, La Trobe University, Melbourne, Australia.

Mountain, Shane, 2002, September. Personal communication.

Munn, Daniel, 1981. Ngati Manu: An Ethnohistorical Account. MA thesis, University of Auckland, Auckland, New Zealand.

Murray, J., 2000. The Role of Women in the CMS, 1799–1917. In *The Church Missionary Society and World Christianity, 1799–1999*, edited by Kevin Ward, and Brian Stanley, pp. 67–90. William B. Eerdmans Publishing Co, Michigan.

Mutu, Margaret, 1999. Tuku Whenua and Land Sale in New Zealand in the Nineteenth Century. In *Voyages and Beaches: Pacific Encounters 1769–1840*, edited by A. Calder, J. Lamb, and B. Orr, pp. 317–328. University of Hawaii Press, Honolulu, Hawaii.

Netting, R., R. Wilk, and E. Arnould (Eds.), 1984. *Households: Comparative and Historical Studies of the Domestic Group*. University of California Press, Berkeley, California.

New Zealand Gazette, 1981. No. 29. Government Printer, Wellington, New Zealand.

Nicholas, John L., 1817. *Narrative of a Voyage to New Zealand*, vols. 1 & 2. James Black and Son, London (undated facsimile Wilson & Horton, Auckland, New Zealand).

Noel Hume, Ivor, 1969. *A Guide to the Artifacts of Colonial America*. University of Pennsylvania Press, Philadelphia.

Noel Hume, Ivor, 2001. *If These Pots Could Talk*. Chipstone Foundation, Hanover.

Nora, P., 1989. Between Memory and History. *Representations*, 26(Spring 1989):7–24.

Ollivier, I., 1985. *Extracts from Journals Relating to the Visit to New Zealand in May–July 1772 of the French Ships Mascarin and Marquis de Castries under the Command of M.-J. Marion du Fresne*. Alexander Turnbull Library Endowment Trust with Indosuez New Zealand Ltd., Wellington, New Zealand.

Oppenheim, R., 1973. *Maori Death Customs*. Reed Books, Wellington, New Zealand.

Orange, Claudia, 1987. *The Treaty of Waitangi*. Allen & Unwin, Wellington, New Zealand.

Orange, Claudia, 1997. The Maori People and the British Crown. In *The Oxford Illustrated History of New Zealand*, edited by Keith Sinclair, pp. 21–48. Oxford University Press, Auckland, New Zealand.

Orser, Charles, 1988. Toward a Theory of Power for Historical Archaeology. In *The Recovery of Meaning*, edited by Mark Leone, and P. Potter, pp. 313–321. Smithsonian Institution Press. Washington.

Orser, Charles, 1996. *A Historical Archaeology of the Modern World*. Plenum Press, New York and London.

Orser, Charles, A.M. Nekola, and J.L. Roark, 1987. *Exploring the Rustic Life: Multidisciplinary Research at Millwood Plantation, a Large Piedmont Plantation in Abbeville County, South Carolina, and Elbert County, Georgia*. National Park Service, Atlanta.

Orton, J., n.d. *Visit to New Zealand*. Micro-ms-90. Alexander Turnbull Library, Wellingotn, New Zealand.

Orwin, C.S., and C.S. Orwin, 1938. *The Open Fields*. Clarendon Press, Oxford, UK.

Owens, J.R.M., 1968. Christianity and the Maoris to 1840. *New Zealand Journal of History*, 2(April 1968):18–40.

Owens, J.R.M., 1974. *Prophets in the Wilderness*. Auckland University Press, Oxford University Press, Auckland, New Zealand.

Owens, J.R.M., 1985. *Missionaries and the Treaty of Waitangi*. Wesleyan Historical Society, New Zealand.

Parsonson, A., 1981. The Pursuit of Mana. In *The Oxford History of New Zealand*, edited by William H. Oliver, and Bridget R. Williams, pp. 140–167. Clarendon Press and Oxford University Press, Wellington, New Zealand and Oxford, UK.

Paterson, Alastair, and Wilson, A., 2000. Australian Historical Archaeology: Retrospects and Prospects. *Australian Archaeology*, 81–89.

Peacock, P., 1972. *Buttons for the Collector*. David & Charles, Devon, UK.

Phillips, Caroline, 2000a. Post-Contact Landscapes of Change in Hauraki, New Zealand. In *The Archaeology of Difference*, edited by Robin Torrence and Anne Clarke, pp. 79–103. Routledge, London & New York.

Phillips, Caroline, 2000b. *Waihou Journeys: The Archaeology of 400 Years of Maori Settlement*. Auckland University Press, Auckland, New Zealand.

Pickmere, Nancy, 1994. *Kerikeri Heritage of Dreams*. Northland Historical Publications, Russell, New Zealand.

Piddock, Susan, 2001. An Irregular and Inconvenient Pile of Buildings: The Destitute Asylum of Adelaide, South Australia and the English Workhouse. *International Journal of Historical Archaeology*, 5(1):73–95.

Pilley, H.M., n.d.a. *Letters*. CMS archives microfilm 79–342, University of Auckland Library, Auckland, New Zealand.

Pilley, H.M., n.d.b. *CMS London Additional Papers Relating to the N.Z. Missions*. MS-0498, Hocken Library, Dunedin, New Zealand.

Plowman, M., 2000. The Archaeological Use of Historic Ceramics as Indicators of Status and Class: His Majesty's Theatre Ceramic Assemblage a Case Study. MA thesis, University of Auckland, Auckland, New Zealand.

Porter, Andrew, 1999. Religion, Missionary Enthusiasm, and Empire. In *The Oxford History of the British Empire: The Nineteenth Century*, edited by Andrew Porter, pp. 222–246. Oxford University Press, Oxford, UK and New York.

Porter, Frances (Ed.), 1974. *The Turanga Journals*. Price Milburn/Victoria University Press, Wellington, New Zealand.

Porter, Frances, 1992. All that the Heart Does Bear. In *Mission and Moko*, edited by R. Glen, pp. 134–151. Latimer Fellowship, Christchurch, New Zealand.

Porter, Frances, and C. Macdonald (Eds.), 1996. *My Hand Will Write What My Heart Dictates*. Auckland University Press, Auckland, New Zealand.

Pratt, J., n.d. Letter to William Hey. *CMS London Additional Papers Relating to the N.Z. Missions*. MS-0498, Hocken Library, Dunedin, New Zealand.

Pratt, J., and E. Bickersteth, n.d. Letter to J. King. *Transcripts of Selected Items from the Four Volumes of Marsden Correspondence*. MS-0057a, Hocken Library, Dunedin, New Zealand.

Prickett, Nigel, 1981. The Archaeology of a Military Frontier: Taranaki, New Zealand 1860–1881. PhD thesis, University of Auckland, Auckland, New Zealand.

Prickett, Nigel, 1994. *Archaeologial Investigations at the Omata Stockade and Warea Redoubt, Taranaki*. New Zealand Archaeological Association Monograph, Auckland, New Zealand.

Puette, Thomas, and Thomas Dye, 2003. *Archaeological Monitoring of Trench Excavation for Electrical Renovation at the Mission Houses Museum, Honolulu, Hawaii*. T.S. Dye & Colleagues, Archaeologists, Inc., Honolulu, Hawaii.

Purchas, H.T., 1914. *A History of the English Church in New Zealand*. Simpson and Williams, Christchurch, New Zealand.

Rhodes, David, 1986. *Lake Condah Project: Post-Contact Archaeological Component*. Unpublished report, Victoria, Australia.

Rhodes, David, 1996. *The History of Ramahyuck Aboriginal Mission and a Report on the Survey of Ramahyuck Mission Cemetery.* Occasional Report No. 47, Aboriginal Affairs, Victoria, Australia.

Rihari, Whakaaropai, 2002 September. Personal communication,.

Robinson, James, 1995. *Recent Excavations at the Seat of New Zealand's First Colonial Government.* Unpublished report, Department of Conservation, Northland Conservancy, New Zealand.

Roenke, K., 1978. Flat Glass: Its Use as a Dating Tool for Nineteenth Century Archaeological Sites in the Pacific Northwest and Elsewhere. *Northwest Anthropological Research Notes, Memoir 4.*

Rogers, Lawrence, 1961. *The Early Journals of Henry Williams 1826–1840.* Pegasus Press, Christchurch, New Zealand.

Rogers, Lawrence, 1998. *Te Wiremu A Biography of Henry Williams.* Shoal Bay Press, Christchurch, New Zealand.

Ross, Ruth, n.d. *Papers.* Ms 1442, Auckland Institute and Museum Library, Auckland, New Zealand.

Rountree, Kathryn, 2000. Re-making the Maori Female Body. *Journal of Pacific History,* 35(1):49–66.

Rubertone, Patricia, 1989. Archaeology, Colonialism and 17th Century Native Americans: Towards an Alternative Interpretation. In *Conflict in the Archaeology of Living Traditions,* edited by R. Layton, pp. 32–45. Unwin Hyman, London, UK.

Rubertone, Patricia, 2000. The Historical Archaeology of Native Americans. *Annual Review of Anthropology,* 29:425–446.

Rubertone, Patricia, 2001. *Grave Undertakings: An Archaeology of Roger Williams and the Narragansett Indians.* Smithsonian Institution Press, Washington.

Russell, M., 2001. Influence of the Ideal. The Archaeology of the Monastic Mission of New Norcia. BA(Hons) thesis, Australian National University, Canberra, Australia.

Salaman, R.A., 1975. *Dictionary of Tools used in the Woodworking and Allied Trades, c. 1700–1970.* Allen & Unwin, London.

Salisbury, Neal, 1992. Religious Encounters in a Colonial Context: New England and New France in the Seventeenth Century. *American Indian Quarterly,* 16(4): 501–509.

Salmond, Anne, 1991a. *Two Worlds: First Meetings Between Maori and Europeans 1642–1772.* Viking Penguin, Auckland, New Zealand.

Salmond, Anne, 1991b. Tipuna – Ancestors: Aspects of Maori Cognatic Descent. In *Man and a Half: Essays in Pacific Anthropology and Ethnobiology in Honour of Ralph Bulmer,* edited by A. Pawley, pp. 343–356. The Polynesian Society, Auckland, New Zealand.

Salmond, Anne, 1997. *Between Worlds: Early Exchanges Between Maori and Europeans 1773–1815.* Viking Penguin, Auckland, New Zealand.

Salmond, Anne, 2000. Maori and Modernity: Ruatara's Dying. In *Signifying Identities,* edited by A. Cohen, pp. 37–58. Routlegde, London, UK.

Salt, Annette, 1984. *These Outcast Women: The Parramatta Female Factory, 1821–1848.* Hale & Iremonger, Sydney, Australia.

Sambrook, P., 1983. *Laundry Bygones.* Shire Album, Buckinghamshire, UK.

Sandos, James, 2004. *Converting California.* Yale University Press, New Haven.

Saunders, Rebecca, 1993. Architecture of the Missions Santa Maria and Santa Catalina de Amelia. In *The Spanish Missions of La Florida,* edited by Bonnie McEwan, pp. 35–61. University Press of Florida, Gainsville.

Saunders, Rebecca, 1996. Mission Period Settlement Structure. *Historical Archaeology,* 30:24–36.

Saunders, Rebecca, 1998. Forced Relocation, Power Relations, and Culture Contact in the Missions of La Florida. In *Studies in Culture Contact,* edited by James Cusick, pp. 402–429. Center for Archaeological Investigations, Southern Illinois University Occasional Paper No. 25, Carbondale, Illinois.

Savage, John, 1973 (1807). *Some Account of New Zealand*. Capper Press, Christchurch, New Zealand.

Schmidt, Matthew, 1996. The Commencement of Pa Construction in New Zealand Prehistory. *Journal of the Polynesian Society*, 105:441–460.

Schrire, Carmel, 1988. The Historical Archaeology of the Impact of Colonialism in Seventeenth Century South Africa. *Antiquity*, 214–225.

Schrire, Carmel, 1992. Digging Archives at Oudepost 1, Cape, South Africa. In *The Art and Mystery of Historical Archaeology: Essays in Honour of James Deetz*, edited by Anne Yentsch and Mary Beaudry, pp. 361–372. CRC Press, Boca Raton.

Schrire, Carmel, 1995. *Digging through Darkness: Chronicles of an Archaeologist*. University Press of Virginia, Richmond, Virginia.

Schuyler, Robert (Ed.), 1978. *Historical Archaeology: A Guide to Substantive and Theoretical Contributions*. Baywood Publishing Company, Farmingdale.

Schuyler, Robert, 1988. Archaeological Remains, Documents, and Anthropology: A Call for a New Culture History. *Historical Archaeology*, 22:36–42.

Schuyler, Robert, 1999. The Centrality of Post-Medieval Studies to General Historical Archaeology. In *Old and New Worlds*, edited by G. Egan, and R. Michael, pp. 10–16. Oxbow Books, Oxford, UK.

Scott, P., and James Deetz, 1990. Buildings, Furnishings and Social Change in Early Victorian Grahamstown. *Social Dynamics*, 16:79–89.

Sharp, Andrew, 1971. *Duperrey's Visit to New Zealand in 1824*. Alexander Turnbull Library, Wellington, New Zealand.

Shawcross, K., 1967. Maoris of the Bay of Islands 1769–1840: A Study of Changing Maori Responses to European Contacts. MA thesis, University of Auckland, Auckland, New Zealand.

Shepherd, James, n.d. *Letters, Journals, Reports 1821–1850*. CMS archives microfilm 79–343, University of Auckland Library, Auckland, New Zealand.

Shoebridge, Tim, 2006. *Waitangi Tribunal Bibliography, 1975–2005*. Waitangi Tribunal, Wellington, New Zealand.

Silliman, Stephen, 2001. Theoretical Perspectives on Labor and Colonialism: Reconsidering the California Missions. *Journal of Anthropological Archaeology*, 20:379–407.

Silliman, Stephen, 2004. *Lost Laborers in Colonial California*. University of Tuscon Press, Arizona.

Silliman, Stephen, 2005. Culture Contact or Colonialism? Challenges in the Archaeology of Native North America. *American Antiquity*, 70(1):55–74.

Silverman, David J., 2003. We Chuse to be Bounded: Native American Animal Husbandry in Colonial New England. *The William and Mary Quarterly*, 60(3):511–548.

Simmons, William S., 1979. Conversion from Indian to Puritan. *New England Quarterly*, 52(2):197–218.

Simmons, William S., 1986. *Spirit of the New England Tribes: Indian History and Folklore, 1620–1984*. Hanover: University Press of New England.

Simpson, H., 1962. *The Women of New Zealand*. Paul's Book Arcade, Auckland, New Zealand.

Sinclair, Keith, 1969. *A History of New Zealand*. Penguin, London, UK.

Sissons, Jeffrey, 2007. Hongi Hika. In *Te Kerikeri 1770–1850: The Meeting Pool*, edited by Judith Binney, pp. 47–50. Bridget Williams Books, Wellington, New Zealand.

Sissons, Jeffrey, W. Wi Hongi, and Pat Hohepa, 2001. *Nga Puriri o Taiamai*. Reed, The Polynesian Society, Auckland, New Zealand.

Skudder, Les. February 2002. Personal communication.

Sleeper-Smith, Susan, 2000. Women, Kin and Catholicism: New Perspectives on the Fur Trade. *Ethnohistory*, 47:423–452.

Sleeper-Smith, Susan, 2001. *Indian Women and French Men: Rethinking Cultural Encounter in the Western Great Lakes*. University of Massachusetts Press, Amherst.

Smith, Bernard, 1985. *European Vision and the South Pacific 1768–1850*. Yale University Press, New Haven, London.

Smith, I. W.G., n.d. *Bottle Glass Identification Guide*. Laboratory manual, Department of Anthropology, University of Otago, Dunedin, New Zealand.

Smith, I.W.G. 1990. Historical Archaeology in New Zealand: A Review and Bibliography. *New Zealand Journal of Archaeology*, 12:85–119.

Smith, I.W.G., 2004. Archaeologies of Identity: Historical Archaeology for the 21st Century. In *Change through Time: 50 Years of New Zealand Archaeology*, edited by Louise Furey, and Simon Holdaway, pp. 251–262. New Zealand Archaeological Association Monograph 26, Auckland, New Zealand.

Smith, I.W.G., 2005a. Retreat and Resilience: Fur Seals and Human Settlement in New Zealand. In *The Exploitation and Cultural Importance of Sea Mammals*, edited by Greg Monks, pp. 6–18. Oxbow Books, Oxford, UK.

Smith I.W.G., 2005b *The New Zealand Sealing Industry*. Department of Conservation, Wellington, New Zealand.

Smith I.W.G., and Atholl Anderson, 2007. *Codfish Island / Whenua Hou Archaeological Project Preliminary Report*. Unpublished report to New Zealand Historic Places Trust and Department of Conservation, New Zealand.

Smith, I.W.G., and Karl Gillies, 1997. *Archaeological Investigations at Luncheon Cove, Dusky Sound, February 1997*. Unpublished report to New Zealand Historic Places Trust and Department of Conservation, Wellington, New Zealand.

Smith, I.W.G., and Karl Gillies, 1998. *Archaeological Investigations at Facile Harbour, Dusky Sound, February 1998*. Unpublished report to New Zealand Historic Places Trust and the Department of Conservation, Wellington, New Zealand.

Snow, D., 1967. Archaeology and Nineteenth Century Missions. *Historical Archaeology*, 1:57–59.

Spencer, Jeremy, 1983. Rangihoua Pa and Oihi Mission Station, Purerua Peninsula. In *A Lot of Spadework to be Done*, edited by Susan Bulmer, G. Law, and D. Sutton, pp. 77–110. New Zealand Archaeological Association Monograph, Auckland, New Zealand.

Spencer-Wood, Suzanne, 1999. The World Their Household: Changing Meanings of the Domestic Sphere in the Nineteenth Century. In *The Archaeology of Household Activities*, edited by Penelope Allison, pp. 162–189. Routledge, London, UK.

Spencer-Wood, Suzanne, 2004. What Difference Does Feminist Theory Make in Researching Households? In *Household Chores and Household Choices*, edited by K. Barile, and J. Brandon, pp. 235–253. University of Alabama Press, Tuscaloosa.

Spencer-Wood, Suzanne, and S. Baugher, 2001. Introduction and Historical Context for the Archaeology of Institutions of Reform. Part I: Asylums. *International Journal for Historical Archaeology*, 5(1):3–17.

Sprague, R., 2000. Glass Trade Beads: A Progress Report. In *Approaches to Material Culture Research for Historical Archaeologists* (2nd ed.), edited by David Brauner, pp. 202–220. Society for Historical Archaeology, Pennsylvania.

Stack, James, n.d. James Stack to Rev. E.G. Marsh. *CMS London Additional Papers Relating to the N.Z. Missions*. MS-0498, Hocken Library, Dunedin, New Zealand.

Stack, J.W., 1937. *Early Maoriland Adventures*. Oxford University Press, Oxford, UK.

Stack, J.W., 1938. *More Maoriland Adventures*. A.H. & A.W. Reed, Dunedin, New Zealand.

Stack, J.W., and E. Stack, 1938. *Further Maoriland Adventures*. A.H. & A.W. Reed, Dunedin, New Zealand.

Standish, M.W., 1962. *The Waimate Mission Station*. Government Printer, Wellington, New Zealand.

Stevens, C., 1994. *White Man's Dreaming*. Oxford University Press, Melbourne.

Stock, E., 1899. *History of the Church Missionary Society*. Church Missionary Society, London, UK.

Stock, E., 1913. *The Story of the New Zealand Mission*. Church Missionary Society, London, UK.

Stocking, George, 1987. *Victorian Anthropology*. Macmillan, New York.

Sutton, Mary-Jean, 2003. Re-Examining Total Institutions: A Case Study from Queensland. *Archaeology in Oceania*, 38(2):78–89.

Swain, T., and D. Rose (Eds.), 1988. *Aboriginal Australians and Christian Missions*. Australian Association for the Study of Religions, Bedford Park, Australia.

Tapp, E.J., 2006. Jones, John 1808/1809? – 1869'. Dictionary of New Zealand Biography. URL: http://www.dnzb.govt.nz/

Tapsell, Phillip, n.d. (1870). *Reminiscences*. MS-Papers-7168. Alexander Turnbull Library, Wellington, New Zealand.

Tasker, J., 1989. *Old New Zealand Bottles and Bygones*. Heinemann Reed, Auckland, New Zealand.

Taylor, G., 1988. Goods and Gods. In *Aboriginal Australians and Christian Missions*, edited by T. Swain, and D. Rose, pp. 438–451. Australian Association for the Study of Religions, Bedford Park, Australia.

Taylor, Richard, n.d. *Journal 1833–1873*. MS 302, Auckland Institute and Museum Library, Auckland, New Zealand.

Thomas, David Hurst, 1990. The Spanish Missions of La Florida: An Overview. In *Columbian Consequences*, edited by David Hurst Thomas, pp. 357–397. Smithsonian Institution Press, Washington.

Thomas, David Hurst (Ed.), 1991. *Columbian Consequences*, vols. 1–3. Smithsonian Institution Press, Washington.

Thomas, David Hurst, 1993. The Archaeology of Mission Santa Catalina de Guale: Our First Fifteen Years. In *The Spanish Missions of La Florida*, edited by Bonnie McEwan, pp. 1–35. University Press of Florida, Gainsville.

Thomson, A.S., 1859. *The Story of New Zealand: Past and Present, Savage and Civilized*. John Murray, London, UK.

Thorne, Susan, 1999. *Congregational Missions and the Making of an Imperial Culture in Nineteenth-Century England*. Stanford University Press, Stanford.

Torrence, Robin, and Anne Clarke (Eds.), 2000. *The Archaeology of Difference*. Routledge, London.

Treadwell, S., 1999. Categorical Weavings. In *Voyages and Beaches: Pacific Encounters 1769–1840*, edited by A. Calder, J. Lamb, and B. Orr, pp. 265–284. University of Hawaii Press, Honolulu, Hawaii.

Trigger, Bruce, 1985. *Natives and Newcomers*. McGill-Queen's University Press, Montreal.

Trigger, Bruce, 1987. *Children of Aataentsic*. Kingston: McGill-Queen's University Press.

Turton, Henry Hanson, 1877–1883. *An Epitome of Official Documents Relative to Native Affairs and Land Purchases in the North Island of New Zealand* (microform). New Zealand Government, Wellington, New Zealand.

Twidale, C.R., 1971. Farming by the Early Settlers. *Tools and Tillage*, 4:205–223.

Twidale, C.R., 1972. 'Lands' or Relict Strip Fields in South Australia. *Agricultural History Review*, 20:46–60.

Twidale, C.R., G.J. Forrest, and J. Shepherd, 1971. The Imprint of the Plough: 'Lands' in the Mt. Lofty Ranges, South Australia. *Australian Geographer*, 11(5):492–503.

Urry, Katharine, 1993. Te Hakari: Feasting in Maori Society and Its Archaeological Implications. Unpublished MA thesis, University of Auckland, Auckland, New Zealand.

Varman, R., 1980. The Nail as a Criterion for the Dating of Buildings and Building Sites (Late Eighteenth Century to 1900). *Australian Society for Historical Archaeology Newsletter*, 10:30–37.

Von Huegel, B.K., n.d. *Diaries: Sydney, New Zealand and Norfolk Island from 10 February to 16 April 1834*. MS-papers-1527. Alexander Turnbull Library, Wellington, New Zealand.

Wade, William, n.d. *CMS London Additional Papers Related to the N.Z. Missions*. MS-0498, Hocken Library, Dunedin, New Zealand.

Wagner-Wright, S., 1990. *The Structure of the Missionary Call to the Sandwich Islands 1790–1830: Sojourners among Strangers*. Mellen Research University Press, San Francisco.

Walker, Ranginui, 1990. *Struggle Without End: Ka Whawhai Tonu Matou*. Penguin, Auckland, New Zealand.

Wallace, Lee, 2005. A House is Not a Home: Gender, Space and Marquesan Encounter, 1833–1834. *Journal of Pacific History*, 40(3):265–288.

Walter, Richard, Ian W.G. Smith, and Chris Jacomb, 2006. Sedentism, Subsistence and Socio-Political Organization in Prehistoric New Zealand. *World Archaeology* 38(2):274–290.

Walton, Tony, 1982. "Such as are seen on land that has been ploughed:" slope lines and ploughing methods. *N.Z. Archaeological Association Newsletter*, 25(2):125–131.

Walton, Tony (Ed.), 1999. *Archaeological Site Recording in New Zealand. New Zealand Archaeological Association Monograph*. New Zealand Archaeological Association, Auckland, New Zealand.

Ward, Alan, 1974. *A Show of Justice*. Australian National University Press, Canberra, Australia.

Warth, E., 1984. *The Shepherd Flock*. Warth, Wellsford, New Zealand.

Watson, Katharine, 2000. A Land of Plenty: Butchery Patterns and Meat Supply in Nineteenth Century New Zealand. MA thesis, Department of Anthropology, University of Otago, Dunedin, New Zealand.

Webster, Steven, 1973. *Maori Adoption*. Department of Anthropology, University of Auckland, Auckland, New Zealand.

Webster, Steven, 1998. *Patrons of Maori Culture. Power, Theory and Ideology in the Maori Renaissance*. University of Otago Press, Dunedin, New Zealand.

Wells, T., 2000. Nail Chronology: The Use of Technologically Derived Features. In *Approaches to Material Culture Research for Historical Archaeologists*, edited by David Brauner, pp. 318–339. Society for Historical Archaeology, Pennsylvania.

Wheeler, D., 1840. *Extracts from the Letters and Journal of David Wheeler while Engaged in a Religious Visit to … and New Zealand*. Harvey and Darton, London, UK.

Whitaker, Anne-Marie (Ed.), 1998. *Distracted Settlement: N.S.W. after Bligh from the Journal of Lieutenant James Finucane*. Melbourne University Press, Melbourne, Australia.

White, Eliza, n.d. *Journals 1829–1836*. Met 011, 012. St John's Theological College Library, Auckland, New Zealand.

Whiter, L., 1970. *Spode A History of the Family, Factory and Wares from 1733 to 1833*. Barrie and Jenkins, London.

Willett, C., and P. Cunnington, 1951. *The History of Underclothes*. Michael Joseph, London, UK.

Williams, Henry, n.d.a. *Williams Family Correspondence*. MS-copy-micro 0209, Alexander Turnbull Library, Wellington, New Zealand.

Williams, Henry, n.d.b. *Letters*. ML CYA 1994. Mitchell Library, Sydney, Australia.

Williams, Henry junior, n.d. *Diaries 1873, 1880–1901*. Micro ms 817 Alexander Turnbull Library, Wellington, New Zealand.

Williams, Jane, n.d. *Journals, August 1842*. MS-papers-1527, Alexander Turnbull Library, Wellington, New Zealand.

Williams, Marianne, n.d.a. *Journal May 25–June 2 1850*. Misc-ms-1102, Hocken Library, Dunedin, New Zealand.

Williams, Marianne, n.d.b. *Journal June 11–October 5 1844; January 28–31 1846*. Qms-2245, Alexander Turnbull Library, Wellington, New Zealand.

Williams, P., and M. Weber, 1986. *Staffordshire Romantic Transfer Patterns*. vol. II. Fountain House East, Jeffersontown.

Williams, William, 1989 (1867). *Christianity among the New Zealanders*. Banner of Truth Trust, Edinburgh, Scotland.

Williment, T.M.I., 1985. *John Hobbs 1800–1883 Wesleyan Missionary to the Ngapuhi Tribe of Northern New Zealand*. Government Printer, Wellington, New Zealand.

Wilk, R., and W. Rathje, 1982. Household Archaeology. *American Behavioral Scientist*, 25:617–639.

Wilson, Anne C., n.d. *My Hand will Write What My Heart Dictates*. MS-papers-3943-1. Alexander Turnbull Library, Wellington, New Zealand.

Wilson, Daniel, n.d. Rev. D. Wilson to John King. *Transcripts of Selected Items from the Four Volumes of Marsden Correspondence, 1814–1815*. MS 0057a, Hocken Library, Dunedin, New Zealand.

Wilson, John, n.d. *Letters and Journals*. CMS archives microfilm 79–349. University of Auckland Library, Auckland, New Zealand.

Wilson, John (Ed.), 1889. *Missionary Life and Work in New Zealand 1833 to 1862: being the Private Journal of the Late Rev. John Alexander Wilson*. Auckland Star, Auckland, New Zealand.

Wilson, Ormond, 1965. Papahurihia, First Maori Prophet. *Journal of the Polynesian Society*, 74(4):473–483.

Winer, Margot, 1994. Landscapes of Power: British Material Culture of the Eastern Cape frontier, South Africa: 1820–1860. PhD thesis, University of California, Berkley.

Winer, Margot, 2001. Landscapes, Fear and Land Loss on the Nineteenth-Century South African Colonial Frontier. In *Contested Landscapes*, edited by Barbara Bender and Margot Winer, pp. 257–272. Berg, Oxford, UK.

Winer, Margot, and James Deetz, 1990. The Transformation of British Culture in the Eastern Cape, 1820–1860. *Social Dynamics*, 16:55–75.

Wordsworth, J., 1981. *Women of the North*. Collins, Auckland, New Zealand.

Wright, Harrison, 1959 *New Zealand, 1769–1840 First Years of Western Contact*. Harvard University Press, Cambridge.

Wyatt, P., 1991. The Old Land Claims and the Concept of "Sale": A Case Study. MA thesis, University of Auckland, Auckland, New Zealand.

Yarwood, A., 1996. *Samuel Marsden*. Melbourne University Press, Melbourne, Australia.

Yarwood, A., and P. Douglas, 1994. *Historical and Archaeological Assessment of the Site of the Reverend Samuel Marsden's Seminary for Maoris at Parramatta*, commissioned by Te Iwi Maori Inc. (N.S.W.), Sydney, Australia.

Yate, William, n.d. *Order for China*. CMS Archives microfilm CN/08(a) 44. Copy from Kerikeri Mission House and Stone Store, Kerikeri, New Zealand.

Yate, William, 1835. *An Account of New Zealand*. Seeley & Burnside, London.

Zwiep, Mary, 1991. *Pilgrim Path: The First Company of Women Missionaries to Hawaii*. University of Wisconsin Press, Madison, Wisconsin.

Index

Printed in the United States of America